VALUE/MORAL EDUCATION:
THE SCHOOLS AND THE TEACHERS

Other books by the same editor:

The inner Crusade: The closed retreat in the United States.
Loyola University Press, 1965.

The high school counselor today. Daughters of St. Paul, 1966.

The interdisciplinary roots of guidance. Fordham University
Press, 1966.

Values and moral development. Paulist Press, 1976.

Value/Moral Education: The Schools and the Teachers

Edited by
Thomas C. Hennessy, S.J.

Papers by:
James J. DiGiacomo
Leo Gold
Thomas C. Hennessy
Richard H. Hersh & Diana P. Paolitto
Harry B. Kavanagh
Frank W. Lewis
Robert J. Roth, S.J.
Norman A. Sprinthall & Joseph E. Bernier
An Interview with Lawrence Kohlberg

PAULIST PRESS
New York/Ramsey/Toronto

Published by Paulist Press
Editorial Office: 1865 Broadway, New York, N.Y. 10023
Business Office: 545 Island Road, Ramsey, N.J. 07446

Printed and bound in the
United States of America

Contents

Introduction

One of the tragedies of modern life is the disparity between individuals' growth in overall general achievements and their personal moral development. Daily newspapers give accounts of individuals who have reached the top ranks in banking, in athletics, in law and in politics and who are accused and often convicted of legal crimes. The educator is inclined to wonder about the personal, moral education and development of these individuals. Did parents and schools so emphasize success that they omitted equal emphasis regarding ethical methods and considerations such as justice to others? Did they presume that moral development would automatically take place along with cognitive development? Was church-going presumed to be enough to assure moral development, with no recognition of Allport's (1954) distinction between the "interiorized" religious persons and those who are "institutionalized" (seeking safety or personal, political or social benefits)? Were churches so intent upon transmitting dogmatic teachings that they did not attempt to initiate a systematic way of developing the young from "do's and don't's" to deeper, more principled thinking?

One of the persons whose history will intrigue the moral and value educator is that of Richard M. Nixon, who resigned the highest office in the United States and lives in disgrace and retirement at his home in San Clemente. Though he offered many exhortations to the young during his presidency, in the end it turned out that his actions belied his words. To offer a minor example, he had spoken eloquently of the importance of avoiding profanity but the release of audio tapes demonstrated that his personal speech wasn't in tune with his professional speech.

In a well-publicized television interview with David Frost, Mr. Nixon demonstrated that he doesn't understand the fact that morality influences all human behaviors, including political ones. He excused his early reaction to the Watergate break-in as "trying to contain it politically. And that's a very different motive (from) attempting to cover up criminal activities of an individual." A moral

1

educator's reaction to this kind of statement is one of surprise that a successful lawyer doesn't see even the legal implications of this kind of behavior; a moral awareness would surely alert one to the fact that one can't separate one's political from one's ethical, legal and moral behavior. Another reaction is that many businessmen have been known to talk and act in substantially the same way: "My personal life and my business are completely separate; in my personal life I keep the Commandments and go to church on Sunday; but the world of business is 'dog eat dog' and I'm not going to be eaten!"

During the same interview, while not admitting to any technical, legal crimes, Mr. Nixon said that he made many bad judgments, including the fact that he "let down my friends. I let down the country. I let down our system of government and the dreams of all those young people that ought to get into government but think it's all too corrupt . . ." Besides admitting many bad judgments, he also asserted that "I said things that were not true." . . . "Some of my mistakes that I regret most deeply came with the statements I made . . . some of the statements were misleading."

Besides the lying, the only expression of real guilt that Mr. Nixon accepted was in regard to the judicial system: ". . . in some cases going right to the edge of the law in trying to advise . . . as to how best to present their cases . . . I came to the edge and, under the circumstances, I would have to say that a reasonable person could call that a cover-up." He also asserted that: ". . . acting as lawyer for their defense, I was not prosecuting the case. I will admit that during that period, rather than acting in my role as . . . the one with the chief responsibility for seeing that the laws of the United States are enforced, . . . I did not meet that responsibility." Somehow these admissions, though hardly the full story, seemed good to hear in the sense that some personal guilt was accepted. So much of the interview marked this man as rationalizing, ego-centered, and "caught up in something (that) snowballed." It was really not his fault as he was blameless "on the big issues" and at fault only on the minor ones!

The moral educator notes the spirit of pragmatism, the level of law-and-order morality that dominated the Nixon interview. There has been no advance to more principled thinking (even that which dominates the spirit of the U.S. Constitution, certainly not that of those sincerely engaged in the quest for justice). The moral educator realizes that this limited stage of moral development is true not only of the former president but also of the vast majority of the population.

If the general population, including those with a high level of educational achievement, has not developed an advanced moral sensitivity, a legitimate question that may be asked is: Why hasn't there been this growth? Who is to blame? All kinds of conflicting responses are made to these questions. There is the sense of futility that followed the Hartshorne and May (1931) researches, the strong sense of pluralistic thinking that followed World War II, the concern among educators that they would undermine the so-called "wall of separation" between church and state if they even seemed to discuss morality in the classroom. Though educators in the public systems during the past several generations felt a strong desire to engage in a systematic approach to moral development, they ended up in frustration at the lack of official sanction of their goals or because of the absence of theoretical and methodological assistance.

While educators lamented their inability to develop specific programs directed toward moral growth, they did take refuge in general statements which seemed to correlate many aspects of the curriculum to the moral growth and uplift of students. For instance, the Board of Education of the City of New York adopted in 1956 a short statement on "The Development of Moral and Spiritual Ideals in the Public Schools" and the National Educational Association and other groups made similar general and rhetorical affirmations. Bulletins of colleges and private schools over the years have also made beautiful claims to adherence to high moral and spiritual ideals. But in practice the grandiloquent language came to naught because of shortages in acceptable theoretical and methodological materials.

The feeling of shock that has accompanied the recent increase in (or awareness of) public crimes has made many people aware of the need for moral education. They are less worried than formerly about the dangers of introducing specific moral education programs into the public schools. A recent Gallup Poll, published in *Phi Delta Kappan* (October 1976), reported that parents felt that the number one area most neglected by parents and also most neglected by schools is "high moral standards." It seems that the climate is right for a new thrust toward development of theories and programs that foster increased moral perception and growth.

The Plan of the Book

This book mainly contains papers in revised form that were delivered during the Fordham University 1976 Institute on Moral Education. While the 1975 Institute emphasized research in the area of moral development, the 1976 program focused on more practical programs and techniques. Hence this book in general looks to effective methods of imparting moral and value education during different levels of schooling, featuring an interview with Lawrence Kohlberg, and two papers that attend to important personalities in the background of the moral development movement.

The "interview" with Lawrence Kohlberg actually represents sections of the presentation he made at the 1976 Fordham Institute on Moral Education, which are printed with his permission. Eight areas are covered: biographical data; philosophical influences; research and its application; the moral dilemmas; moral stages and behavior applied to moral education; Miligram's experiment in obedience to authority; and current resurgence in interest in moral education. Kohlberg, the Harvard social psychologist who directs the Center for Moral Education, is the major figure behind most of the pages in this book. It is essential that the reader grasp the key ideas that Kohlberg proposes, and the editor suggests that readers make use of the excellent introduction to Piaget and Kohlberg by Duska and Whelan (1975), as well as *Values and Moral Development* (Hennessy, 1970).

A major portion of the book contains the papers that describe and explain programs, techniques and practical approaches to moral education. Papers by R. Hersh and D. Paolitto, J. DiGiacomo, R. Roth, H. Kavanagh, N. Sprinthall and J. Bernier, and T. Hennessy are included in this section.

The Hersh-Paolitto chapter serves as an excellent introduction to the current condition of the moral education scene. Brief summaries of the critically important views of Piaget, Kohlberg and Selman are presented; there is a survey of the intervention research and an explanation of the implications of the research for teacher and classroom use. Conditions of the school environment that foster moral growth are analyzed. Suggestions are given for a methodology to guide the teacher functioning as a discussion leader in moral problems.

The DiGiacomo chapter provides reflection about work in moral education with youth in a Catholic high school and gives a picture of the successful moral educator in action in the classroom. The reader almost feels present in the classroom as the teacher goes to the board to evoke from students the group analysis of the film that has just been shown. Then the use of Socratic dialogue in group work is described with a wealth of real-life, current moral problems. The problems, if not the advantages, of the teaching challenge in the religiously oriented school, are analyzed.

A blueprint for value and moral education at the college level is outlined in the Roth chapter. He summarizes the historical background of value education in the United States and fits the Fordham College tradition into that perspective. The background of the current program involved the group efforts of a committee composed of administrators-faculty-students. Essentially, the program brings together (in tandem courses) faculty and students who work together in value-moral perspectives in the usually separated disciplines: a wide range of courses taken together from different disciplines has been worked out as companion experiences. Evaluation procedures (which aren't "hard" enough in statistical measurements for the satisfaction of this editor) have been planned and are currently being carried out.

The Kavanagh paper is oriented toward the moral education of students in the elementary school. He describes, discusses and applies certain preconditions for moral behavior in regard to practices of parents and teachers. Then he analyzes certain aspects of moral behavior, including moral judgment, future orientation, moral personalism, moral tolerance, moral creativity and empathy. Kavanagh considers each of these factors in its application by teachers in the elementary school setting and also by parents.

The moral and cognitive development of teachers is of vital importance for the attainment of the ideals of moral education, and the Sprinthall-Bernier article focuses on the need for specific attention to this area. They point to the general inadequacies in teacher education in both theory and practice. They suggest Harvey's model as most helpful for the curing of the current ills in teacher education. Recommended practices include the sharing of leadership and responsibility in classrooms and the learning of specific skills including counseling, supervision and sensitive, individualized instruction. The learning of skills involves a term of practicum. Evaluation of the work with teachers showed that the practices produced good results. The Sprinthall-Bernier paper opens up an area for more extensive planning, practice and research if educators are widely convinced of the need for moral education.

Many counselors and other personnel workers have become interested in the recent moral and value growth movement. But due to the earlier commitment of many professionals to the permissive, non-directive views of Carl Rogers, there has been confusion with regard to the integration of their former approach with the newer one. Hennessy's paper integrates elements of the Kohlberg cognitive-developmental theory with the practices of the counselor. He recommends welcoming, not flight from, moral discussions;

focused discussion on moral-value issues; cognitive emphasis; exercises for growth and measurement of moral development; and use of models for moral growth. The final section of the paper reviews Rogers' counseling method as shown in a filmed interview with a client named Gloria. Hennessy finds that Gloria was asking to help in moral growth, an aspect of the interview that Rogers neglected. Suggestions are made for the moral-value counselor's handling of the Gloria-type interview.

The second section of the book contains the papers that describe the specific ideas of three important personalities in the area of moral development: Kohlberg, Adler and Piaget.

The paper by Lewis is meant to be both an explanation of and a tribute to Jean Piaget whose work is often praised by moral educators (and indeed, these days, by most educators). The paper covers four topics: Piaget's conclusions about learning and the learner, specific teachings about cognitive development that pertain to moral education, moral developmental research data and implications of the data for moral educators.

An important writer who is often neglected in the literature of moral education is Alfred Adler. The Gold paper takes care of this situation. The core concept of usefulness to society and social interest are emphasized. Adler urged a democratic approach and positive motivation in his counseling and in his views on education. The importance of the teacher's commitment to these values is brought out. The educational application of the Adlerian doctrine is spelled out and illustrated in the practices of the Family Education Centers and in schools such as Oskar Spiel's school in Vienna and in Elk Grove, California.

The Heinz Dilemma

Kohlberg developed a series of moral dilemmas that were presented to individuals and groups to determine their moral stage and to stimulate discussion and thinking. The most well-known of these dilemmas is that of Heinz and the wonder drug. This story-dilemma is summarized here as there will be references to it in the course of the book. The story has as its background the fact that a druggist had discovered a radium-based wonder drug, and he was determined to make a great deal of money from the drug. So when a certain man named Heinz appeared to purchase the drug for his very ill wife, he was surprised to learn that the price for a small dose was $2,000. Heinz went to everybody he knew to borrow the money, but he could raise only about half the price. So Heinz went to the druggist and begged for a cheaper price or a chance to pay in full later on. But the druggist was adamant saying, "No, I discovered the drug and I'm going to make money from it." Heinz did not know what to do. But later he became desperate and broke into the man's store to steal the drug for his wife. (At this point in interviews, the listener is asked: Should the husband have done that? Why?)

In the scoring and evaluation of the reports of the interviews, Kohlberg was not concerned with the actual solution offered to the moral issue but with the "why" response. The emphasis on the reasoning rather than the preferred kind of action is characteristic of Kohlberg's approach and is a basis for its acceptability to various elements of a pluralistic society. No religious or humanistic group feels that preferential treatment is afforded another group in the fundamental thrust of the moral growth paradigm.

The reader who wishes to review the Kohlberg moral stages and levels is referred to the Hersh-Paolitto article. The reader who seeks an introductory explanation of the Kohlberg and Piaget views on moral education should read Duska and Whalen (1975).

In Conclusion

In concluding this introduction it seems appropriate to offer some definitions that may be helpful to the reader. The words to be defined are *moral education* and *values*.

Moral education is the deliberate process in which the young members of society are assisted to develop from a naive self-orientation concerning their rights and obligations to a broader view of self-in-society and to a deeper view of self and all other reality (which for the religious person preeminently includes God).

Values as used in this book could be defined along the lines offered by Raths, Harmin and Simon (1966) as beliefs, attitudes, activities or feelings that are freely chosen after due reflection from among alternatives; they are prized and cherished, publicly affirmed, incorporated into actual behavior and are repeated in one's life. The emphasis is upon the free choice of values rather than the unreflective acceptance of values common to one's group.

A concluding note and prayer. May this book help young and old, teachers and students, counselors and clients, clergy and laity to grow, gradually but consistently, by conscience-raising efforts, to Teilhard's vision of point Omega.

The Teacher as Moral Educator

Richard H. Hersh & Diana Pritchard Paolitto

Introduction

A constant problem for teachers is consideration of values and moral issues in the classroom. The problem has been intensified in recent years as the effects of racism, Viet Nam, Watergate, and illegal corporate payoffs have caused the public to clamor for an educational solution. The Gallup Poll's latest annual report on American education showed that nearly eighty per cent of the people surveyed favored instruction in the schools that would deal with morals and moral behavior (*Newsweek*, March 1, 1976).

The work of Lawrence Kohlberg has gained widespread attention in the search for such a solution. In addition to a voluminous research literature attempting to validate Kohlberg's moral development efforts, there has been a myriad of articles, speeches, and conferences attempting to convince teachers of the necessity of becoming moral development agents. People seem too willing to jump onto the bandwagon. But the "bandwagon" effect, the usual fate of educational theory made popular by the demand for short-term results, causes a premature rush to practice and results in the simplification of the theory such that it (a) is reduced to the point of nonrecognition, (b) is packaged as if a mechanistic approach will produce a desired change, (c) results in a creation of expectations for the practitioner and consumer which no operational definition could fulfill, and (d) causes people, frustrated by the complex task of applying a simplified version of a complex theory, to reject the theory. Lest such a bandwagon fate devour moral education we hope to make clear the explicit complexity of Kohlbergian moral development research and its uses and limitations in practice.

It is critical to recognize that moral education is broader than moral development. Kohlberg's work in moral development is a

9

major but not a sufficient component in the construction of a moral education program. While others such as Scriven (1975), Peters (1971, 1974), Crittenden (1972, 1975), and Lickona (1976) acknowledge the informing nature of Kohlberg's thinking, they nevertheless point to inadequacies and demand further research and explanation. Indeed, Kohlberg has never claimed that his theory is sufficient to the task of moral education:

> We are not, however, considering all kinds of situations which might be said to fall under the general category moral. It is customary to distinguish three basic concepts which together, combined and interpreted in a variety of ways, constitute all systems or theories of morality, namely, the right, the good, and the moral worth. When we speak of "moral" development, "moral" judgments or deliberation, and "moral" situations, we are focusing primarily on the first of these concepts as central. We are not describing how men formulate different conceptions of the good, the good life, intrinsic value, or purpose. Nor are we discussing how men develop certain kinds of character traits and learn to recognize these traits in judgments of approbation and disapprobation. Instead, we are concentrating on that aspect of morality that is brought to the fore by problematic situations of conflicting claims, whether the conflict is between individuals, groups, societies, or institutions, and whether the source of the conflict lies in incompatible claims based on conceptions of the good, beliefs about human purpose, or character assessments. In short, we intend the term "moral" to be understood in the restricted sense of referring to situations which call for judgments involving deontological concepts such as right and wrong, duty and obligation, having a right, fairness, etc., although such judgments may (or may not) involve either or both of the other two basic concepts or their derivatives. (Boyd and Kohlberg, 1973, p. 360.)

Yet Kohlberg's work is prone to acceptance as sufficient. It is to this concern that this article is addressed.

A full explanation of Kohlberg's work and its critique is not the purpose of this effort. Nor will this paper explain Kohlberg's notion of "just community" theory and its implementation as it relates the moral development of individuals to opportunities for social responsibility and moral action on behalf of others in one's school community (Kohlberg, 1975; Kohlberg, Wasserman, and Richardson, 1975; Wasserman, 1976). Such explanation may be obtained from articles cited in the bibliography. Rather, the purpose here is to articulate a conception of the teacher's role implied by moral development research. Such research, as noted below, rests upon a strong empirical base of theoretical studies begun by Kohlberg and colleagues. The data provide evidence that one does not have to discard the best of teaching practice already in existence. The data are insufficient, however, to reach closure on many heuristic issues. Hence, one must be mindful of the need for further intervention research. But practice cannot await perfect knowledge. James Rest emphasized this need in his review of Kohlbergian research when he noted:

> Clinical or teaching skills necessary to facilitate these developmental processes need to be specified. This review has called attention to the crucial role played by group discussion skills, and other pedagogical skills in the programs now underway. This component should not be underplayed just because it is not the special province of developmental psychology. If the hope is to develop prototype programs that can be replicated, details must be available on goals and assessments, curriculum and activities and pedagogy. (1974, p. 257.)

The present article attempts to address the issue of pedagogy. Specifically, we will attempt to answer the question, "What should teachers be able to do to facilitate the moral development of students?" The answer to this question requires that one not conceive of the teacher's role as the giver of "truth," either in the "facts" or "values" sense. Rather, *the teacher must primarily (a) create "conflict"* —the type of conflict which facilitates cognitive developmental structural change in students—and (b) *stimulate students' ability to take the perspective of others beyond themselves*. Such a role requires that one understand certain psychological and philosophical assumptions rooted in Kohlberg's research, such as those of Jean Piaget.

Piaget: Adaptation as Meaning Making

While an understanding of the characteristics of intellectual reasoning at each stage within Piaget's theory of cognitive development is important in relation to Kohlberg's developmental progression of stages of moral reasoning, more important is the process, or mechanisms, of development which underlie every stage of development in both theories. The basic Piagetian concepts which form the psychological foundations of Kohlberg's work in moral development are "assimilation," "accommodation," "equilibration," and "structural change." These four processes are most critical to the notion of the teacher as a creator of cognitive conflict in the minds of students.

As a biologist Piaget is interested in how humans adapt to the environment. Such adaptation occurs as we try to make sense out of our interaction with the environment through the processes of assimilation and accommodation. Assimilation means structuring the environment to fit into one's present intellectual organization; that is, to construe reality in terms of one's existing cognitive structure (Flavell, 1963). Accommodation refers to the process of change which requires not that the reality be made to fit into a person's existing pattern of thinking, but rather that one's mode of thought becomes restructured to incorporate the encountered experience. Assimilation and accommodation are complementary processes. Through continuous interaction they cause cognitive growth—an increasing ability to cope with a more complex environment through an increased ability to differentiate and integrate one's encounter with reality.

When a balance between assimilation and accommodation has been accomplished, a state of "equilibrium" has been established. This balance may be viewed as a "harmony" between the individual and the environment (Muss, 1975). As one interacts with the environment, however, the balance is disturbed (disequilibrium) and a new process of assimilation and accommodation begins. After many such repetitions of this process equilibrium is re-established at a higher level, and the cognitive organization of ideas (structure) is qualitatively changed. This is what is meant by "development." Critical in the process is the recognition by Piaget that the person is an active agent in his own development. Cognitive and moral development are dependent upon the quality and quantity of one's experiences—interaction with the social environment and the process of successive re-equilibrations:

> In the case of moral development, the kind of interaction most important for the transition from an immature "morality of constraint" to one of "cooperation" is the child's growing intercourse and solidarity with his social peers. It is through such experience that he emerges from his egocentrism and becomes aware of his own thought, learns to take another's point of view, and comes to understand that reciprocal moral behavior is necessary for the stability of social relationships. These general cognitive changes underlie the shifts in the child's specific judgments about justice, responsibility, punishment, and the nature of rules.
>
> In short, although Piaget recognizes physical and nervous maturation as contributors to development, he does not attribute changing moral orientations to genetic programming. Rather he explains moral development as a process of self-equilibrated cognitive changes precipitated by the individual's social-intellectual experience. (Lickona, 1969, pp. 338-339.)

Kohlberg: Moral Development as an Aim of Education

Kohlberg is concerned with the traditional prohibition of schools from teaching values or "morality" normally felt to be the province of the home and church. In keeping family, church, and school separate, however, educators have assumed naively that schools have been harbors of value neutrality. The result has been a moral education curriculum which has lurked beneath the surface in schools, hidden as it were from both educators and the public. This "hidden curriculum," identified by Jackson (1968), has effectively been described by Holt (1964), Kozol (1967), and Dreeben (1968) in their analyses of schools. The hidden curriculum, with its emphasis on obedience to authority ("stay in your seat, make no noise, get a hallway pass"; and the feeling of "prison" espoused by so many students), implies many underlying moral assumptions and values, which may be quite different from what educators would call their conscious system of morality. Schools have been preaching what Kohlberg calls a "bag of virtues" approach—the teaching of a particular set of values which are peculiar to this culture or to a particular subculture, and which are by nature relativistic and not necessarily more adequate than any other set of values. But the teaching of particular virtues has been apparently proven to be ineffective (Hartshorne and May, 1928-30; Jones, 1936). Kohlberg wishes to go beyond this approach to moral education and instead to conceptualize and facilitate moral development in a cognitive-developmental sense—toward an increased sense of moral autonomy and an understanding of the concept of justice.

Moral development, as initially defined by Piaget (1932) and then refined and researched by Kohlberg (1958, 1969), does not represent an increasing knowledge of cultural values; rather it represents the transformations that occur in the child's *form* or structure of thought. Kohlberg has found that the content of values varies from culture to culture; hence the study of cultural values cannot tell us how the person interacts with his social environment, or goes about solving problems related to his social world. This requires the analysis of developing structures of moral judgment, which Kohlberg found to be universal in a developmental sequence across cultures (Kohlberg, 1970).

In analyzing the responses of longitudinal and cross-cultural subjects to hypothetical moral dilemmas presented in his Moral Judgment Interview, Kohlberg postulates that his research has demonstrated that moral reasoning develops over time through a series of six stages. The concept of stages of cognitive development as used by Piaget (1960) and Kohlberg refers to the structure of one's reasoning and implies the following characteristics:

1. Stages are "structured wholes," or organized systems of thought. This means individuals are consistent in their level of moral judgment.

2. Stages form an invariant sequence. Under all conditions except extreme trauma, movement is always forward, never backward. Individuals never skip stages, and movement is always to the next stage up. This is true in all cultures.

3. Stages are "hierarchical integrations." Thinking at a higher stage includes or comprehends within it lower stage thinking. There is a tendency to function at or prefer the highest stage available.

Kohlberg's stages of moral development are defined by those characteristics in Table 1.

Table 1

I. Preconventional Level

At this level, the child is responsive to cultural rules and labels of good and bad, right or wrong, but interprets these labels either in terms of the physical or the hedonistic consequences of action (punishment, reward, exchange of favors) or in terms of the physical power of those who enunciate the rules and labels. The level is divided into the following two stages:

Stage 1: The punishment-and-obedience orientation. The physical consequences of action determine its goodness or badness, regardless of the human meaning or value of these consequences. Avoidance of punishment and unquestioning deference to power are valued in their own right, not in terms of respect for an underlying moral order supported by punishment and authority (the latter being Stage 4).

Stage 2: The instrumental-relativist orientation. Right action consists of that which instrumentally satisfies one's own needs and occasionally the needs of others. Human relations are viewed in terms like those of the marketplace. Elements of fairness, of reciprocity, and of equal sharing are present, but they are always interpreted in a physical, pragmatic way. Reciprocity is a matter of "you scratch my back and I'll scratch yours," not of loyalty, gratitude, or justice.

II. Conventional Level

At this level, maintaining the expectations of the individual's family, group, or nation is perceived as valuable in its own right, regardless of

---

immediate and obvious consequences. The attitude is not only one of *conformity* to personal expectations and social order, but of loyalty to it, of actively *maintaining*, supporting, and justifying the order, and of identifying with the persons or group involved in it. At this level, there are the following two stages:

Stage 3: The interpersonal concordance or "good boy—nice girl" orientation. Good behavior is that which pleases or helps others and is approved by them. There is much conformity to stereotypical images of what is majority or "natural" behavior. Behavior is frequently judged by intention—"he means well" becomes important for the first time. One earns approval by being "nice."

Stage 4: The "law and order" orientation. There is orientation toward authority, fixed rules, and the maintenance of the social order. Right behavior consists of doing one's duty, showing respect for authority, and maintaining the given social order for its own sake.

III. Postconventional, Autonomous, or Principled Level
At this level, there is a clear effort to define moral values and principles that have validity and application apart from the authority of the groups or persons holding these principles and apart from the individual's own identification with these groups. This level also has two stages:

Stage 5: The social-contract, legalistic orientation, generally with utilitarian overtones. Right action tends to be defined in terms of general individual rights and standards which have been critically examined and agreed upon by the whole society. There is a clear awareness of the relativism of personal values and opinions and a corresponding emphasis upon procedural rules for reaching consensus. Aside from what is constitutionally and democratically agreed upon, the right is a matter of personal "values" and "opinion." The result is an emphasis upon the "legal point of view," but with an emphasis upon the possibility of changing law in terms of rational considerations of social utility (rather than freezing it in terms of Stage 4 "law and order"). Outside the legal realm, free agreement and contract is the binding element of obligation. This is the "official" morality of the American government and constitution.

Stage 6: The universal-ethical-principle orientation. Right is defined by the decision of conscience in accord with self-chosen *ethical principles* appealing to logical comprehensiveness, universality, and consistency. These principles are abstract and ethical (the Golden Rule, the categorical imperative); they are not concrete moral rules like the Ten Commandments. At heart, these are universal principles of *justice*, of the *reciprocity* and *equality* of human *rights*, and of respect for the dignity of human beings as *individual persons*. (Kohlberg, 1971, pp. 164-165.)

Given that people have the psychological capacity to progress to higher (and therefore more adequate) stages of moral reasoning, Kohlberg and Mayer (1972) have argued that the aim of education ought to be the personal development of students toward more complex ways of reasoning. This philosophical argument is based on the earlier contributions of John Dewey. Like Piaget, Dewey's idea of development does not reflect an increase in the *content* of thinking (e.g., cultural values) but instead, qualitative transformations in the *form* of the child's thought or action. Kohlberg has elaborated this basic distinction:

> What we examine in our work has to do with form rather than content. We are not describing or classifying what people think is right or wrong in situations of moral conflict, for example, whether draft-evading exiles should be given amnesty or thrown in prison if and when they return to this country, or even changes in what individuals think as they grow older. Nor are we assuming that we can specify a certain behavioral response as necessarily "moral" (in the descriptive or category sense, as distinguished from non-moral), for example, "cheating," and then discuss moral development in terms of the frequency with which individuals engage in this behavior as they grow older, perhaps in different kinds of situations ranging from spelling tests to income tax. As distinguished from either of these two avenues of research that might be said to be dealing with moral content, our work focuses on the cognitive structures which underlie such content and give it its claim to the category "moral," where "structure" refers to "the general characteristics of shape, pattern or organization of response rather than to the rate of intensity of response or its pairing with particular stimuli," and "cognitive structure" refers to "rules for processing information or for connecting experienced events." From our point of view it is not any artificially specified set of responses, or degree of intensity of such responses, which characterizes morality as an area of study. Rather, it is the cognitive moral structurings, or the organized systems of assumptions and rules about the nature of moral-conflict situations which give such situations their meaning, that constitute the objects of our developmental study. (Boyd and Kohlberg, 1973, pp. 360-361.)

Based on this crucial difference between form and content, it is Kohlberg's argument that the aim of moral education is to stimulate people's thinking ability over time in ways which will enable them to use more adequate and complex reasoning patterns to solve moral problems.

The Teacher as Creator of Disequilibrium

Conflict Inducement

Kohlberg's definition of moral education as the facilitator of moral stage change has major implications for the role of teacher.

The first principle for classroom intervention of Kohlberg's research is that ways of thinking at each stage of development cannot be directly taught. The evidence shows that stage thinking is self-generated in interaction with the environment and changes gradually. This means that teachers must provide conditions for such self-generation as the main focus of education rather than trying to teach only the stages themselves. When a person is confronted with experiences that cannot be understood adequately, he attempts to change his way of thinking to "accommodate" the new information. The new experience interacts with the previously established cognitive structure and the building of a new structure begins. Hence, an essential condition for moral development is to provide students with experiences which "stretch" their existing thinking and thus initiate the process of defining a more adequate means for dealing with more complex experience.

Moral development results from the dialogue between the child's structures and the complexity presented by environment. This interactionist definition of moral development demands an environment which will facilitate dialogue between the self and others. The more students encounter situations of moral conflict that are not adequately resolved by their present reasoning structure, the more likely they are to develop more complex ways of thinking about and resolving such conflicts. The process of moral development involves both stimulation of reasoning to higher levels and an expansion of reasoning to new areas of thought. That is, cognitive development occurs both vertically and horizontally. Successive experiences in vertical stimulation result in structural change to the next higher stage of reasoning; and a variety of opportunities in horizontal stimulation, or *decalage* in Piaget's terms, eventuate in the application of one's present reasoning ability to different categories of cognitive and social problems.

The stimulation of moral development requires that the teacher create the conditions for specific modes of classroom interaction. Such interaction requires that students go beyond the mere sharing of information; they must reveal thoughts which concern their basic beliefs. The theory of moral development demands self-reflection stimulated by dialogue. The teacher within this framework must be concerned with four types of interaction: (a) student dialogue with self, (b) student dialogue with other students, (c) student dialogue with teacher, and (d) teacher dialogue with self. Ultimately the interaction-dialogue process is intended to stimulate reflection upon one's own thinking process. It is the student's dialogue with self that creates internal cognitive conflict. The need to resolve such conflict eventually results in development.

The teacher initiates those conditions necessary to all subsequent interaction that develops at the teacher-student, student-student, and student-with-self levels. This prerequisite does not imply that the teacher is the center and controlling force of the moral education classroom. Rather, the teacher enters the moral education classroom with deliberate and systematic pedagogical skills and acts as a catalyst whereby interaction leading to development may take place. These interactions expose students to stages of thinking about their own and thus stimulate them to move beyond their present stage of thinking.

Social Role-Taking

Exposure to social interaction is necessary for active cognitive restructuring and stage change. Such exposure must be such as to require that the student "see" the other person's point of view. Taking the perspective of others is a necessary pre-condition for moral development (Kohlberg, 1969). Selman notes that the linkage between cognitive development and moral development may be found in the ability of a person to take an increasingly differentiated view of the interaction between oneself and others (Selman, 1976). Selman suggests that role-taking ability develops in a progressive sequence prior to parallel stages of moral development.

Table 2 Parallel Structured Relations Between Social Role-Taking and Moral Judgment Stages	
Social Role-Taking Stage	**Moral Judgment Stage**
Stage 0—Egocentric Viewpoint (Age Range 3-6)*	*Stage 0—Premoral Stage*
Child has a sense of differentiation of self and other but fails to distinguish between the social perspective (thoughts, feelings) of other and self. Child can label other's overt feelings but does not see the cause and effect relation of reasons to social actions.	Judgments of right and wrong are based on good or bad consequences and not on intentions. Moral choices derive from the subject's wishes that good things happen to self. Child's reasons for his choices simply assert the choices, rather than attempting to justify them.

Social Role-Taking Stage	Moral Judgment Stage
Stage 1—Social-Informational Role Taking (*Age Range 6-8*)	*Stage 1—Punishment and Obedience Orientation*
Child is aware that other has a social perspective based on other's own reasoning, which may or may not be similar to child's. However, child tends to focus on one perspective rather than coordinating viewpoints.	Child focuses on one perspective, that of the authority or the powerful. However, child understands that good actions are based on good intentions. Beginning sense of fairness as equality of acts.
Stage 2—Self-Reflective Role Taking (*Age Range 8-10*)	*Stage 2—Instrumental Orientation*
Child is conscious that each individual is aware of the other's perspective and that this awareness influences self and other's view of each other. Putting self in other's place is a way of judging his intentions, purposes, and actions. Child can form a coordinated chain of perspectives, but cannot yet abstract from this process to the level of simultaneous mutuality.	Moral reciprocity is conceived as the equal exchange of the intent of two persons in relation to one another. If someone has a mean intention toward self, it is right for self to act in kind. Right defined as what is valued by self.
Stage 3—Mutual Role Taking (*Age Range 10-12*)	*Stage 3—Orientation to Maintaining Mutual Expectations*
Child realizes that both self and other can view each other mutually and simultaneously as subjects. Child can step outside the two-person dyad and view the interaction from a third-person perspective.	Right is defined as the Golden Rule: Do unto others as you would have others do unto you. Child considers all points of view and reflects on each person's motives in an effort to reach agreement among all participants.
*Stage 4—Social and Conventional System Role-Taking*** (*Age Range 12-15 +*)	*Stage 4—Orientation to Society's Perspective*
Person realizes mutual perspective taking does not always lead to complete understanding. Social conventions are seen as necessary because they are understood by all members of the group (the generalized other) regardless of their position, role, or experience.	Right is defined in terms of the perspective of the generalized other or the majority. Person considers consequences of actions for the group or society. Orientation to maintenance of social morality and social order.

(Selman, 1976, p. 309.)

  *Age ranges for all stages represent only an average approximation based on Selman's studies to date.

  **Higher stages of role taking and their relation to Kohlberg's Stages 5 and 6 have been defined by Byrne (1973).

A theoretical understanding of the function of role-taking is important as a basis of teacher and student behavior in the classroom. Moral conflict results from being able to take the perspective of others. The "cognitive dissonance" described by Kohlberg occurs as a result of one's own point of view being confronted by a different perspective. This conflict requires resolution. The individual realizes that his own answers to the problem are inadequate. If a person could not assume the role of another, he would see no conflict. Hence, teachers must create classroom conditions which call upon the student to practice taking the perspective of others. This involves helping students to perceive others as similar to themselves but different in respect to their specific thoughts, feelings, and ways of viewing the world. Also important is the development of the ability to see oneself from the viewpoint of others. For example, the following moral dilemma designed for elementary school children poses questions both of moral judgment and of social reasoning, or role-taking:

> Holly is an eight-year-old girl who likes to climb trees. She is the best tree-climber in the neighborhood. One day while climbing down from a tall tree, she falls off the bottom branch but doesn't hurt herself. Her father sees her fall. He is upset and asks her to promise not to climb trees any more. Holly promises.

> Later that day, Holly meets Shawn. Shawn's kitten is caught up in a tree and can't get down. Something has to be done right away or the kitten may fall. Holly is the only one who climbs trees well enough to reach the kitten, but she remembers her promise to her father.

> Role-Taking Questions:
>   1. Does Holly know how Shawn feels about the kitten?
>   2. How will Holly's father feel if he finds out she climbed the tree?
>   3. What does Holly think her father will do if he finds out that she climbed the tree?
>   4. What would you do in this situation?
> (Selman, 1976, p. 302.)

> Moral Reasoning Questions:
>   1. Should Holly rescue the kitten or should she keep her promise to her father? What is the right thing for her to do? Why?
>   2. Was it fair for Holly's father to ask her to promise never to climb trees? Why? Can you think of a promise that would be more fair to Holly?
>   3. Suppose that Holly's father asks her if she broke her promise; what should Holly say? Why?
> (Kohlberg, Selman, and Lickona, 1972, pp. 8-10.)

The teacher's understanding of role-taking is important for another reason. The development of reciprocity forms the basis of the concept of justice in Kohlberg's theory. Equality through reciprocity is conceived of at the highest stages of moral reasoning by an idealized role-taking between self and others in the social environment.* The individual's network of social relationships and social interaction forms the basis of his primary role-taking opportunities. The family, the peer group, and school are the major social institutions in which children have the opportunity to consider the viewpoint of others in making decisions and in understanding the implications of their decisions on others. The more the structure of the group is democratic, the more the individual learns to experience taking the perspective of others.

In a moral education class the teacher becomes the primary role-taker in the group. The ability of the teacher to take the perspective of each student is a vital "skill." It is all too frequent that during any teacher-student dialogue, the teacher is unaware of where the student "is coming from," or the structural characteristics of the pattern of the student's response or question. This failure often leads to a belief on both the student's and teacher's part that each is not listening to the other. But in another sense this problem is a case of misunderstanding, of not being able to make sense of the differences in the way in which the other person reasons about the same problem. The onus of failure in this regard, however, must be placed on the teacher, since developmentally the teacher will most often be in a better position to take the perspective of the student rather than the reverse. At the same time the teacher needs to create conditions in which student-student dialogue helps individuals to develop an increasingly more differentiated and integrated social role-taking perspective. This notion of taking another's perspective is especially crucial in the teaching of social science and literature; for concepts and events in this area require one to be able to make value judgments about the efficacy of social events as a result of the ability to "see" reality from as many points of view as possible.

The review of moral education studies below provides the teacher with suggestions as to how to provide opportunities in the school setting to facilitate moral development by (a) creating cognitive conflict, and (b) exploring different social perspectives. Four questions should be kept in mind in reading the summary of intervention literature:

    1. In what arrangements do teacher and students interact? (Small

---

*See John Rawls, *A Theory of Justice*, for an understanding of the Stage 6 notion of ideal reciprocal role-taking.

groups, homogeneous groups, discussions, practicums, seminars, communities, etc.)

2. What is the curriculum? (What materials or experiences are provided or structured by the teacher?)

3. What is the teacher's role? (How are students' tasks defined and supported by the teacher? What skills are important for the teacher to have?)

4. How does one assess progress? (How are overall effects measured?) (Adapted from Rest, 1974, p. 246.)

Review of Intervention Literature

A review of the research conducted in classrooms with children and adolescents at different stages of moral reasoning indicates that the prerequisite conditions for classroom interaction (i.e., conflict inducement and social role-taking), and the pedagogical methods successful in stimulating moral development are similar across groups at different ages and levels of moral reasoning. The type and structure of classroom activity which encourages cognitive dissonance necessary for stage change, however, varies considerably.

Intervention research has focused on the two critical transition periods which Kohlberg (1969) has identified as theoretically "open" periods for stimulating movement to the next stage of moral reasoning. These are development from the pre-conventional to the conventional level (around ages 10-13), and from the conventional to the post-conventional level (around ages 15-19 and into adulthood).

The basic research in moral development by Turiel (1966) and Rest (1970) also helped to form the basis for intervention studies. In analyzing the "preference" choices of subjects in responses to hypothetical moral dilemmas, these researchers found that individuals preferred reasoning that was one stage higher than their own characteristic pattern of thinking about moral dilemmas. Their results also demonstrated that individuals rejected lower stages of reasoning as inadequate to their own characteristic way of thinking. In students' preferences for stages that were two or more stages above their own, however, they tended to translate or "corrupt" the reasoning of those higher stages to fit into their own level of understanding (Rest, 1970). The implications for teacher intervention are that the teacher must: (a) understand the child's current stage of moral reasoning, (b) focus on the reasoning process in discussions, (c) help to stimulate the child's thinking, and (d) create experiences with the type of conflict that leads to awareness of the greater adequacy of the next stage (Kohlberg, Selman, and Lickona, 1972).

In addition, when children are challenged to perceive contradictions in their own thinking, they will try to generate new and better solutions to moral problems (Turiel, 1969). Turiel further explains that schools play an important role in the moral development process in that they can (a) induce "cognitive conflict" in the child's internal organization at the appropriate time and in the appropriate way, and (b) provide the proper guidance in the resolution of that conflict toward an internal reorganization at the next level of conceptualization (Turiel, 1973).

In utilizing the results of this basic research in moral development, Blatt (1970; Blatt and Kohlberg, 1975) tested the possibility of stimulating moral development through systematic educational intervention during these two "open" periods. His discussion pedagogy, based on the research on Turiel, Kohlberg, and Rest, provided the foundation for subsequent classroom research in what has become known as "leading moral discussions." Over a three-month period in each of the two studies, Blatt found that experimental groups of twelve- and sixteen-year-olds from middle-class and working-class backgrounds showed significant development in their moral reasoning ability in pre-test, post-test comparisons over non-treatment groups. This significant change as measured by the Kohlberg Moral Judgment Interview was maintained after a year.

This initial research suggested that the teacher's role in leading moral discussions was critical if students' moral development was to be affected. Further, Blatt's specific teaching techniques were systematically designed and practiced to create cognitive dissonance and to stimulate students' thinking toward the next higher stage of moral reasoning:

> [The teacher] tried to establish an atmosphere in which there was protection of freedom of expression and in which understanding of alternative views was encouraged. This involved drawing a clear line between understanding someone's point of view and agreeing with it and clarifying the issues of disagreement. . . . The experimenter made it a point to leave as much of the argument to the children as possible; he stepped in to summarize the discussion, to clarify, add to the argument and occasionally present a point of view, himself. In addition, he tried to encourage higher level children to point out why the stages below were incomplete or inadequate. (Blatt and Kohlberg, 1975, p. 133.)

Blatt's method consisted of presenting a series of moral conflicts, in the form of "classical" hypothetical moral dilemmas. As teacher, his most important contribution was to present moral reasoning at the next higher stage to that of the majority of students in the class, and on occasion to individual students whose reasoning was typically reflective of a stage different from the majority of students.

These first studies in moral education were important for several reasons. They showed: (a) that moral development could be promoted through systematic classroom discussion of moral dilemmas; (b) that stage movement could occur during the two transitional ages identified in theory as periods open to developmental change; (c) that both middle-class and disadvantaged individuals might benefit from moral discussions; and (d) that the school and peer group were effective social institutions in which to promote moral development. These efforts were the beginning of systematic curriculum development in moral education based on Kohlberg's theory.

Subsequent research has both incorporated the basic research findings of Blatt's original work and moved away from Blatt's narrow definition of teaching content (i.e., hypothetical, "classical" dilemmas) and process (i.e., posing "plus one" stage arguments).

Intervention Research with
Late Adolescents and Young Adults

The first series of moral education research which followed Blatt's studies focused on the high school adolescent and young adult. One direction of this research was the extension of Blatt's moral discussion format for the purpose of stimulating cognitive conflict. Sullivan (1975) began his review of moral education studies with a commentary on both the merits and the drawbacks of Blatt's "moral discussion" approach:

> It seems clear that a comprehensive series of educational experiences aimed at stimulating moral development would have to include moral discussions conducted in the manner described by Blatt. Both developmental theory and the empirical evidence of the Blatt studies argue for the use of such discussions.

> But in considering the Blatt approach one is struck by the singular nature of the curriculum materials employed. Brief written dilemmas obviously are useful. One may question how many such dilemmas students (or teachers) will sustain before they lose interest. More imaginative, engaging materials may also be available. (Pp. 60-61.)

In his study with adult male prison inmates Hickey (1972) introduced into such discussions "personal" moral dilemmas which related to the daily problems of prison life. With high school students Sullivan (1975) used videotape of television programs and such feature-length films as *Serpico* and *The Godfather* as vehicles for moral discussions. DiStefano (1976) combined using videotapes and films along with "personal" dilemmas in her high school psychology curriculum, which was designed to relate ethical problems to personal and sexual relationships among adolescents.

The second and most sustained effort surrounding moral education programs for adolescents involved an emphasis on psychological processes which are related to social role-taking ability. In these courses the teacher's role was to help students develop their ability to listen and communicate to others, to increase their capacity for empathy, to stimulate self-reflection, and to facilitate the movement from egocentric thinking about the self toward more differentiated patterns of thinking about self and others. The notion of egocentrism (Elkind, 1967) theoretically accompanies the transition to Piaget's stage of formal operational thinking during adolescence. Egocentric thinking causes the adolescent to be self-consciously occupied with himself, and to feel unique (and hence alienated) in regard to his specific thoughts and feelings.

The goal of affecting the moral development of adolescents by designing educational experiences based on these four psychological processes was related to a larger purpose, the stimulation of various aspects of personal development. In advocating "deliberate psychological education" for all students in school, Mosher and Sprinthall (1970, 1971) initiated with their doctoral students (Atkins, 1972; Dowell, 1971; Greenspan, 1974; Mackie, 1974) a series of systematic courses as part of the academic curriculum of the high school in response to the alienation of adolescents from school, described by Goodman (1964), Holt (1964), Jackson (1968), Kozol (1967), and others; and the failure of the "new curricula" of the 1960's (e.g., Harvard Project Social Studies, Illinois mathematics) to address the "hidden curriculum" (Silberman, 1970). Mosher and Sprinthall criticized the failure of the schools to address the personal concerns of students:

> One example of what we mean by reformulating education is a curriculum in *personal* and *human* development; a comprehensive set of educational experiences designed to affect personal, ethical, aesthetic, and philosophical development in adolescents and young adults. We believe that a powerful intellectual, social, and psychological argument can be made for such education and that the need is neither age, race nor class specific. The development of morally and emotionally sensitive human beings is by no means an exhaustive education, but it is desperately missing in our present institutions and curricula. (1971, p. 9.)

A major intention of these courses was to focus on the human life cycle, with particular emphasis on young childhood and adolescence in order to generate self-reflection and meaningful interaction with peers and adults for the purpose of affecting the student's development.

Two types of programs that were a part of these first efforts to promote psychological education in high schools were found to have an effect on adolescents' moral development: courses in peer counseling and cross-age tutoring. Both of these curricula involved experiences in which adolescents could try out responsible roles to facilitate an understanding of the perspective and feelings of others. Kohlberg's theory supports the notion that "role-taking opportunities" have the potential to affect the moral development of adolescents:

> Each state is both a cause and a result of a wider and more adequate process of taking the perspective of others, personal and societal, upon social conflicts. (1974, pp. 34-35.)

> Processes responsible for social development are theoretically different from those responsible for development of physical concepts because they require role-taking. Since persons and institutions are "known" through role-taking, social-structural influences on cognitive-structural aspects of social development may be best conceived in terms of variations in the amount, kind and structure of role-taking opportunities. (1969, p. 414.)

In their peer counseling courses Dowell (1971) and Mackie (1974) highlighted several important psychological processes related to role-taking ability: (a) listening and communication skills, (b) the recognition of conflicting thoughts and feelings, and (c) the ability to experience empathy for the feelings of another person. Effective teaching strategies designed by Dowell and Mackie to relate closely to these psychological processes included personal self-introductions by students and the teacher, role play (by students taking the roles of counselor and client), and the analysis of tape recordings of simulated and real peer counseling sessions. Dowell extended the counseling of real problems among students in the course to include the opportunity to counsel junior-high and high school students outside the class as well.

Trying out real roles was an integral part of cross-age tutoring courses which were also designed to stimulate adolescents' moral development through role-taking. The high school adolescents in Atkins' (1972) course, for example, tutored young children in primary school for one semester and discussed their tutoring experience in weekly seminars.

A third area of research in moral education has involved designing curricula with specific attention to the ethical and philosophical foundations of Kohlberg's theory of moral development. A major purpose of such studies is to stimulate late adolescents to think beyond the conventional level of moral reasoning by considering moral principles, which form the foundation for post-conventional reasoning. Two studies centering on the teaching of ethics and moral philosophy to high school students (Beck, Sullivan, and Taylor, 1972) and college freshmen and sophomores (Boyd, 1976) showed that an ethics course which stresses that students practice *reasoning* about complex moral problems can be important for affecting the difficult transition to post-conventional thinking that seldom reaches full maturity in adulthood.

Sullivan (1975) combined the most significant educational experiences gleaned from all three of these approaches into a year-long psychology course, for the purpose of stimulating both the ego and moral development of high school adolescents. Both the stimulation of cognitive conflict and adolescents' ability to take the perspective of others were stressed as important teaching strategies. Basing his rationale on the significant impact of moral discussions, real role-taking (i.e., peer counseling and cross-age teaching), and the study of ethical theory and philosophy, Sullivan designed a carefully conceived sequence of educational experiences for a group of fourteen juniors and seniors. He began his course with personal introductions by students, during which Sullivan highlighted the ethical aspects of the students' autobiographical presentations. The second segment of the course included the discussion of moral dilemmas in such feature-length films as *Serpico*, *On the Waterfront*, *The Godfather*, and short excerpts from older film classics like *Abandon Ship* and *I Never Sang For My Father* ("Searching for Values," Learning Corporation of America). This format was an attempt to apply the pedagogical techniques of Blatt to high-interest and "personal" dilemmas. The third phase of the course was training in peer counseling, designed as preparation in listening and communication skills to facilitate a practicum in leading moral discussions with elementary school children later in the course. Fourth, Sullivan organized an introduction to moral philosophy which included a presentation of Kohlberg's theory of moral development. Understanding the theory was an important preparation for the practicum, which was the last part of the curriculum. Sullivan himself attended many of the discussion sessions in the sixth-grade classrooms, in which his students showed filmstrips (Guidance Associates) depicting unresolved moral dilemmas and then led moral discussions with the young children. The high school students then evaluated their teaching and in their psychology class speculated on the level of the children's moral reasoning. Sullivan underscored the value of this practicum experience for the adolescents:

> In summary, the adolescents encountered many of the same problems which beginning teachers experience, e.g., getting students to interact with one another and not the teacher all the time, maintaining discipline, asking specific questions, listening to and understanding children, etc. Since they were also leading moral discussions, they had an additional set of skills to learn, e.g., how to recognize stage arguments, how to make arguments one stage above a child's, how to probe for moral reasoning, how to keep the children from avoiding the dilemma, etc. (p. 173.)

Another vital developmental experience for the students in the course was the spontaneous organization of the students to create a board of appeals in their high school. Sullivan identified the importance of the adolescents' opportunity to experience meaningful interaction with the major institutions of their society as well as to heighten their awareness of moral issues if they were to be stimulated to reason beyond conventional levels of moral reasoning. Since the consistency between judgment and action is more likely at Stage 5 and 6, which are based on moral *principles* (Kohlberg and Turiel, 1971), the adolescent's opportunity to practice commitment to an ideology is an essential experience for moral development during late adolescence (Kohlberg, 1972).

Sullivan's (1975) work pointed to the significance of the cumulative effect of all four types of experiences for adolescents over a year's time. Moral discussions, the opportunity to try out real roles, learning about ethical theory, and participation in affecting the institutions of which they were a part, were effective experiences for adolescent development. The results of his study were highly significant (p. <.001) both in the development of students' moral reasoning and in their ego development.

In summary, the studies which were designed as systematic developmental experiences for late adolescents and young adults demonstrated that moral development could be stimulated through a variety of meaningful activities, carefully conceptualized in close relationship to cognitive developmental theory. The discussion of moral dilemmas moved away from Blatt's original presentation of hypothetical dilemmas to the discussion of personalized dilemmas, drawn from both the real concerns and problems of students, and fictitious case studies and film which closely simulated autobiographical moral conflicts. The experience of trying out new roles which demanded responsibility to others and to the society at large was another effective activity which stimulated moral development (and often ego development as well) during adolescence. *The psychological processes which these experiences affected were the stimulation of cognitive dissonance through the interaction of different levels of complexity in students' patterns of thinking, and the expansion of the adolescent's ability to understand the perspective of others through empathy and taking the role of others.* "Roletaking" involved both real social experiences and what Kohlberg (1974) calls "vicarious symbolic role-taking opportunities." For the latter, students are asked hypothetically to take the perspective of each character in a dilemma, to imagine what each character thinks the other people in the dilemma should do, and finally to place oneself in the framework of mediator among all characters' rights and claims in the situation.

These studies also suggested that educational experiences which affected adolescents' moral reasoning often had a parallel effect on other strands of development, especially ego development (Dowell, 1971; Sullivan, 1975). Additional aspects of moral development which were noticed as outcomes of these courses were suggested in the discussion of descriptive findings: students' heightened awareness of moral issues in their lives, the interrelationship between that heightened awareness of those issues and the stimulation of moral reasoning, the development of awareness and practice of taking the perspective of others, and the initiation of "moral action," or responsibility taken on behalf of others.

Intervention Research at the Elementary and Junior-High School Levels

Curricula designed for children and early adolescents at the transition from pre-conventional to conventional moral reasoning at Stages 2 and 3 centered around moral issues related to friendship, the peer group, family, and dyadic or small-group interaction (Grimes, 1974; Paolitto, 1975), as opposed to more abstract notions of obligations to institutionalized rules and societal norms, which were appropriate to high school adolescents at the conventional level of moral reasoning. Educational activities designed by curriculum developers for upper-elementary and junior-high school students, therefore, reflect the researchers' knowledge of these developmental differences. Blatt's basic moral discussion format, first tested with twelve- and thirteen-year-olds, was modified considerably by Grimes and Paolitto to encompass experiential, activity-oriented components.

Based on the research of Holstein (1969), Grimes (1974) recognized the influence of the family in the moral education of the elementary school child. In her study with 53 middle-class families, Holstein found a significant correlation between the mother's level of moral reasoning and that of her pre-adolescent son or daughter. Grimes was interested in comparing the effect of teaching moral discussions to a group of eleven-year-old children who were at the transitional period to conventional moral reasoning, to the effect of teaching a similar course to children of the same age whose mothers also participated in the course. She compared these two classes to a third non-treatment group from the same school. Grimes found that children in the mother-child course showed even more significant development in their moral reasoning from pre-test to post-test on Kohlberg's Moral Judgment Interview than those children in the moral education course without their mothers. The non-treatment group showed no statistically significant growth in moral reasoning. Grimes' study indicated the effectiveness of training mothers to be moral educators to promote the cognitive development of their children.

The curriculum in Grimes' study centered around the stimulation of cognitive conflict and perspective-taking through moral discussion and role play. Many dilemmas used during her course were designed by mother and child together, often with the help of other family members. "The Ice Cream Dilemma" is one such example:

> You know the ticket for the free ice cream you get from Baskin-Robbins [an ice cream chain] for your birthday? . . .
>
> Well, I wrote my name down just once to get one and I got three in the mail. The moral problem is should I keep them or should I bring the two extra ones back. This is a real one. It happened to me. I have them at home. (Grimes, 1974, p. 63.)

An example of how the inducement of cognitive conflict can lead to moral stage change over time occurred during the discussion of this dilemma. When presented with several examples of Stage 3 solutions to this dilemma, a boy who had primarily used Stage 2 thinking to resolve the dilemma "became quite agitated":

Leader: "Why switch, you liked your reason a minute ago."
David: "I still like my reason but I like her reason more."
Leader: "Why?"
David: "Her reason is bigger and so it includes my reason."
(Grimes, 1974, p. 65.)

During the last part of her course the children became actively involved in writing and producing "morality plays," in which both mothers and children took the roles of characters in various dilemmas which they designed. They spontaneously "acted out" the dilemmas by portraying each character's point of view, feelings, and solution to a given moral problem. Grimes' study indicated that role play was an effective way to engage in role-taking.

In designing a one-semester moral education program at the junior-high level, Paolitto (1975) also focused on the importance of role-taking experiences which would be appropriate developmental experiences for early adolescents. In the first segment of the course, Paolitto introduced students to the discussion of both hypothetical and "personal" moral dilemmas through small-group discussion, film, journal writing, and role play. In the second part of the curriculum the students learned to communicate moral issues to each other by role playing, writing their own dilemmas, and learning to conduct interviews based on those student-designed dilemmas. The last part of the course involved the core of the "role-taking opportunities." Students conducted interview discussions of the moral dilemmas they designed specifically for people in various school roles, including custodian, principal, cafeteria worker, house master, and guidance counselor. One such student-designed dilemma that was discussed with the custodian was:

The custodian gave a boy a key to the teachers' room to buy a coke, but when the custodian got the key back, he found there was some money missing from the teachers' room.

Questions:
1. What should the custodian do? Why?
2. Who is responsible for the money being taken—the boy, the custodian, or the teacher who left it there? Why?
3. What is the importance of trust in this situation? What does trust mean to you?
4. What does the boy think the custodian is thinking? What is the custodian thinking? (Paolitto, 1975, p. 366.)

Next they discussed moral decisions which faced representatives of various institutions which affected the students' lives in a direct way in their neighborhood community. These people included a nun, pediatrician, waitress, juvenile lawyer, and fireman.

All these discussions centered on the importance of learning to take the perspective of each person in the dilemmas, as well as the students' own ways of solving the conflicts. Paolitto concentrated on the importance of planning and evaluation through the use of tape recordings and role play, and the development of effective group interaction to generate self-reflection and cognitive conflict. A pre-test, post-test comparison showed a significant difference at the .01 level of significance in the group's movement from pre-conventional to conventional moral reasoning over that of a non-treatment class from the same population, also taught by Paolitto.

Grimes and Paolitto designed their moral education programs around the developmental theory and research of this younger age group. Structured role play was identified by both researchers as particularly important to expand the ability of students to understand the perspective of others. Social perspective-taking in the younger child is limited to understanding the point of view of one or two other people simultaneously (or a small group at the most), rather than the perspective of a whole group or society in general, as in adolescence and adulthood (Byrne, 1973). Since the development of role-taking is a necessary prerequisite for a parallel development in moral reasoning (Selman, 1969, 1971), the opportunity to expand one's perspective at this age level is important to prevent fixation of moral development at lower stages.

Implications of Intervention Literature

The careful design, implementation, and evaluation of pilot research in moral education has been cautious but optimistic in order to lay a substantial foundation for the expansion of developmental education programs in schools. A review of this literature at the young adult, high school, junior-high, and elementary levels indicates that the initial intervention research has been conducted by university faculty and advanced doctoral students who have a sophisticated knowledge of moral development theory and psychology, teaching and counseling skills, and subject-matter expertise in the related disciplines of social science and philosophy. The question must therefore be asked if it is possible for the "average" classroom teacher to develop and teach curriculum which is effective in the stimulation of the moral development of students.

The first important issue to consider regards the research methodology of these initial studies. The pilot research has combined quantitative methods of pre-test, post-test design with one or more comparison groups, along with descriptive evaluation methods which combine clinical and formative evaluation procedures. Although research based on a statistical comparison between only two or three groups limits the generalizability of such studies, other methodological factors suggest similar developmental effects across different studies. The various curriculum interventions suggest that it is possible to stimulate the moral reasoning ability of students through classroom learning for these reasons: (a) nearly all research interventions showed significant group mean differences at the .01 level, (b) the same pedagogical techniques (e.g., moral discussion, peer counseling) were successfully employed by many different experimenters, and (c) these same intervention strategies were tested with groups at different ages, with different racial and socioeconomic backgrounds, and in different settings (e.g., schools and prisons).

In addition to the measurement of moral judgment, careful documentation of the pedagogical techniques and the effect of curriculum activities on students through clinical evaluation procedures meant that actual student-teacher interactions were recorded and critically analyzed for application in future work. Teacher and student journals, audio-visual tape recordings, systematic observations by participant recorders, written curriculum evaluations, and a variety of unobtrusive measures have been the rich sources of valuable data on the process of interaction that occurs in a moral education classroom.

One of the major outcomes of the extensive planning and evaluation procedures of this pioneer work in moral education has been the realization of the need to link other strands of developmental theory (e.g., ego and social development) to moral education curricula to foster a broader conception of intervention toward affecting human development (Sullivan, 1974; Mosher, 1975). Careful documentation of the teaching process as it affects students' moral development will hopefully provide valuable insights into the most effective ways to stimulate other areas of human development.

There exists the potential for public school teachers and counselors to practice moral education in the schools à la Kohlberg. Such activities as role play and interviewing, highlighted in the review of intervention research, remind us that these teaching techniques are currently within the repertoire of competent, creative teachers whose classrooms are not the focus of moral education programs to date. Further, the most recent approach to stimulating moral development through systematic intervention is in the area of integrating the discussion of moral dilemmas into existing curricula, rather than through the development of separate psychology or social studies courses (Ladenburg, 1977). Currently, courses in English literature, American history and social studies, and guidance are being revised in the Boston area (Brookline, Cambridge, Hyde Park); Pittsuurgh; Tacoma, Washington; and Toronto Public Schools to add the Kohlbergian moral discussion approach to other already existing goals and learning methods.

Kohlberg, Colby and Fenton (1975), for example, conducted an initial pilot study in American history classes in the Boston and Pittsburgh areas. After a one-week teacher education workshop to introduce the theory and pedagogy of moral education to teachers in the study, each teacher participant led moral discussions in the context of their history curriculum over the course of twenty weeks. In a pre-test, post-test design with an equal number of comparison groups from the same school districts, the results indicated a significant increase in the students' stages of moral reasoning in the experimental classes. A significant finding of this study was the fact that probing questions by teachers was a critical behavior in causing stage change (Kohlberg, 1975).

Besides stimulating the moral development of adolescents, this preliminary research suggested (a) that the tenets of rational discussion can be taught effectively to teachers, (b) that the inductive moral discussion approach can be integrated into an existing social studies curriculum by adding a non-indoctrinaire approach to moral issues in American history and government, and (c) that the humanities provide a teaching area compatible with developmental goals. Curriculum developed by so-called moral education "experts" as well as by more traditional subject-matter "experts" both have the potential to be effective in stimulating the moral development of adolescents.

At the elementary school level Kohlberg, Selman, and Lickona (1972) have made these pedagogical techniques available to teachers through a series of filmstrips which pose concrete but open-ended moral dilemmas of concern and interest to young children. Dilemmas such as the following example are presented to young children in a filmstrip format for small-group discussion with the teacher for the purpose of eliciting the children's way of reasoning:

Alex has been visiting Russell on his farm for a week during school vacation. Every day the boys have gone horseback riding. Russell has been riding King and Alex has been riding Midget, the little pony. Russell has promised Alex that if he practices riding on the pony all week, he can try riding the big horse, King, on the last day of his visit. However, Russell's older brother, Zack, needs King to compete in a horse show. What is more important—Russell's promise to Alex or Zack's 4-H Club competition? (Kohlberg, Selman, and Lickona, 1972, p. 8.)

Based on Blatt's initial pedagogy, Kohlberg, Selman, and Lickona have suggested developmental teaching strategies adapted for this younger age group. These include preserving the moral conflict, focusing on reasons, encouraging role-taking, modifying the dilemma to elicit higher stages of reasoning, encouraging children who are undecided, and helping children to develop group listening and communication skills.

An initial pilot study to test the effects of this filmstrip-discussion approach was conducted with sixty-eight second graders from working- and middle-class families to determine both (a) whether such filmstrips and follow-up discussions were effective methods for stimulating moral reasoning, and (b) whether the children's stage change was greater in the groups led by teachers who were experienced in a cognitive developmental framework as compared to those groups having a "lay teacher who has only read the manual and instructions" (Selman and Lieberman, 1975, p. 713). Although the change scores on Kohlberg's Moral Judgment Interview of the two experimental groups were significant over a third comparison group, the results indicated no significant difference between the groups with the two different types of teacher expertise. These results suggested "that the process of group discussion, and not the knowledge of cognitive developmental theory, is of greater importance" (Selman and Lieberman, 1975, p. 716). *Both* teacher competency and moral discussion pedagogy are suggested as important for stimulating students' moral reasoning ability.

The possibility that competent teachers and counselors in the mainstream of public school education can effectively implement programs in moral education raises the question of what successful teacher behavior has been identified from all these pilot studies which would contribute to the likelihood of wide dissemination of these programs.

A Concept of Teaching

The review of literature suggests various developmental strategies for teaching to stimulate moral development: moral discussions, role playing, peer counseling, discussing ethical philosophy, cross-age tutoring, and interviewing. Common to each of the intervention strategies is a prior conception of teaching which led to subsequent steps of an approach to planning and implementation. This conception is based on the notion of teacher as developmental educator wherein conflict inducement and social role-taking are constructs important to the teaching process in order to facilitate development. The research indicates that the teacher who intends to stimulate moral development needs to do some careful thinking along several main dimensions. As in any area of teaching, the moral educator needs to acquire a certain body of knowledge; in this case, knowledge of the theory of moral development and of applied research in the pedagogy known to stimulate moral development. Unlike other fields of teaching, however, the moral educator becomes more than a specialist in a specific body of knowledge. *The teacher's knowledge of development is the starting point and the means by which interaction is stimulated between what is inside the student's head and what exists in the world.*

The teacher's task is to empower developmental theory with substantive meaning for a specific population who are at a certain period in their development. In other words, the teacher needs to think about the developmental characteristics of a particular group of children or adolescents with whom one is working (Mosher, 1975). The more that a teacher's developmental knowledge about a particular group of children or adolescents is specific and defined, the more likely will educational experiences designed to stimulate development be effective. The junior-high school teacher working with children at the transition to conventional moral reasoning ability, for example, will be thinking about educational experiences effective in stimulating their development to a conventional moral reasoning. These consist of moral conflicts surrounding friendships, family, or other small groups of people which tend to elicit Stage 3 reasoning. An example of such a moral dilemma follows:

A father and his son were watching a professional hockey game on T.V. They were supporting different teams. The son said to the father, "I bet that team X will win." The father said, "No, team Y will win. I will bet ten dollars." So they both agreed to bet. If the father wins, he will take away his son's allowance; if he loses, he will double it.

The father lost, but he refused to give his son ten dollars. The father said that he needed the money to fix his car.

1. Does the father, because of his authority, have the right to break his promise?
2. Which is worse, father breaking his promise to a son, or son to father?
3. Why should a promise be kept?

(Grimes, 1974, p. 125.)

On the other hand, the teacher working with high school seniors, who are likely to be at the conventional level of moral reasoning, needs to consider situational conflicts which are very different. Issues focusing on the law and the right to life, for example, relate to the developmental stages of this group of adolescents, who are ready to take an abstract perspective from a legal or societal point of view. One such dilemma might be:

Mr. and Mrs. Jones belonged to a religious group called the Christian Scientists. They believed that if someone was sick or was going to die it was God's will and they should not question it. As a result, they did not believe in going to a doctor or in taking medicine even when someone was dying.

One day their son Mark, who was nine years old, got a terrible stomach pain while he was in school. The school doctor rushed Mark to the hospital where it was learned that Mark had appendicitis and needed an operation immediately. However, Mark's parents would not consent to an operation. The doctor knew that he could go to court and get the court to sign the consent papers, but by that time Mark might be dead. If he didn't go to the court and operated on Mark, he would be breaking the law.

1. What should or what would be right for the doctor to do? Why?
2. Should the parents have the right to make the decision in this case? If the answer is no, why does the law exist that says the parents must give their permission for the operation?
3. Is it right that a court order can override the parents? Why?
4. Should the doctor consider what Mark wants? Why?
5. What should be the right of the parents? What decisions should they be able to make for their children? In making this decision, consider how you would feel (1) as a parent, (2) as a child, and (3) as a doctor.

(Blatt, Colby, and Speicher, 1974, "Parents' Rights.")

But even prior to the design of such classroom activities appropriate to the developmental level of students is a fundamental assumption underlying effective moral education classrooms: *that establishing an accepting classroom atmosphere in which fairness, trust, respect, and empathy are intentionally fostered is a precondition to stimulating moral development.*

Preconditions for Moral Development in the Classroom

The stimulation of moral development requires a focus on skills which help the teacher create the conditions for specific modes of classroom interaction. Such interaction requires that students go beyond the mere sharing of information; they must reveal their thoughts and feelings about basic beliefs. Moral development results from self-reflection and dialogue. An atmosphere is required in which self-disclosure may take place.

The dialogue process is in reality creative confrontation with self and others. Such a process involves a high degree of risk taking, on the part of both the teacher and the student. Teachers who have been used to operating as THE AUTHORITY, not sharing their beliefs or reasons for those beliefs openly, might find it difficult to accept such an atmosphere. No less threatening might such a classroom seem to students who are oriented toward teacher-approved behavior, and who in the process also worry about their classmates' opinion of them. Miller (1972) characterizes this attitude:

> Not only is the teacher-student relationship often an impersonal one, but institutional pressures encourage lack of communication among the students. Because the emphasis in many classes is on discipline and control, the students learn not to communicate with one another except in the manner prescribed by the teacher. As Jackson puts it, "In a sense, then, students must try to behave as if they were in solitude, when in point of fact they are not." (p. 113.)

Jules Henry further illustrates the nature of the problem in a fifth grade arithmetic class.

> Boris had trouble reducing $12/16$ to the lowest terms, and could only get as far as $6/8$. The teacher asked him quietly if that was as far as he could reduce it. She suggested he "think." Much heaving up and down and waving of hands by the other children, all frantic to correct him. Boris pretty unhappy, probably mentally paralyzed. The teacher quiet, patient, ignores the others and concentrates with look and voice on Boris. After a minute or two she turns to the class and says, "Well, who can tell Boris what the number is?" A forest of hands appear, and the teacher calls Peggy. Peggy says that four may be divided into the numerator and the denominator. (1963, pp. 295-296.)

Henry then comments on this observation:

> Boris' failure made it possible for Peggy to succeed; . . . his misery is
> the occasion for her rejoicing. This is the standard condition. . . .
> School metamorpheses the child, giving it the kind of Self the school
> can manage and then proceeds to administer to the self it has made. (p.
> 296.)

This phenomenon of student isolation and eventual withdrawal
may also be understood through Kohlberg's moral development
framework. Conditions which inhibit social interaction in the classroom are not conducive to moral development. Although it is possible to facilitate the development of post-conventional or autonomous moral reasoning in adolescence (Stages 5 and 6) (Beck, Sullivan, and Taylor, 1972; Boyd, 1976), it can be asserted that forcing
students into merely passive receptors of "truth" from the authority
called "teacher" creates conditions which reinforce students to operate at pre-conventional (Stages 1 and 2) and conventional (Stages 3
and 4) levels. Henry's observation above exemplifies the problem
that schools teach students to succeed at another person's expense.
This practice encourages a Stage 2 notion of justice, one which
causes a person to view others in terms of one's own needs. When
schools demand adherence to external authority as the sole arbiter
of moral decision-making, they can be said to thwart movement
toward post-conventional development. "In sum, an institutional
morality which supports instrumental hedonism and action in accor-
dance with external expectations is not conducive to moral development and the eventuality of autonomy" (Miller, 1972, p. 113).

In contrast, several conditions are fundamental to an environment which will stimulate moral development: fairness, trust, respect, and empathy. These fundamentals have been part of the
classroom components identified with effective teaching in general
(Hunt and Metcalf, 1968; Lewin, 1948) and are not restricted only to
classrooms which provide stimulation of students' moral reasoning.
An analysis of each of these preconditions is precluded by the scope
of this article.* Several statements can be discussed, however,
which relate to the importance of these prerequisites in the context
of a developmental classroom.

First, a classroom with these prerequisites does not simply

---

*A detailed review of these classroom conditions can be found in Chapters 25
and 29 of Lawrence Kohlberg's *Collected Papers on Moral Development and Moral
Education*, Volume II, 1975.

"happen" as a result of students and teacher being together over time. The teacher is instrumental in creating an accepting atmosphere by modeling specific behaviors from the very first teacher-student interaction that takes place. Students are often not accustomed to participating in discussions which center on listening to one another's opinions. It may take, for example, five minutes or more to help and encourage all students to maneuver their chairs to be seated as members of a circle. In addition, students sometimes "yell out" their responses and impulsively interrupt each other without realizing it. Time must be taken as part of the core of the moral education classroom to teach listening and communication skills.

Second, it takes time for these accepting conditions to develop in a moral education classroom, especially among students who are at the pre-conventional level of moral reasoning. That is to say that *development* takes time. Certain activities, like role plays and interviews require the group to cooperate in order to organize themselves effectively in deciding what to do and what is fair to expect of each other in accomplishing a task. For students to learn to evaluate their own dilemmas, role play "productions" and videotaped discussions means that critical self-reflection and evaluation of others are encouraged in relation to developmental goals.

Third, understanding what the students in the class are experiencing *from their point of view* is a critical aspect of all four of these preconditions. By virtue of the teacher's own developmental difference as an adult, he or she has a different social perspective, personal and emotional perspective, and probably a different moral reasoning level than the students. The teacher brings interpersonal and pedagogical skills into the classroom which hopefully reflect this more complex developmental pattern. Recognition of this difference is fundamental to all other areas of creating an accepting climate within which student development can take place, since the teacher needs to be able to comprehend the perspectives of the students and thereby stimulate their thinking to more complex levels. The reverse of this process is not likely to be true, however. That is, the students may not have the ability to take the cognitive perspective of the adult. In this very crucial sense, the teacher is therefore a "first among equals" (Sullivan, 1975), not simply one among equals.

The development of these qualities of fairness, trust, respect, and empathy is basic to establishing an atmosphere which stimulates cognitive conflict and social role-taking ability. Assuming that these core conditions are established in a moral education classroom, what might a teacher do differently from a "traditional" classroom teacher who has also established these fundamentals? Such a difference may be seen in the analysis of the discussion of moral dilemmas.

The Teacher as Moral Discussion Leader

As the review of literature indicates, moral discussions may act as primary catalysts for dialogue, conflict inducement, the stimulation of perspective-taking, and eventually structural development. The teacher needs to develop enough competence to facilitate a discussion among students which elicits different stages of moral reasoning:

> Regardless of the specific techniques used in conducting a moral discussion, however, the processes of confronting a dilemma, taking a tentative position, and examining and reflecting on the reasoning behind various positions remain essential activities. Crucial, too, are the student-to-student interaction, the constant focus on moral issues and reasoning, and the emphasis on a supportive trusting, informal classroom atmosphere. The extent to which the teacher can direct the entire process without assuming an expository or authoritarian role largely determines the success of a moral discussion. (Beyer, 1976, p. 200.)

In other words, the teacher must learn to keep in mind the various stages of reasoning reflected in the students' discourse. This approach also includes the fact that students often move between different stages in their thinking and that they often seek to avoid issues or entangle themselves in a web of hypothetical complexity which may result in frustration.

The discussion of moral dilemmas is a new experience for most children and adolescents in a moral education environment (Grimes, 1974; Paolitto, 1975; Sullivan, 1975). Dilemmas are often not perceived as such by students because parents and teachers make decisions for students before situations have the potential to become those of conflicting obligation or choice. In addition, children at the first level of moral development (Stages 1 and 2) respond to external rules in making moral decisions and therefore do not see a separation of self from external sources of judgment. Moral conflict often does not exist at Stage 1 because, after all, "It's wrong to steal, period." Confusion is also evident when students create moral dilemmas out of non-moral situations. As one thirteen-year-old described, "Of course whether to paint your bike blue or green can be a very important moral dilemma! I'd paint my bike from green to blue any day to hide it if I stole it!"

In the initial phases of leading moral discussions, the teacher must be very active in teaching a process of inquiring into moral issues. Helping students to recognize that they are indeed thoughtful reasoners and to articulate elements of conflict in a situation are important first steps for students to experience. The teacher's role as questioner to elicit moral reasoning is evident in the following moral dilemma discussion with eighth graders. In this excerpt a group from the class have just finished role playing for the other students a dilemma concerning whether a policeman ought to arrest a friend of his whom he sees on the road as a drunken driver:

Ruth:	(Narrator) What would be the best and most important reason for the policeman not to report his friend?
Ramon:	(Audience) 'Cause he'd lose the friendship!
Jeff:	(Audience) Yeah.
Peter:	(Audience) Yeah, if they put him in jail overnight, what would happen to his wife?
[Teacher]:	Are there any other reasons not to arrest him?
Angela:	(Audience) No! He should be.
[Teacher]:	What would be the best reasons to arrest him?
Patty:	(Policeman) For drunken driving—.
Brian:	(Audience) 'Cause the police chief said so.
Patty:	Disturbing the peace—.
Brian:	He didn't disturb the peace yet!
[Teacher]:	Brian, what do you think is the best reason?
Brian:	'Cause the chief told him to arrest drunken drivers.
[Teacher]:	And if you don't?
Brian:	The policeman could get in trouble.
Sarah:	(Audience) He won't get into trouble if he doesn't follow the car, but still, if you get the job as policeman, you're still expected to.
Mei-ling:	(Audience) If he gets into an accident or something, it's kind of his responsibility. It's kind of his responsibility for not stopping him.
[Teacher]:	Responsibility in what way?
Mei-ling:	It's kinda like if a bartender kept giving someone a drink when he's drunk, it's *his* responsibility.
Teacher:	I'm kind of thinking, too, of a comment Luther made the first week when we talked about pulling a chair out

from somebody, and you said, Luther, it was the responsibility of the *group*, not just the teacher and the
two students who were fighting. Is this sort of similar,
Mei-ling?

(Silence; everyone listening closely.)
Mei-ling: Yeah—. . . .

(Paolitto, 1975, pp. 237-239.)

Posing questions that provoke cognitive conflict as a result of
exposure to more complex ways of seeing the world than the students' own (i.e., a higher stage of reasoning) is a second stage in the
teaching process. The teacher has the responsibility of insuring that
students are exposed to the stage of reasoning above their own. This
the teacher may do by either utilizing his or her own higher stage
arguments. In addition, since classrooms normally contain students
at a variety of stages of reasoning, the teacher can elicit those same
higher-stage arguments from students as well. In a later part of the
same discussion with the eighth-grade students above, both teacher
and students posed a higher-stage response to Brian's Stage 1 reason:

Brian: [Mei-ling] said it would be Patty's [policeman in the
            role play] responsibility because she didn't stop and
            take him in, but if she stopped him and put him in a cab
            and told the cab driver not to stop but to take him
            home, then the cab driver's not drunk—so there
            wouldn't be an accident.

[Teacher]: What if the police chief found out?

Brian: He could say, "Well, at least you didn't let him go, and
            you *did* send him home—.

[Teacher]: He wouldn't be in as much trouble? [Referring to
            Brian's reason of avoiding trouble given earlier, re-
            flecting Stage 1.]

Brian: Yeah, instead of if he just said, "Go on, I'm not going
            to stop you."

[Teacher]: What if he said, in talking to the police chief, "Well, I
            didn't do it this time, but if you let me go and not report
            me or take my salary away," and the police chief says
            to the policeman, "OK, but the next time I'll have to
            report it—, in other words, if you do this favor for me
            this time, the next time I'll do it as a favor for you—?"
            [Stage 2 argument.]

Brian: But it's not really a *favor*—I mean it's just that if the
              guy didn't do nothin'—.
Sarah: You could get *fired* for it!
Brian: But he didn't do nothin' wrong yet, except that he was
              drunken driving. He could send him home; it's just like
              takin' his keys away and givin' 'em back in the morn-
              ing. [Suggestive of Stage 2.]
Mary Ann:(Audience) But what's to prevent him from going out
              again and doing it again? [Pointing out the inadequacy
              of a Stage 2 solution.]
Ramon: Yeah!
Angela: But why would he go out drinking? There's no reason
              for it.
Brian: His wife is very sick!
Maria: (Audience) Isn't he under strain?
Angela: But that's no way to solve it.
Brian: But it makes you feel better.
Teacher: True enough. Time for one more comment.
Mary Ann:But if Patty [policeman] goes up to the police chief and
              says, "Come on and do me a favor" and everything;
              well, if you're just talking about Patty and the police
              chief . . . but then what about if the *Mayor* finds out?
              Then Luther [the police chief] is also tied in and gets
              responsible. He's letting Patty off 'cause Patty's let
              him off. That's easy not to say anything and drop the
              whole matter. Then if Kathy [the Mayor] found out,
              Kathy might get mad at Luther or something and just
              get a whole big chain reaction if she lets him off the
              hook. [Also pointing out the inadequacy of a Stage 2
              argument by suggesting a Stage 3 notion of responsibil-
              ity.]
Luther: (Police Chief) Well, first of all, if she did come up and
              say that, I *doubt* if I would make a deal with her, but if
              I did, how would he ever find out in the first place?
[Teacher]: Why would you not make a deal with her?
Luther: Because it was her job to do that in the first place and it
              was my job to enforce hers.

                                          (Paolitto, 1975, pp. 239-240.)

   In this dialogue the students showed a high interest in Brian's
solution to the dilemma, and more importantly, in his *reasons* be-

hind that solution. They, not the teacher, in fact took major responsibility for maintaining the focus of the discussion as well as for pointing out the limitations of his logic by taking the perspective of other people in the dilemma (e.g., mayor, police chief) beyond the policeman alone who was faced with the dilemma. It takes time, though, for students to become the initiators of the developmental teaching process in which they too stimulate cognitive conflict and perspective-taking in one another.

When leading moral discussions for the first time, teachers often experience a disappointment that accompanies a simple "Yes" or "No" answer to a "Should" question, or a mere "Because" reply to a "Why?" question. A paucity of response is particularly true from students who are not highly articulate or verbal. The sequencing of qualitatively different types of questions and comments is therefore important for the teacher to consider:

(1) *Asking "Why?" questions.* Asking why somebody should resolve a certain moral conflict in a particular way helps students identify situations as dilemmas which require resolution from a conflict of choice. Such questions also, of course, elicit one's level of moral reasoning more easily than most other types of questions. Questions like, "Why do you think your solution to the dilemma is a good one?" or "What is the main reason you decided to resolve the problem as you did?" are two examples.

(2) *Complicating the circumstances.* Adding new situations to the original dilemma increases thoughtful, differentiated responses to a problem, and often stimulates higher stages of reasoning. This strategy also helps students to avoid "escape hatches." "Escape hatches" involve changing the nature of the facts of the dilemma, thereby effectively solving the dilemma by eliminating it as a conflict situation. For example, in a dilemma concerning the decision to throw certain people overboard from an overcrowded lifeboat drifting at sea, students commonly avoid confronting the dilemma by asking to tie the extra people to the side of the boat with ropes. To help students face the moral question in this case, the teacher might say, "Suppose there were no ropes in the lifeboat." The teacher might also complicate the dilemma in this instance: "Suppose holding the ropes would sink the lifeboat—if you had to choose between a mother and her eighteen-year-old son, who should be cast overboard?"

(3) *Presenting "personal" examples.* Such examples give students the realization that moral dilemmas are a part of their daily social interaction, as well as the source of many problems and solu-

tions in the society at large. "Personal" in this sense implies situations within the experience of students and the teacher. A dilemma in the news or on a television program is as much a personal one in this context as a "personal problem." If a dilemma is personal, then there is likely to be high interest and emotional investment on the part of students. Such situations give a person pause to think about daily problems in new ways. Conflicts over different people's rights in the cafeteria, corridors, and classroom are especially fruitful sources of personal dilemmas. Real dilemmas can be written and presented by students themselves, such as this example co-authored by two eighth-grade girls:

> One table of girls constantly leaves their trays on the table. Because of this the cafeteria workers say that everyone who eats that period can't have ice cream until those trays and a few other scattered trays start getting cleared on a regular basis.
>
> Unfortunately, the girls at that table don't buy ice cream anyway, so they don't care.
>
> Should everyone get deprived of ice cream because of a few people? Why or why not?
>
> What should they do now that they know the ice cream punishment isn't working? For instance, should they punish each individual who doesn't clean his or her tray, individually? Why would the solution you choose be a good one? (Paolitto, 1975, p. 362.)

(4) *Alternating real and hypothetical dilemmas.* This format helps to expand the range of the students' notion of what constitutes a moral problem. This variation also takes into account the range of student interests in the class.

Hypothetical dilemmas are imaginary conflict situations which highlight and often polarize particular rights or obligations to dramatize the *moral* components of a problem. "The Desert" (Blatt, Colby, and Speicher, 1974) is one such dilemma:

> Two people had to cross a desert. When they started, both had equal amounts of food and water. When they were in the middle of the desert, one person's water bag broke and all his water ran out. They both knew that if they shared the water they would probably die of thirst. If one had the water, that person would survive.
>
> What should they do? Give your reasons. ("Why?" question)
>
> Suppose the two people are husband and wife. Should that change the issue and the decision? (Complicating the circumstances)

Hypothetical dilemmas in early sessions of the class also help students to develop trust through sharing the common experience of discussing crucial situations. At the same time, students do not feel prematurely "pushed" toward self-disclosure before the group is ready to respond at a level of personal acceptance.

For adolescents in particular, a combination of hypothetical and real, personal dilemmas makes sense developmentally and "works" in the classroom (DiStefano, 1976). For those at the beginning stages of formal operational thinking, or Piaget's conception of abstract reasoning ability, the intriguing aspect of hypothetical dilemmas may be the abstract dimensions which they entail. Part of this development of abstract intellectual thinking involves the ability to be self-reflective. Real, personal dilemmas, therefore, can complement hypothetical dilemmas, since they stimulate reasoning about the self in relation to others. Given the self-consciousness that accompanies the discovery of self, it seems important to provide a variety of opportunities for adolescents to move between the hypothetical and the real.

The four above considerations constitute the "core" of the introduction to moral dilemma discussions. They involve an exposure to the breadth of the notion of moral dilemmas. How long the teacher concentrates his or her efforts on teaching students to consider the range of moral considerations in conflict situations depends on the nature of the particular group of students.

The second phase of a moral discussion format involves a *focus in depth*. The teacher's questioning techniques parallel this change in effort.

(1) *Presenting few questions.* Fewer questions means a sustained focus through a resolution of conflict. Questions should probe many sides of the same issue. A "Why?" question is not sufficient at this point. Students need to hear extended arguments from each other so they can understand the reasoning and challenge each other's logic. Beyer (1976) offers five types of probing questions:

1. Clarifying probe—anything from Why; to What do you mean by . . ., or Then are you saying . . .?
2. Issue-specific probe—asks student to examine their own thoughts about one of the major issues identified by Kohlberg—obligation, contract, authority.
3. Inter-issue probe—asks what to do when two issues conflict, e.g., loyalty to President vs. loyalty to Constitution; loyalty to friend vs. obligation to the law.
4. Role switch probe—asks student to put self into position of someone in the dilemma in order to get them to see other side.
5. Universal consequences probe—asking person to consider what would happen if such reasoning were applied to everyone.

Probing usually involves role-taking questions that are effective in pursuing motives, intentions, and personalities of characters in dilemmas. Spontaneous role plays when students are "stuck" trying to resolve a certain issue can be tremendously helpful. Students are ready to role play when trust and acceptance have developed in the group. Concentration in depth also alleviates the problem of escape hatches. We assume that this in-depth period of questioning is the part of the moral discussion process where sustained cognitive dissonance leads to structural change.

(2) *Referring to the history of the group.* The teacher can link the present discussion with earlier discussions to help students see commonalities and differences. It is especially important to refer to earlier solutions of particular students. This helps students become aware of changes in reasoning in themselves and their classmates. (See Teacher's last comment on first dialogue of drunken driving dilemma above.)

(3) *Clarifying and summarizing.* The teacher's role changes to that of clarifier and summarizer, rather than that of major initiator of topic questions. Students by this phase of discussion have learned how to approach questions of moral conflict; *they* can ask "Why?" questions. The teacher therefore becomes a more active listener in order to link crucial elements of discussion.

Conclusion

Teachers, like their students, are moral philosophers. Teachers too must ask questions of what is right and what is good before walking into the classroom as well as during actual classroom interaction. The classroom itself confronts teachers and students with a myriad of potential dilemmas surrounding issues like cheating, truth telling, and keeping promises. As a philosopher, the teacher needs to realize that children have the capacity to reason philosophically and to become aware of themselves and others as reasoners. The teacher must also be a developmentalist. This does not mean that a teacher necessarily needs to become an "expert" in the theory of moral development (Selman and Lieberman, 1975). Rather, the developmental perspective is a rationale for education and demands that teachers become competent not only in knowledge and skills in their content area, but also in the ability to create the conditions for social interaction that are conducive to structural change. As a developmentalist, the teacher wants to stimulate children's thinking to the next higher level of moral reasoning. In performing the developmentalist's function as teacher, one must also be able to take the social perspective of each of the stages of development represented by one's students, and create an environment in which students are brought into contact with those differing perspectives.

The teacher who engages in a cognitive developmental approach to moral education, therefore, is not only a moral discussion leader. The teacher is responsible for creating a classroom which will stimulate in students cognitive conflict and the ability to take the perspective of other people. The essence of moral education is that the teacher creates the opportunity for students to organize their own experience in more complex ways. The moral educator is actually teaching the students a cognitive developmental approach for pursuing their own education after the formal educational process has ended. To learn by reasoning, as well as to see the world in the eyes of another—these are the fundamental experiences of moral education.

Ten Years as Moral Educator in a Catholic High School

James J. DiGiacomo, S.J.

Young people in their teen years are faced with certain basic tasks in their growth as persons. They must find out who they are, what they believe in, and what kind of people they want to be. They must decide what kind of world they want to live in, and how they are to be a part of that world. Toward these ends, it is desirable that they consciously choose a set of values, interiorize them, and through choices and repeated acts strive to live in a manner consistent with those values.

That's a big order. Many people succeed in these tasks, and we recognize them as integral, fully functioning persons. Many others apparently fail in these developmental tasks. They don't know what they believe in, and the standards they actually live by (pleasure, power, security, greed, etc.) are not consciously chosen. They don't decide; they drift. Instead of deciding what kind of world they want to live in, they accept unquestioningly the world as it is or as they perceive it. Rather than choose their values, they let others choose for them by manipulating their appetites, prejudices, and fears.

The Problem with Freedom

Education should help people make free, responsible choices of the ideas and the values by which they live. If liberal education means anything, it must mean at least that. Of course, if we're really serious about liberating people, we must face the fact that we are then confronted by the same problem that God faced on the sixth day of creation. That was when he made a creature that was *free*. In doing so, he let loose a force which not only enhanced the potential of the universe but also provided infinite possibilities for mischief. When God made human beings free, he endowed them with the capacity to assist in the completion of his world, but he also gave them the power to say *no* and thus to unleash destructive forces of evil.

You all know what happened. As the Garden of Eden myth says so well, people said no to God and continue to say no. They persist in choosing death instead of life. Their rejection of the good leaps out from the pages of our newspapers and assaults daily our sensibilities on television and radio news broadcasts that depress and discourage us. One result has been a sharp drop in the Creator's popularity rating. Think of how many people have chosen to be atheists because they cannot believe in a God who permits such things. Think of sensitive people like Richard Rubinstein and Eli Wiesel who, after the Holocaust, felt compelled to reject the God of their fathers. Think of Ivan Karamazov, whose reaction to a God who permits evil was somewhat more nuanced. "I don't deny that God exists," says Ivan. "I simply reject his world. And I most respectfully return him the ticket."

If, as my students say, God catches so much static for letting people choose their own world, then teachers must expect no better treatment. When you free people to choose, you take the risk of having them choose badly, sometimes with devastating consequences to themselves and others. This is the danger that impels authoritarian societies and institutions to deny their subjects the freedom they might misuse. Let's face it: one of the most attractive features of Fascist governments is their comparative success in making the streets safe. (How can you be against safe streets?) The military promises to "make a man of you" by, among other things, removing the need and the opportunity to think or choose for yourself. (Military schools seem to be in the same business, if we correctly read between the lines of their advertisements and brochures.) And every school has to face the dilemma: Do we loosen the reins, give students the chance to fail, and live with a certain amount of academic inefficiency, or do we protect them from their laziness, insulate them from the consequences of their lack of self-discipline, and take upon ourselves a responsibility too heavy for the shoulders of the young? Parents face this troublesome choice every day from the earliest years of their children's lives. It takes a great deal of wisdom to know when you're giving children neither too little nor too much room to grow. If you don't let out enough rope to a growing child, you strangle her; let out too much, and she'll hang herself.

Of course, one way to cut the Gordian knot is to admit that people are going to choose, anyway . . . that children are going to take their freedom whether we give it to them or not, so we may as well surrender gracefully and at least save face. This is a very specious solution, especially at a time when ghetto walls are crumbling and when community forces like church, school, and home are unable to exert the social pressures they once commanded. When custom loses its clout and pluralism becomes a fact, we can no longer teach through indoctrination nor punish deviants with group disapproval or ostracism. We know times have changed when we read news items like this one:

SALT LAKE'S FIRST BABY
BORN OUT OF WEDLOCK*

SALT LAKE CITY (AP)—The city's first baby of 1977, winner of a merchants' "diaper derby," was born out of wedlock. The mother and grandmother say they are happy and don't expect the child to carry any stigma of illegitimacy.

"It's a new generation," said Rosie Coulter, 21, from her bed at Holy Cross Hospital a few hours after her 9-pound, 13-ounce girl was born, at 12:14 a.m.

"I feel great. It's the best thing that could happen," she said.

Her mother, Charlotte Coulter, said her generation wouldn't have so readily accepted an illegitimate child. "It's something that you hate to happen. But afterwards it's just one of those things," she said.

. . . Miss Coulter said the baby's father, a steel worker, visited the mother and child after the birth but she would not give his name.

"We don't live together. We're just really still close to each other," she said, adding that they have no plans to marry.

"Hurrah!" cries the liberal. "We're winning the war against puritanism. We're free." The conservative growls: "See what happens when society becomes too permissive."

They both miss the point. To be sure, we've come a long way from Hester Prynne. It's a bad year for Scarlet Letters. But what does it all *mean*?

Before you conclude that young people who have cast off the shackles of intimidation by parents, school, and church are now free to choose their own values and lifestyle, listen to that much-maligned and much-misunderstood creation of Ivan Karamazov, the Grand Inquisitor. When the latter tells Christ to leave people alone, he gives a reason that we may not want to hear but one which we

*Corpus Christi Caller & Times, Jan. 2, 1977, p. 1.

must take seriously and which we ignore at our peril. People, says the Inquisitor, don't really want to be free. They don't want the agony of responsibility, the burden of choice. They prefer the neurotic assurance of rules, the security that comes with approval by the Others, to whom they surrender their wills.

When we look around us today, it might seem, at first blush, that the Grand Inquisitor has finally been refuted. Aren't men and women rejecting the norms laid down by society? Look at the massive rejection of authoritarianism in the Roman Catholic Church. See how children resist indoctrination. The civil rights revolution, the women's liberation movement and gay liberation attest to a growing refusal by men and women to be defined and dominated by others. And the sexual revolution is a spectacular example of the failure of group pressure in the face of individual choice.

Alas, the Grand Inquisitor is alive and well and looking better every year. If you don't believe it, consider the following sequence of events which takes place in my classes several times a year. The students are eleventh and twelfth grade boys, a group of varied racial, ethnic and economic backgrounds from various points in and around New York City. I show them a film* which debates the pros and cons of premarital sex, in which Albert Ellis makes the following statement:

> I would like to see them really stop and think for themselves and ask themselves why they should or should not have intercourse or any other type of sex relations before marriage—not because their parents or other authorities told them not to but because they can figure out for themselves the advantages and the individual disadvantages in each of their particular cases.

A Classroom Discussion

When I solicit student reactions to Ellis' view, the comments are invariably approving, even enthusiastic. So I ask them: who are these authorities who are trying to make you do it their way? Together, we list them on the chalk board:

Parents
School
Church ·

---

*"Merry-Go-Round," National Film Board of Canada, 1966.

Someone usually adds "other kids." And with a little prodding on my part, we come up with a whole new team, which I write in the second column:

I	II
Parents	Peers
School	Music
Church	TV
	Radio
	Magazines
	Movies

Are the people in column II "authorities"? You bet. And do they give you the same advice, send out the same signals, and promote the same values as those in column I? Hell, no. Well, which group do *you* listen to? Now you're getting close to the knuckle. Albert Ellis is a smart man, but he said a dumb thing. He helped reinforce the illusion that when people throw off a tyrant, they are free. He ought to know that most revolutions just substitute one oppressor for another. So it is with the sexual revolution. Young people have successfully freed themselves from the authority of parents, church, and school. Now they live under the not-so-benevolent tyranny of peers, disc jockeys, and unscrupulous script writers who make money by manipulating a whole generation's fear of the ultimate put-down—sexual inadequacy.

When ghetto walls come down and pluralism becomes a fact of life, and indoctrination becomes impossible, what is left? Personal conviction, and free choice. We can no longer impose our beliefs or our morals on our children. What fills the vacuum? I wish I could say that now my students live by conviction and choice. I can say that about some of them, who are admirable young people, caring and free and growing in ways that I envy, remembering my own youth with its unquestioning loyalty, its uncritical acceptance of a thousand dogmas I should have challenged. But of many I can only say that they live in a cultural desert devoid of conviction and paralyzed of will. For puritanism, they have substituted hedonism; for dogmatism, they have substituted amorality. Or rather, they have let others make the substitution for them.

Teachers and Parents Can Contribute

In such a situation, what is a teacher or a parent to do? Abdicate responsibility, pretend not to notice, support by silence the illusion that all is well? Or withdraw into the castle and pull up the draw-bridge? Is there no other way?

There is. If the young cannot accept our convictions on our word, we can extend a hand and help them find their own. If we cannot make them believe what we believe or choose what we choose, we can help them learn to choose. With eyes wide open, without overestimating their wisdom or their strength, we can second their stumbling efforts to be free. If the bird insists on leaving the nest before it knows how to fly, and will not heed our admonition to wait, then we can fit it for a pair of wings. It is a risky business, setting people free, and it is fraught with danger. But for most of them, there is no other way.

Recently I asked four successive groups of young men the same question, and had the unusual experience of receiving the same one-word answer from the first volunteer in each group. The question, put in somewhat simpler language, was: "In one word, what is the sexual identity that our culture tries to impose on you as a young male?" The answer was, four times running—can you guess?—*Stud*. That's a sobering reply, but it shouldn't surprise any of us who don't have our heads buried in the sand. In a way it's reassuring. For it shows that they have some grasp of how those other authorities are trying to limit their freedom. Into such an opening, you can drive a wedge.

Sexual morality is not the only ground on which this battle is waged. But let's stay with it a little longer. In the face of a culture which debases sexuality and drains it of responsibility and significance, how do we transmit to our young an ethic that calls for commitment, for restraint and sacrifice in the name not of puritanism but of responsible, unselfish love? Threats and prophecies of doom are ineffectual. We must let them know the choices that are available, the options that are open to them, and the advantages and dangers that accompany the choices they make. Show them the games people play and the stakes involved. If they say that love makes it right so long as no one gets hurt, encourage them to find what love is and how many ways people can be hurt. When they call adults hypocrites, show them how dishonest they can be with themselves and others. Challenge them to take their own ideals seriously. And if they have no ideals, hold up before them a mirror in which they can get a glimpse of their true selves. But don't leave them there. Offer them a vision of the kinds of persons they can be. If we don't believe in them, they can hardly believe in themselves.

Some Difficulties . . . Some Possible Solutions

Of course there are problems with such an approach. I have been describing a kind of dialogue with youth, a dynamic interaction wherein we take them seriously, challenge their premises, examine options, and help them to make free, responsible choices. Even before Lawrence Kohlberg shared with us the results of his research, we knew that such a process poses many difficulties. If a person operates habitually at the preconventional level of moral maturity, basing judgments and decisions purely on fear and self-interest, such a conversation is difficult to carry on and has limited prospects of success in the short run. (This handicap operates not only in discussions of sexual morality, but also in such areas as honesty. How do you persuade preconventional people not to lie, cheat, or steal?) Even with young people who have been socialized to the point of operating at the conventional level, difficulties abound. Stage Three people are too vulnerable to peer pressure, and Stage Four law-and-order persons are confronted with a society which does not send out clear, unambiguous signals in matters of sex. Conventionally moral people are those who listen to the Others, but here is one area where they receive contradictory and confused messages.

Real as these problems are, they should not make us despair. The logical conclusion seems to be that we must help prod young people along toward post-conventional moral levels at a somewhat faster pace than we have done up 'til now. That's a hard saying, but what are the alternatives? When men and women live in a pluralistic society where authoritarianism is rejected and social pressures are blunted, the individual bears a heavier burden of choice. If he does not yield to manipulation by subtle group pressures, he must choose, in terms of his own values, among the many possibilities open to him. But that is a fair description of an *adult* way of doing things. Moreover, if Kohlberg is correct in his judgment that most adults do not advance beyond Stage Four moral thinking, the picture is even more bleak. But not hopeless. Not if we start, boldly and with determination, to educate the young not for conformity but for responsible freedom. Let's face it: that would be a new way of doing things. And maybe something new and good could happen. It does, in fact, happen often enough to raise our hopes of doing it more often.

How can we stimulate the process of growth toward post-conventional moral maturity? By structuring learning situations and creating a process that encourages such growth. For several years now my students and I have been engaged in this enterprise, and the interaction produced in the classroom has been occasionally disheartening, sometimes puzzling, often encouraging, and always enlightening.

The day I penned these lines, I completed a series of encounters with 55 high school boys in eleventh and twelfth grade. The sessions took place in small groups of ten to twenty for about six weeks and twelve meetings, a little over seven clock hours. Our experiences are worth describing in some detail and deserve analysis and evaluation.

Group Encounters with Youth

Basically, we studied and engaged in Socratic dialogue concerning several real-life people who in the present and recent past have had to struggle with conflicts between their loyalty to nation, institutions, and laws, and their personal feelings and convictions about right and wrong. Through reflection on their struggles, occasional role-playing, and group discussion, we try to assimilate in a personal way the mentality and the values of those who act for reasons of integrity, and to understand and sympathize with those who are unable to take a critical stance toward authority. The goal is to assist the students not only to understand and appreciate, but also to move toward interiorizing a moral style based on principle and personal conviction rather than blind obedience, peer pressure, or selfishness.

The first case concerns two Russian citizens who silently demonstrated in Red Square, Moscow, against their government's brutal suppression of freedom in Czechoslovakia in the summer of 1968, and were given sentences of banishment to Siberia. Was their gesture totally futile, or did it have meaning? The policeman who arrested them said, "You fools! If you had kept your mouths shut you could have lived peacefully." Most of the students disagree with the policeman, but some of their more pragmatic peers feel that he has had the last word. This first disagreement tells the boys something about themselves, the values they espouse, and perhaps their level of moral maturity. To the preconventionals, the demonstrators' action is the height of folly: why get in trouble? But they hear from their more idealistic classmates who express admiration of the deed and insist it is not useless.

Disagreements in the group become more pronounced when we

try to compare the two Russians with American draft evaders and resisters during the Vietnam war. Both groups dissociated themselves from what they considered immoral actions by their governments. How far can we equate them? Is America more free than Russia? If we condemn the Soviets for exiling dissidents, can we approve our government's exiling of men who in the name of conscience refused to kill? Needless to say, the students reach very different conclusions here. Some exhibit a fixation at Kohlberg's Stage Four by being quite unable or unwilling to grasp the motives of genuine conscientious objectors. Sometimes the clash between students helps sharpen issues and lends a note of urgency to the whole moral enterprise.

Before the amnesty debate bogs down and positions harden, the group's attention is diverted to a peacetime personality. Rosa Parks is a black woman who broke a law of the city of Montgomery (Ala.) a little over 20 years ago when she refused to surrender her seat on a bus to a white man. Her arrest sparked a protest and bus boycott led by a then obscure young Baptist minister, Martin Luther King, and culminated in the successful civil rights revolution of the 1960's. We role-play the incident and then discuss the issue of civil disobedience. Is it ever right to break a law? Under what circumstances? What values are involved? If it is sometimes right to disobey unjust laws, who decides which laws are just?

Now the students are ready to consider the B-52 bomber pilots interviewed by a reporter in Vietnam. On being asked whether they considered themselves justified in carrying out their missions, they referred him to their commanding officers, who made up the schedule and who—according to them—bore the sole responsibility. One dramatic exception is Michael Heck, a much-decorated flyer who on Dec. 26, 1972 informed his C.O. that he would fly no more missions because he could no longer find moral justification for them. Nearly all the students praise Heck for his stand and criticize the others, calling them "robots." But when we role-play and appoint them make-believe Air Force commanders, and ask them to "appoint" assistants, most of them reject Heck as unreliable and express a preference for the pilots who will follow orders without question. This latter phenomenon is subject to varying interpretations, since the role-player often expresses not his own convictions, but the attitudes of those whom they are imitating. But by this time a good number of the boys are torn between conflicting values of efficiency and moral integrity. So it's time for a trip to Nuremberg.

The war crimes trials afford a new perspective on the issues we have been dealing with. To avoid being abstract or theoretical, we do something they did at the Nuremberg trials: show a film documenting the horrors of the German concentration camps. This moves us out of the realm of intellectualization and into strong feelings of horror and revulsion. However, when asked "who was responsible?" some have difficulty answering. They somehow presume that all the war criminals must have acted under threats to their own lives, and are reluctant to assign responsibility to anyone except "higher-ups." This phenomenon is ambiguous, but it seems to betray a preconventional bias: don't condemn anyone who was "under pressure." The same thing happens when we discuss cheating in school. They tend to excuse anyone who is "under pressure" to get good grades. And the same pattern will emerge when we confront the Mylai massacre. Don't be too hard on the American soldiers who wantonly slaughtered hundreds of defenseless old men, women, and children. They were "under pressure." Anyone who listens to this kind of talk has to conclude that many of our young people lack any moral strength, anything like conviction or a sense of honor. It lends credibility to the harsh judgment of John Rouse that the emerging youth ethic is one of hedonistic amorality.* For them, anything that demands sacrifice is unreasonable, and anything done to avoid pain is justified. It sounds harsh again, but the conclusion is inescapable that they would make "good Germans," not out of any exaggerated sense of loyalty but because they lack the inner strength that is needed to offer even minimum resistance to intimidation. Of course, it doesn't stop them from denouncing the war resisters who left the country just to avoid getting shot at by the Vietcong. That kind of "pressure" doesn't count. Well, at least we know now that hypocrisy is not limited to those thirty years old and over.

This pessimistic view is confirmed by the next exercise, which centers around the Mylai massacre. At the close of the film detailing the horrors of the Nazi concentration camps, the narrator remarks that too many people think these things happened long ago, at a certain time in a certain place and are a thing of the past. They deceive themselves, he says, for "the monster is still alive, and in our midst." This cryptic statement elicits no clear reaction until we view a disturbing documentary film, an interview with five American soldiers who were at Mylai. This has by far the greatest impact on the groups as a whole, and produces a whole spectrum of emotional reactions, debates and discussions for weeks after.

*"The Death of Willie Baxter," *Media*, Nov. 1967, p. 13.

As the five veterans describe, objectively and dispassionately, what happened on that day of shame, they repeatedly bear witness to the utter needlessness of the slaughter. Time and again we are told by eyewitnesses and participants that there was no resistance, no return fire, no threat to themselves on the part of the villagers. They remark on how many of the men were actually *enjoying* themselves, taking out their anxieties and frustrations in savage reprisal against helpless civilians. Some of the students are shocked, angry, and ashamed, as any sensitive person would be. These now perceive that "the monster" was not annihilated at Nuremberg, but lives on in our own people, in young American men who, if they had never gone to war, would probably have led normal lives free of violence and savagery.

For these students, this experience appears to be either a turning point or a moment of confirmation in their progress toward post-conventional thinking. It would be unwise to set too much store by a few weeks in a classroom, but I get the definite impression that this process, touching them not only intellectually but also emotionally, can have a significant impact on impressionable young minds and hearts. It is not just the violence of the slaughter that moves them, but the chilling rationalizations of one particular G.I. who says, over and over again, that this is what a soldier is trained to do, that he need not consider the morality of orders unless he is an officer, that orders must be carried out without question. They heard these same words uttered by the defendants at Nuremberg in pitiful justification of sickening war crimes. I like to think that when my students put all those things together, they will be much less docile and manageable if they are ever called upon to commit "legal" crimes in the name of duty or loyalty.

There are other valuable results of the Mylai lesson. In assessing the moral dimensions of the event, we consider William Calley's apologia, published eighteen months later:

> Maybe if I were president, I could change things. Till then, I'll be like anyone else and I'll carry my orders out. I'll do everything the American people want me to. That's what the Army's for. . . . Even if the people say, "Go wipe out South America," the Army will do it. No question about it. Majority rules . . . and if a majority tells me . . . "Lieutenant, go and kill one thousand enemies" . . . I'll do as I'm told to. I won't revolt. I'll put the will of America above my conscience always. I'm an American citizen.*

*Esquire Magazine, Nov. 1970.

This remarkable manifesto is juxtaposed with a similar statement by a civilian:**

Q. What is your concept of loyalty?
A. "Having deep-seated belief in the principles of our country and being willing to defend them. Stephen Decatur stated it best when he said: 'Our country! In her intercourse with foreign nations may she always be in the right; but our country, right or wrong!' "

Here is a rich mine indeed for the moralist, young or old. When I ask the boys what religion these two men profess, they offer guesses like Protestant or Catholic. But I reject this as a purely conventional description. What is their *real* religion, unconsciously professed, in terms of ultimate commitment, unconditional loyalty? It is, of course, nationalism. And in the light of the First Commandment given to Moses, this kind of pseudoreligion is idolatry. Many in the group now begin to see, for the first time, that the religion of Moses and Jesus precludes unconditional commitment to anything less than God himself . . . that our relation to God, properly grasped, relativizes every other loyalty. As I told the cadets at the Air Force Academy a few years ago in a similar context: "Gentlemen, I am a Christian first and an American second. If that be treason, make the most of it." Until young people hear this sort of thing, they may be very fuzzy about what belongs to Caesar and what belongs to God. We may encourage them to be "for God and country," so long as we maintain the clear distinction and the proper subordination between the two.

Results of the Group Encounters

I wish I could report that only these positive results emerge from the study of Mylai. Alas, the outcomes are much more ambiguous. There are students who bring to the experience such strong nationalistic bias that they cannot hear what the veterans are telling them with brutal frankness. They have swallowed a thousand cliches and rationalizations, and these block out enlightenment. "I heard that children used to walk up to our soldiers and blow them up with concealed weapons." "The communists did much worse things than we did." "Civilians often booby-trapped our men." "The soldiers

**Inquiring Photographer, New York News.

had to do what they were told; they had no choice." One lad gave the matter much thought, and carefully wrote the following:

> I don't like to admit it, but I think I would have done the same thing as those men who killed all the Vietnamese at Mylai.
> As I grew up, I used to read the paper and watch the news every day. Every day I saw pictures of dead bodies lying in fields and everywhere else. Every day they gave the American death casualties. Even without being in the war, I began to develop a deep hatred for all Vietnamese people. I can understand how the soldiers in the war must have felt . . . I don't know if I would have killed little babies, but children wouldn't make a difference. The children are the ones who helped plant all the land mines . . .
> I'd know what I was doing was wrong, but I think, after being put through everything those soldiers went through, I would have opened up on everything in sight.

And so it goes. These are the kids who, if born forty years earlier on the other side of the Atlantic, would have made good Hitler Youth. For them, the Americans *have* to be the good guys (what else do they have to believe in?). Their minds are made up, and you can't confuse them with facts.

There is another reaction to the Mylai revelations which is even more disturbing. It is the inability of many students to react at all. This is one of those phenomena that Kohlberg does not help me to evaluate. It has nothing to do with rationalization. It is a failure to *feel*. There is a curiously low-key quality about young audiences' emotional reactions to films which shock their elders. I am not speaking of the kind of shock that is produced by the merely outspoken or unconventional. Too many adults are shocked by too many harmless things, and the youngsters don't need *that* kind of sensitivity. No, I mean the healthy kind of shock and dismay that normal persons experience when they witness violence and brutality. When one of the veterans tells us that he "figured he might as well get some target practice" during the massacre, I am horrified. When another, explaining the murder of the children, says "the guys figured they'd just grow up to be Vietcong anyway, so why not kill them now?" I am repelled. Most adults react the way I do. But not the young people . . . not all of them . . . not by a long shot. Maybe they have seen so many thousands of make-believe murders on television, so much brutality and torture in movies that leave nothing to the imagination, that they are no longer capable of normal, healthy reactions to such stimuli.

I am not being dogmatic in thus explaining my students' apparent insensitivity. The causes may well be much more complex. And I am trying not to make the mistake of expecting immature young-sters to respond with adult depth and intensity. I am simply sharing my disquiet at a social phenomenon that can no longer be ignored. How do you socialize children whose capacity for feeling has been severely limited? Moral formation has to offer more than guidance in how to think, as important as that is. Of what use are intellectual considerations of justice, when the subject is insensitive to the pain and suffering inflicted on others? How do you enlist the moral con-cern of people whose capacity for indignation has been stunted?

Sensitivity: Feeling and Thinking

With each passing year, I find myself, after viewing a powerful documentary film with my classes, first asking the boys not what they think about the film but what they feel. I very rarely get an answer expressing emotion. Usually they proceed to tell me what they think. Well, adults do this, too, but in a different way. My contemporaries tend to intellectualize because most of them have not been taught or encouraged to get in touch with their feelings. *But the feelings are there*, waiting to be dredged up, brought out into the open, and dealt with. With the young, it's a different story. I get the eerie but definite impression that they can't express their feelings because they don't have any. Maybe their circuits are overloaded. Maybe they've been exposed to too much too soon, through visual media. Does this sound paranoid? Then spend an hour with a group of teenagers, trying to elicit and deal with basic human emotions like pity, indignation, enthusiasm, fear, admiration. It can be very dif-ficult, and after a while you get the feeling that the problem is not with the medium but with the subjects. They are curiously passive and apathetic, like prematurely burnt-out cases. Whatever the ex-planation, the implications for moral education are not encouraging. How do you cultivate moral perception without a foundation of basic sensitivity?

Despite these problems and setbacks, or rather because of them, we push on. We cannot end our journey at Mylai. Those who work with youth must always close on a note of hope. A word of idealism, of heroism, must be the last thing they hear. The young need more than information, shocks, and self-knowledge. They need heroes and heroines, people who embody the ideals we want our children to look up to and strive for. So our tale ends not in Vietnam but in Germany, where two young men, Franz Jaggerstatter and Joseph Schultz, restore our hope in people and their capacity for authentic existence.

On the Other Hand . . .

Franz Jaggerstatter was the young husband and father of three small children who was executed by the German government during World War II for refusing, on grounds of conscience, to be drafted into the German army. A devout Roman Catholic, he received neither encouragement nor understanding from clergy or laity in his religious community. He went alone to his death, a solitary martyr to conscience in the face of institutionalized evil. My students are presented with this theoretical problem: suppose Franz had escaped from the Nazis just before his scheduled execution and slipped over the border into Switzerland, where he stayed for the duration of the war. A few years after the armistice, he hears that children are taught in German schools that the war was immoral, that the nation's head of state was a monster, and that Germany's defeat was a blessing for the world. Rejoicing that his countrymen have finally reached his own level of awareness, he applies for permission to return from exile. Should they take him back? Of course, the boys reply. But what about the men who did their duty, who fought and died at Stalingrad and in the Ardennes? What about their families? Are we going to say their deaths were in vain? If we take this draft-dodger back, what's going to happen the next time we're in a war? I think Socrates would like that.

Joseph Schultz went along with his country much further, all the way to the Yugoslav village of Orahovica. There, on July 21, 1941, he was assigned to a firing squad and ordered to execute a group of civilians. There, in that remote corner of Europe, he finally drew the line of personal conscience. He laid down his arms, was lined up with the hostages, and was shot on the spot. The story of this extraordinary man is told in a short film which recreates the incident with maximum impact. It is difficult to assess the students' reaction to this experience. They are not very articulate. Most of them have no vocabulary with which to express admiration for integrity or to pay tribute to heroism. You don't pick up such words or such categories of thought or feeling on a steady diet of Clint Eastwood and Starsky and Hutch. There is that passivity and apathy, too. And the unwritten code that commands them all to Stay

Cool. But I hope that the story of Joseph Schultz will pierce the crust of insensitivity, jolt a few, inspire a few, and strike a blow for personal integrity. Anyway, it can't hurt.

The Religious Setting

An important and lengthy postscript to these different problems of war and peace and loyalty and conscience and amnesty is possible within my particular school setting, which is explicitly Christian within a Roman Catholic framework. Before sharing with them those official documents which embody the Church's enlightened teaching on these matters, I surprise them with this significant little item of recent, easily forgotten history. It is a page from a religious instruction book, *Catholic Action*, printed in 1960 and used with high school seniors in various parish communities:

> God knew from all eternity that in our day communism would be his great worldly enemy.
> When our country was born, He made it a great stockpile so that in the twentieth century it might be used against communism. America's acceptance of Russia's challenge and your participation in (military) service are certainly taking place under God's providence. You can have great certitude when you "fall in" for the first time that this is precisely where you should be; that God wants you there; that you have a role in keeping atheistic communism at bay; and that if you were in any other place you would not be in the place that God wanted you to be . . .
> God knew from all eternity that your number would be called, that you wouldn't have much to say about it, and that your chance for eternal glory is, at least in part, bound up with the service. Your participation in military training, therefore, should be viewed in perspective of God's providence. For actually it is God as well as your country asking you to help prevent Communism from achieving its proclaimed goal of world domination. It is not merely the United States against Russia that you are defending, but Christianity against Communism, God against the devil's enslavement.

The boys are amazed at the simplistic naivete of this page from the American church's recent past. An explanation of the mood of 1960 America is provided to help them understand how so many Americans (including their teacher!) could uncritically swallow so much political and religious confusion. They begin to get an inkling of how we became trapped first in our own rhetoric and then in Indochina. Some may accuse us of cheap-shot debunking here, but we like to think of it under the heading of Learning From History.

By contrast, the church documents of the next ten years are illuminating and encouraging. The Second Vatican Council's teaching on Just War, with its strict limitations on legitimate defense and its condemnation of indiscriminate killing, is explained, as well as the recognition of the right of Catholics to embrace pacifism as one expression of Christian idealism. Then there is the Catholic Bishops' unheeded appeal to the United States government in 1968 to amend the Selective Service Act in favor of selective conscientious objectors. These teachings are presented not as easy solutions but as sober, honest attempts by our religious leaders to give responsible moral guidance to those who have had to deal, in real life, with the issues we study in the classroom.

Since I teach in a Roman Catholic school, I cannot leave the issue of conscience and authority without dealing with the role of individual conviction within the church. This is a delicate question, hard even for adults to handle; all the more difficult is it for young people who are not always capable of nuanced thought and the fine distinctions necessary for anyone who seriously wishes to do justice to the legitimate demands both of church authority and of individual conscience. Prudence and skill, clarity of thought, and genuine humility are required of the adult Catholic who would explain to the young how they are called to grow up responsible adults in a religious community which claims divine sanction for its exercise of leadership.

The adolescent mind, left to itself, tends to think in black-and-white, either-or categories, e.g., are you going to follow the church or your conscience? Some too easily accept the popular misconception of Catholic moral life as a no-win proposition in which only two choices are available: either abdicate responsibility in the name of obedience, or reject all authority in the name of freedom. This inadequate view is not limited to teenagers. Many adult Catholics have not achieved a dynamic synthesis of the roles of conscience and authority in their personal lives; some of these even make their living as priests and bishops. But we refuse to be discouraged. There is hope for the future, and its name is youth. It is well worth the risk and the trouble to explain to young adults that as grown-up Catholics they will be responsible for their own existence, that no authority can lift from their shoulders the burden of choice. Being a Catholic is a great blessing, for those who exercise the teaching office are obliged to guide and challenge us in the name of Christ. For our part, we are obliged in his name to heed their voice, to stand humbly before God, to listen to his Spirit in scripture, in prayer, and in dialogue with the Christian community. But then *we* must decide, for we are free with the freedom of the sons and daughters of God. To put it in Kohlbergese: Yes, Virginia, there is a place for postconventional people in the Catholic Church.

*   *   *   *   *

Looking back on this whole series of learning situations, which I have structured for my classes, the reader may have perceived one particular facet of my overall strategy. Young people labor under a serious handicap in their attempts to acquire skills in moral decision-making. They lack experience on which to base personal choice. In a post-ghetto situation, they are unable or unwilling to base their choices on adult experience and adult interpretation of that experience. So I offer them vicarious experience through film, news items, historical vignettes, and other media. Then it is up to them to interpret that experience, with the help of an adult guide operating on a Socratic model. In reliving and evaluating the experiences of people like Heck, Calley, Jaggerstatter, and Schultz, we "try on" various identities, sift moral attitudes and value systems on the level of feeling and of intellect, and get some idea of the possible and likely consequences of different kinds of behavior. This is not to deny that direct experience is the best teacher; only to insist that it is not the *only* teacher. Some kinds of experience are just too expensive in human terms. Getting "busted" for shoplifting, becoming pregnant outside marriage, being used and dumped by a boy friend who doesn't "love" me anymore, are very effective learning experiences. But they can leave a person with deep, long-term scars. Vicarious experience and reflection can be almost as effective and much less painful.

This process which I have described also raises a question which I encourage readers to ask for themselves. Would you call this kind of moral education a strictly *religious* enterprise? As I pointed out, it goes on in a Roman Catholic school, under the heading of religious studies; and from time to time explicitly religious issues are addressed. But most of the exercises confront problems of universal concern, in terms neither specifically Christian nor even explicitly religious. Questions like premarital sex, civil disobedience, abortion, honesty, and amnesty are not the private preserve of any religious group. Moreover, it is inadequate to try to solve any of these problems by appealing to church dogma. The reflective, responsible adult cannot reject abortion just because "the Catholic church is against it." If premarital sex is wrong, it cannot be simply because "we have a commandment against it." The Second Vatican Council can't *make* saturation bombing wrong by condemning it. Lying, cheating, and stealing aren't immoral because "they're against my religion."

The sophisticated reader may consider this belaboring the obvious, but the popular mind has always been bedeviled by a kind of Suarezian voluntarism, in which authority "makes" morality and hence becomes the ultimate measure of right and wrong. In Kohlbergian terms, this is a Stage Four cop-out. For this mentality, religion becomes the arbiter of morals, and church membership is a short-cut to enlightenment by way of the unexamined life. Dogmatism in any form is unacceptable to the post-conventional mind, and should be.

So we come full circle, to the point at which we began this essay. It was our contention that moral education, far from constricting people, should set them free—not only free from external, arbitrary influences, but from inner restraints as well. I have described one educator's attempt to make this actually happen in the lives of his students. Without a doubt, it could be done better. Some of my underlying premises may well be vulnerable. And my sociological and psychological interpretations are surely limited, subject to correction by those with more expertise in these areas. They are offered merely as food for thought to those who take a serious interest in the moral development of youth.

Conclusion

For the last ten years I have been engaged in the moral education of young men between the ages of 13 and 18. After thousands of hours of encouraging them to grow toward moral maturity, I have attempted to share with you some impressions, some convictions, and some questions about how children grow into responsible, sensitive, liberated adult human beings.

One inescapable conclusion is that humanity is not a given, but an achievement. Personhood is a task, and morality is an accomplishment. This is not as self-evident as it may seem at first sight. Some people think that we are naturally good, and that rascals are people who went wrong. It seems more accurate to say that wicked people are those who have failed the task of growth. Criminals are not deviants, but dropouts from the school of life.

Observant educators never cease to wonder at the extraordinary range of moral maturity and sensitivity among youngsters the same age and with similar background and with so little experience of life. The degree of differentiation is astounding. In the same classroom students who are endowed with an impregnable sense of honor sit next to others apparently devoid of anything like personal integrity. Unselfish, compassionate adolescents rub elbows with callous, self-centered classmates. They read the same books, go to the same churches, attend the same schools, play in the same neighborhoods; but they might as well live on different planets. Their world of concern, their self-image, their way of relating to other human beings is so diverse that they present the moral educator with an enormous problem and a marvelous opportunity.

The research of behavioral scientists helps us to understand the factors that contribute to this diversity of moral development. They show us how environment shapes the individual. They are to the educator what Hegel was to Marx. The latter proclaimed that Hegel helped us to understand the world, but it was his (Marx's) task to change that world. The educator is summoned to create and shape an environment calculated to assist moral development. This is done by structuring learning situations that will promote the growth of authentic, fully functioning, responsible human beings. Parents don't send their children to school just to have their behavior analyzed; they want them to be influenced and changed for the better. Schools probably cannot succeed in opposition to familial influences which are nearly always stronger. But they can support and supplement and even make up for some of the deficiencies in home training.

In authoritarian societies those charged with the socialization of youth may attempt to accomplish this through indoctrination. Values and standards of behavior are imposed and backed up by social pressure and threats of punishment. Such tactics may succeed for a time with subjects who operate at a preconventional or conventional level of moral maturity, but only in a ghetto or similar closed society. A minority of today's youth, seeking a painless route to instant identity, seek to create such societies in rigid, fundamentalistic communities which specialize in thought control and offer total security to anyone willing to become a zombie. They haunt street corners and bus terminals and airports, harassing bystanders and offering "free" religious trash in exchange for a "contribution." They are pathetic and deserve our concern, but they are outside the mainstream of American life. Most of our growing children are marching to far different drummers.

To these young people, growing up in a confusing culture that features a babble of voices and unprecedented powers of manipulation, education should offer the chance to grow up responsible, sensitive, and free. Those who would engage in such a task need large stores of wisdom, inventiveness, courage, and conviction. This essay has been a modest attempt to add to the supply.

Moral Education at the College Level: A Blueprint

Robert J. Roth, S.J.

The purpose of this chapter is to provide a blueprint for a moral education program at the college level. By way of illustration, I shall use the program being developed at Fordham College. At the risk of indulging in semantics, I would have to say that the word "blueprint" may not fully indicate what I am attempting to do, though it may be the best term available at the moment. By this I mean that the program which I shall describe is in various stages of development. Parts of it are still on the drawing board, parts are in the process of being built, and parts are already in place. Prudence would seem to dictate that it would be better to wait until the program is completed before giving an account of it. But I am persuaded against a delay for two reasons. First, as will be explained shortly, colleges and universities are becoming more and more interested in such programs and unfortunately there isn't much at hand that they can turn to for guidance. Hence the experience of one institution may be of some assistance. Secondly, the decision to wait until a program is completed seems to assume either that it will fail or that it will soon outlive its usefulness. In either case, we would be assisting at the program's obsequies. My own hope is that the kind of program herein described will succeed, though that hope will have to await the empirical evidence. And my judgment is that the need for a values program will be around for some time. Hence we are dealing with an open-ended ongoing process that can be viewed in many moments of its course.

At first I thought that writing this paper would be a simple task. I would merely have to provide some factual details regarding the program and give a list of the courses offered. But it turned out to be a much more complex affair than that. For if a program is planned with any degree of care, it involves a number of presuppositions regarding the need for such a program, the ways in which the program is to meet those needs, and the reasons for choices made regarding its structure. Moreover, the assumptions made at the outset depend largely on how those making the assumptions view the role of institutions of higher learning in contemporary society and especially how they assess the situation at the particular institution in which the program is developed.

It can be seen, then, that if a particular program is to be understood properly, and especially if it is to be helpful to others, a good deal of background explanation will have to be given. For this reason, I propose to discuss the following topics:

1. Historical Perspectives on Moral Education in American Colleges
2. Historical Background and Rationale of Fordham College's Values Program
3. Procedures in Developing the Program
4. The Values Program
5. Evaluation Procedures

1. Historical Perspectives

The February 23, 1976 issue of *The Chronicle of Higher Education* carried a rather surprising headline: "Colleges' Concern Grows over Ethical Values." The ensuing article written by Gael M. O'Brien states that "values" has become one of the most popular topics on American campuses and adds:

> Colleges and universities have always talked about values in their institutional philosophies and included them in philosophy courses. Now, however, educators are becoming increasingly concerned over what role institutions of higher education should play in helping students to think through ethical questions and to make responsible personal and professional decisions (p. 5).

In citing *The Chronicle*, I called the title of the article "surprising." It may not be so for those who are already working in the area of values and moral education. But if we look at the broad spectrum of higher education today, we will realize that, after a long period of relative unconcern, it is only very recently that American colleges and universities are beginning consciously to turn their attention in this direction. To help us appreciate this course of events, I would like to give a brief survey of moral education in American higher education. I do not pretend to write a history in the literal sense, for this would entail a carefully researched account. To my knowledge, no such work has as yet been written and it is sorely needed. It would require perhaps a team of writers who would have to trace the history of American higher education with particular attention to moral education from the early colonial colleges to the present day. One would have to comb through presidential addresses, faculty publications, and college catalogues for statements of institutional aims and of courses and programs. But all this may in the end reveal little of the intellectual and moral atmosphere in which administrators, faculty, and students have lived and breathed in the classrooms, corridors, and campuses of these institutions. This section, then, is not a strict historical account but rather a record, perhaps impressionistic at times, of one person's experience in higher education for twenty-five years. It may also serve to indicate those areas that would have to be researched by our hoped-for historian.

On the eve of the American Revolution, there were nine colonial colleges—Harvard, William and Mary, Yale, New Jersey (Princeton), King's (Columbia), Philadelphia (Pennsylvania), Rhode Island (Brown), Queen's (Rutgers), and Dartmouth—all fashioned after Oxford and Cambridge (Rudolph, 1962, p. 3). It is widely assumed that the colonial colleges, especially Harvard and Yale, were founded to train clergymen. This is quite incorrect, as shown by the statements issued by their founders. It is true, however, that between 1642 and 1700, 266 out of 543 Harvard graduates became clergymen, and that in 1774, of the 500 Congregational ministers in New England at that time, about 300 were educated at Harvard and 200 at Yale (Morison, II, p. 562; Bainton, p. 80). It is also true that, at least until the Civil War and even afterwards, not only at Harvard and Yale but at other American colleges as well, a large part of the curriculum was devoted to religion. Moral philosophy was taught in senior year by the president of the college who was frequently a clergyman.

During the nineteenth century, the influence of theology in the curriculum gradually declined. There are various reasons for this trend. One powerful influence was the liberalizing tendencies within orthodox theology itself. This could be traced quite easily in institutions like Harvard and Yale. Again, colleges which from the very beginning were church-related began to lose their religious affiliation, and colleges with no ties to a religious sect were founded. This is seen especially in the proliferation of state colleges. Nonetheless, one discerns a strong moral stance among the colleges, especially in official statements of college presidents and catalogues.

From the 1930's on, there was a rapid decline in interest in moral education in our colleges and universities. This no doubt is a generalization that can be refuted in particular cases. But I am speaking of a general trend. Several reasons can be given for this decline.

1. The change in church-related schools and the rise of schools that were not church-related. This has already been noted above. Also, added to the liberalizing influence of theology, we witness the introduction into America of a wide variety of European philosophical currents. This trend had begun as far back as the early eighteenth century, but its influence, at first relatively weak, increased considerably in the late nineteenth century.

2. Concomitant with, perhaps even consequent upon, #1 above, there is a blurring of the "sense of mission" that was quite common in earlier times. Though in many colleges official statements retain the high purpose claimed for these institutions, one suspects that there are wide discrepancies between sonorous rhetoric and hard reality. In many instances, too, even these statements of purpose become muted as institutions show a greater hesitancy, or perhaps greater difficulty, in articulating precisely what stance the institution assumes.

3. Change in curriculum. The heart of the college curriculum from earliest times had been liberal and humanistic education where moral questions were either directly or indirectly discussed. However, as early as 1869 Charles William Eliot, President of Harvard, launched a vigorous and public campaign in favor of the elective system. It subsequently had a long and difficult history, and colleges bought into it in varying degrees. But by the 1930's, and even earlier, it was sufficiently influential in most colleges to diffuse the integrating and humanistic effect of the liberal arts curriculum. Within the philosophy curriculum, though courses in ethics continued to be taught, they lost their privileged position and were in many cases no longer required. Of course, a full picture of the dramatic changes made in the college curriculum would have to include the rise of the land-grant colleges which were instituted in 1862 by the Morrill Federal Land Grant Act. The terms of this act provided for at least one such college in every state. These colleges had a purpose quite different from the traditional American college for they were designed to provide students with agricultural and mechanical training to meet America's agrarian and industrial needs (Rudolph, pp. 247-263).

4. The rise of the universities. The opening of Johns Hopkins in

1876 began the trend toward the university fashioned after the German model, with full-scale doctoral programs. The first Ph.D. had been awarded in 1861 by Yale (Jencks and Riesman, p. 13), but Johns Hopkins began a new era in American higher education. The emphasis would now be placed, not so much on teaching as had previously obtained, but on research and publication. Moreover, colleges became more oriented to graduate schools and there resulted an increased specialization in various disciplines and the division of faculty into separate and more-or-less autonomous departments. In addition to graduate schools of arts and science, there also emerged schools of medicine, law, education, social service, business, and so on. In such institutions, the college became diminished in stature and importance, so much so that today when students receive the baccalaureate degree, they claim to be graduates of such-and-such *university*, not college.

While colleges were being turned into universities, there was also a dramatic growth in the universities themselves, both in the number of universities and in their enrollments. It should be remembered that in the mid-1800's the colleges were very small by current standards, with graduating classes of less than a hundred. In Ohio, for example, there were twenty-two colleges in 1859 with an average college enrollment of eighty-five (Rudolph, p. 219). In 1865, Columbia numbered only 150 students, and in 1872 only 116. In 1890, Yale's total enrollment was not yet 1500, with Yale College much smaller. In 1895, Nebraska numbered 1000 and in 1900, it had 2000. In 1909, only six American universities had more than 5000 students, and only one of these was a state university (Veysey, pp. 99, 234, 339, 356). Compare these figures with the enrollment of many universities across the country today, especially state universities, which number their students in the tens of thousands. This is a far cry from the small rural colleges whose students numbered several hundred and where an overall goal could be clearly articulated and implemented. Of course, it goes without saying that small colleges continued to exist in the 1930's, as they do today, but they usually suffer the effects of departmentalization and specialization which were caused by the direction taken in higher education generally toward university training.

5. The rise of "value-free" education. It is difficult, if not impossible, to assign a precise date when "value-free" became an accepted concept in higher education. Even if one could, it would not mean that it was accepted everywhere or in the same way. But roughly from the 1930's onward, it became common to hear ar-

guments voiced in favor of keeping education and the objective search for knowledge free from the intrusion of value judgments. There were several reasons for this change, particularly the increasing importance of natural science and the dramatic development of academic specializations.

The first reason I suggest for the growth of "value free" education was the rise of science and its clash with religion and theology from the middle nineteenth century onward. America was to repeat the opposition between religion and science that erupted in Europe about the seventeenth century. The rise of evolution is a classic example of the disputes that arose. I have always felt that both the theologians and the scientists were at fault in exacerbating the dispute, and that neither side exerted enough effort to understand the other's position.

In any event, the scientists and especially the evolutionists have had reason to feel uncomfortable, since extremists in religion tried to ignore or even refute science on theological grounds. The result was a heightened sensitivity and an exaggerated defensive stance on the part of the scientists. The cry for objectivity in science was voiced not only regarding theology but also regarding any attempt to inject value or moral questions in any of the academic disciplines.

The second reason I suggest for the growth of "value free" education was the rise of academic specialization. This has already been mentioned in the discussion regarding the rise of the universities. It deserves attention here since the cry for "value-free" education was not confined to the sciences. Most disciplines, as they became more technical and specialized, made the same claim to objectivity and became more and more sensitive to any erosion of that objectivity.

In recent decades, then, one witnesses in American colleges and universities various attitudes toward moral education, ranging from unconcern, through uneasiness, to open hostility. Hence I have called "surprising" the *Chronicle* article which reports an increased interest in ethical values. How widespread this trend is, it is difficult to say. The article mentions the following institutions by name: Kenyon, St. Olaf, Notre Dame, Fordham, Eckerd, Seattle Pacific, and the thirteen liberal arts colleges in the Associated Colleges of the Mid-west. I myself have received inquiries from fifteen colleges regarding Fordham's program.

It is encouraging to note that high level administrators are beginning to underscore the need for more attention to moral education. Writing in *The New York Times*, Ernest L. Boyer, Chancellor of the State University of New York, stated that in the light of national and global problems education must give renewed attention to the question of moral development. Hence he proposes "a 21st-century version of a liberal arts education, which draws on the wisdom of the past, organizes our present knowledge of the world, and then focuses sharply on alternatives for the future" (1975, p. 98). In his 1974 Faculty Convocation address, James C. Finlay, President of Fordham University, invited the faculty to rethink the connection between academic and professional training and professional responsibility. While noting that value-free research is a requisite for scholarly investigation, he pointed out that alone it is inadequate for the integration of learning with life. He felt that considerably more effort and attention, examination and expression must be devoted to an elaboration of an ethical or moral code within which our research and teaching can find their meaning. Likewise, Theodore M. Hesburgh, President of Notre Dame, stated that values that bear on global justice, professional values, and such personal values as honesty, integrity, justice, and compassion for others are too important for the university to take a chance that students will not be exposed to them (*The Chronicle*, p. 5). Furthermore, Derek C. Bok, President of Harvard, states that "there has rarely been a time when we have been so dissatisfied with our moral behavior or so beset with ethical dilemmas of every kind" than the present. Hence he advocates that universities develop problem-oriented courses in ethics (1976, p. 28). All these are indeed encouraging signs and give hope of a wider interest for the future.

The Chronicle cites three reasons for the renewed interest in ethical questions. Others could be added, I am sure, but these three pretty well sum up the situation.

1. No doubt the ethical questions raised by Vietnam, Watergate, and current issues such as abortion and euthanasia have been strongly influential. One could also add the problems of our contemporary, especially technological, society, such as world hunger, urban poverty, the pollution of our natural resources, moral issues raised by the life sciences, mass media, and racial and social injustice. The academic community is beginning to realize that the solution of these pressing problems needs the resources provided by the academic disciplines of the University, more obviously mathematics and the sciences, psychology, philosophy, theology, law, medicine, history, economics, political science, sociology, and communications. Less obvious but certainly important are the contributions of literature and the fine arts. Academicians are slowly becoming

aware that they can no longer insulate and isolate themselves, their disciplines, or indeed the university from these problems, though few as yet know exactly what their role is to be.

Coincidentally, in the issue of *The Chronicle* already cited there appears an article entitled "History as a Moral Science," by Gordon Wright, Professor of History at Stanford University. Professor Wright laments the fact that in the face of today's moral confusion many historians suppose that dispassionate, value-free history will automatically lead those studying it to sensible and judicious conclusions. While not advocating that we return to "19th-century pieties and platitudes," or to the indoctrination of students, or to a downgrading of the search for truth, Professor Wright states:

> If one purpose of historical study is to broaden and enrich the minds of students so that they can shape their own values and arrive at their own judgments (as I think they should), that purpose is likely to be best served if they are offered not only raw data and quantified facts, but also broad exposure to various mature interpretations of the past . . . for some of us, at least, our search for truth ought to be quite consciously suffused by a commitment to some deeply held human values. The effort to keep these two goals in balance may be precarious; but if we can manage it, perhaps we will be on the way to re-establishing history's role as one—and not the least—of what we might fairly call the moral arts (p. 24).

2. *The Chronicle* states that, since outside money is becoming more available for values programs, some small liberal arts colleges are becoming interested in order to survive. No doubt survival is a factor, but I would also like to think that the interest shown by these agencies and by the colleges which have applied for funds indicates an appreciation for the intrinsic importance of the programs.

3. Church-related schools are said to be interested in values programs in order to recapture a "sense of mission." In the case of many colleges this contention is true as will be made clear in the following section. Therein we discuss the background of a particular college, and what is related of it could apply with only slight modification to many other such institutions. Actually colleges and universities, whether church-related or not, are being forced to reflect upon themselves in order to articulate their purpose. Fiscal stringencies impose upon such institutions the heavy burden of setting priorities as to what schools or programs should be discontinued and priority-setting cannot be done intelligently without some overall goal. Outside agencies, too, stimulate the consideration of such goals. Thus in preparing for re-evaluation by the Commission on

Higher Education of the Middle States Association of Colleges and Secondary Schools in order to obtain a reaffirmation of accreditation, universities are required to include a statement of purpose. "The Bulletin of the (New York) Regents 1976 Plan for the Development of Postsecondary Education" requires a statement of the mission of the institution in clear and precise terms. "Declarations of institutional mission, as presently listed in college catalogues or planning documents, are often couched in general platitudes which encompass a broad range of philosophical aspirations" (1975, p. 7). Such statements are also required at times by funding agencies. For example, the National Science Foundation in accepting proposals for comprehensive assistance for undergraduate science programs requires a mission statement of the university for undergraduate education. The same is true of the National Endowment for the Humanities in its requirements for institutional grants for comprehensive improvement and development of humanistic programs.

The task facing the university in identifying its goals is extremely complex. Besides the sectors mentioned above, there are other constraints affecting the university, as Clifton Conrad has shown. Among these are the professional norms and values set by the faculty in defining their autonomy, state government and Boards of Trustees, the federal government, the publics such as alumni, parents and local communities, and student interests (1974, pp. 504-516). In the face of these pressures, one can only hope that the imperious demands of contemporary moral problems will somehow be heard.

2. Background and Rationale of Fordham College's Values Program

As already noted, before the program of a particular college can be meaningfully discussed, it is necessary to appreciate the situation in which the college found itself at the time that it began to develop a moral education program. It is also necessary to understand why it felt it ought to move in that direction. Fordham College was founded in 1841 as a private church-related school and in 1846 it was placed under the direction of a Religious Order, the Society of Jesus. Throughout its history it has maintained its Christian, specifically Catholic, tradition. Fordham today intends to be neither narrowly sectarian nor secular. It seeks to maintain an openness to students and faculty with diverse beliefs, does not require any religious test for admission or appointment, nor does it seek to indoctrinate. As a consequence of its tradition, however, religious ideas, perspectives, and values hold an important place in the curriculum. Religion is deemed to be an important subject requiring serious intellectual study.

Fordham College went through the kind of development and expansion that has already been described as taking place in other American colleges. In 1902 there were 420 students, and in 1904, 480. In the same year, it began the move toward university status with the opening of departments of medicine (discontinued in 1921) and law which were established as separate Schools in 1907. Other Schools were added in rapid succession until it reached its present state of some 14,000 students in ten Schools on two campuses. Through all this development, Fordham College has remained a liberal arts and sciences college with a present enrollment of some 3100 students and a faculty of some 265. It is this college that is the subject of our discussion.

The liberal arts have always formed the central part of Fordham College's curriculum. Nevertheless, its curriculum developed as it did everywhere else, and for many decades it has included the usual variety of departments and disciplines. Moreover, the curriculum has become more flexible, for though Fordham College never moved to a completely elective system, it does offer the student a considerable amount of choice.

A concern for moral values and moral education has been an integral part of Fordham's educational philosophy from its very origins. There were required courses in philosophy and theology and attempts were made to stress the links between learning and life and the importance of both intellectual and moral growth. In the past, its perspective was perhaps too narrow. This perspective has widened considerably, though Fordham still commits itself to challenging the students, whatever their religious belief, to face the moral issues that will arise in their personal and professional lives. For this reason, though Fordham's faculty has long engaged in the free and objective search for knowledge in all disciplines, it has not adopted as a group the strong affirmation of "value-free" education that has been emphasized at many institutions.

In many respects, the picture as described would seem to fulfill all the requirements of any kind of moral education program that one could devise. No changes would seem necessary, and as a matter of fact there was for a long time general satisfaction with this curriculum. Within the last few years, however, voices of discontent began to be heard. Administrators, faculty, and students began to feel that Fordham College's focus had become blurred and that the once clearly articulated purpose and direction had become less clear.

Several factors contributed to this change of view. One has already been indicated above in our discussion of the article from *The Chronicle*. It is the major moral questions that have arisen in contemporary society. A further dimension of these questions is the fact that they arise with greater rapidity and intensity today than in any other period in our history. As a result, one does not easily find at hand the resources necessary to face these issues.

Another factor is the realization that students who enter universities are less prepared by family, Church, and school to confront these issues. And lastly, the departmental structures which now characterize colleges and universities tend to isolate faculty and prevent them from coming together in order to bring to bear on contemporary dilemmas the resources supplied by their respective disciplines in a unified way.

3. Group Procedures in Developing the Program

As a faculty member at Fordham, I had heard the reservations voiced regarding the curriculum. When I became Dean in the summer of 1974, I felt that the time had come to initiate plans for alleviating the situation. The matter was brought to the Academic Council of the College and approval given to begin plans for a Values Program. In the spring of 1975 a grant was obtained from a private foundation and a Committee on the Study of Values was appointed. The Committee consisted of two Assistant Deans, three faculty, and one student.* The Committee engaged in a five-week Workshop during the summer of 1975. In November, it submitted its Report to the College Council and to the whole faculty.

The Report consisted mainly of three parts. The first part sets down the rationale for beginning a Values Program. It describes the background of Fordham College and the reasons why a new program should be initiated. All this has been explained in the preceding section of this paper. The second part of the Report proposes the

*The Committee members were: Deans P. Lacy and J. McGowan; faculty members V. Cooke (Philosophy), P. Gerson (Fine Arts), and J. Kelly (Sociology); the student was G. Syrek, '76. I draw heavily on their *Report of the Committee on the Study of Values at Fordham College*. I could never adequately express my appreciation to the members of this Committee for all that they did.

program for moral education which will be discussed in the following section of this paper. The third part of the Report discusses evaluation procedures. These procedures will be explained in the final section of this paper. The entire Report was discussed at a meeting of the College Council and at an open meeting of the faculty. In February, 1976, I met with each Department in order to explain the plan more fully, answer questions, and invite all faculty interested in participating to submit appropriate course titles and descriptions. Over forty faculty responded, far more than could be fitted into the program in its first year. Finally, twenty-seven faculty were selected to teach in the program, either in the fall or spring of 1976-77, with some teaching in both semesters.

The original Committee which had worked through the summer of 1975 had quickly seen that for any interdisciplinary program to succeed, the faculty involved must be specially prepared. It has been my observation that new programs frequently fail because the faculty have not had the time or opportunity to discuss the program, plan the courses, and meet together as a group during the semester. Hence the Committee made the strong recommendation that the faculty involved in the Values Program should engage in a Two-Week Workshop. This recommendation was followed in early summer of 1976.

During the first week, the twenty-seven faculty engaged in general meetings and seminars to discuss various aspects of the program, for example, its objectives and the relationship of these to certain theories of developmental psychology and various approaches to moral education. The faculty were also introduced to the research and literature in the field of moral education, and they were provided time to read and discuss this material. During the second week, the faculty who were teaching together met to prepare their courses for the following fall and spring.

Through long discussion and sometimes heated debate, and against a background of differences of opinion, the faculty were able to lay the foundations for a statement of goals and purposes for the Values Program. This statement was developed and refined during the remainder of the summer by a Coordinating Committee which was elected from the group. The faculty also appointed a Committee to work out evaluation procedures.* In addition, the faculty made

*The members of the Coordinating Committee are: Associate Dean J. McGowan, and faculty members J. Doyle (English), J. Fitzpatrick (Sociology), C. Kelbley (Philosophy), E. Kraus (Philosophy), and M. Parvin (Economics). The members of the Evaluation Committee are: Associate Dean J. McGowan, M. Fergus (Political Science), J. Macisco (Sociology), and J. Phelan (Communications). All these, like the members of the original Committee, deserve the highest praise.

good progress in preparing their courses so that they began the academic year with a sense of confidence.

4. The Values Program

There is a wide spectrum of views on the meaning of moral education, coming from cognitivists, developmentalists, cognitive-developmentalists, affectivists, values clarificationists, and so on. The whole issue of *Kappan*, June, 1975, is devoted to a discussion of these views. I shall here describe the viewpoint adopted by those involved in the program at Fordham College.

Moral Education

Moral education, as here understood, is an effort to stimulate the development of the student's capacity for reasoned moral judgment.

> Moral education stresses the intellectual component in moral reasoning and recognizes both the priority of the search for truth in academic life and the destructive artificiality resulting from the severance of the pursuit of knowledge from the moral dilemmas of personal and civic choice. It consists in part of a consideration of values and conflicts within a pluralistic society and aims to assist the student in the development of a moral code (*Report*, p. 6).

Expressed in terms of the mission, goals and objectives of the values program to be discussed later, moral education is the effort to promote a reflective awareness of the individual and social values which are manifested in human actions and to develop the critical skills with which to appraise those values, so that appropriation or rejection of those values may be conscious, deliberate, and informed.

Moral education is not indoctrination. It should not, therefore, have for its purpose the acceptance by the student of a particular moral code through forceful instruction, the suppressing of other viewpoints, and so on. It does not mean, either, that the instructor must remain morally neutral, either publicly or privately, on every moral issue. For example, in teaching an ethics course, the instructor should not be required to suppress his or her own opinion. But this opinion should be presented in such a way that the students may challenge it with counter-arguments and the students themselves should be ready to meet counter-arguments from the instructor and fellow students.

The stress on the intellectual component, however, does not exclude a very crucial and as-yet insufficiently discussed aspect of moral education in higher education, namely, the school environment. This has to do with the setting, atmosphere, "ambience," as it were, which is or is not conducive to the study of moral values, as are also the public statements and actions of the administrators and faculty. Derek Bok (1976) has pointed out that universities can accomplish more toward building character in students by what goes on outside the classroom than by the curriculum itself.

> For example, the moral aspirations of Harvard students undoubtedly profited more from the example of Archibald Cox than from any regular course in ethics. Moreover, if a university expects to overcome the sense of moral cynicism among its students, it must not merely offer courses; it will have to demonstrate its own commitment to principled behavior by making a serious effort to deal with the ethical aspects of its investment policies, its employment practices, and the other moral dilemmas that inevitably confront every educational institution (p. 29).

Nonetheless, Bok insists on the need for courses that give the opportunity for "carrying on an active discussion in an effort to encourage students to perceive ethical issues, wrestle with the competing arguments, discover the weaknesses in their own position, and ultimately reach thoughtfully reasoned conclusions" (p. 28).

Freshman Program

The Freshman Program brings together two courses into a "cluster." Each cluster involves thirty students. The same students register for both courses and are together for all classes in the cluster. The courses are unified around a common theme, decided upon by the instructors and centered on important human values. The cluster concept is a variation of the team-teaching system. That is, each course is separately taught, though the two faculty members meet together with the class on a fairly regular basis. In some cases, the faculty attend each other's classes. And, of course, the faculty have already prepared their cluster together during the Workshop of the preceding summer. Below is the list of clusters that were offered in the fall and spring of 1976-77. It will be noted that two of the clusters in the fall of 1976 involve three courses:

Fall 1976
1. *Social and Religious Dimensions of Man*
   Sociology—Introduction to Sociology—J. Fitzpatrick
   Theology—Man and His Religious Experience—A. Grady

2. *Man: Alive, Personal, and Responsible*
Biology—Biological Concepts—M. Hegyi
Philosophy—Introduction to Problems of Morality—A. Varga
Philosophy—The Person: In Nature and Community—L. Feldstein

3. *Puritanism to Paganism: Values in America*
Philosophy—American Philosophy—E. Kraus
Communications—The Search for American Values—R. Schroth
History—The Shaping of Modern America   R. Himmelberg

4. *The Shaping of Human Experience: Philosophy and the Visual Arts*
Art History—Gods, Myths, & Mortals in Art through the Ages—I. Jaffe
Philosophy—The Problem of Man—J. Chethimattam

5. *What is Man? Religious and Psychological Resolutions*
Psychology—Personality—M. Massimo
Theology—Belief and Unbelief—D. Moore

Spring 1977
1. *Symbolism in Poetry and Religion*
English—Poetry—J. Doyle
Theology—Symbols and Sacraments: Encounter with God—S. Babos.

2. *Politics and the Literary Imagination*
English—Fiction—J. Christie
Political Science—Introduction to Politics—W. Baumgarth

3. *Responsible Use of Society's Resources*
Economics—Introduction to Micro-Economics—E. Dowling
Chemistry—Natural Science—R. Rozett

4. *The Image of Man: Implications for Public Policy*
Sociology—Introduction to Sociology—J. Macisco
Theology—Religion East and West—E. Rushmore

5. *Social and Religious Dimensions of Man*
Sociology—Introduction to Sociology—J. Fitzpatrick
Theology—Man and His Religious Experience—A. Grady

The Freshman Program aims at a general introductory study of moral values in the light of a unified moral issue. It is rather broad-based and sometimes indirect in its approach to value questions. It proposes to raise the consciousness level of both faculty and students regarding moral dilemmas. This need not involve major changes in course content, though the individual teacher may decide to make such changes. In any case, the faculty have taken great pains not to change the course so substantially that it becomes something quite different from what it was. The real challenge here, as it is in the Junior Program, is to steer a middle position between two extremes, that of leaving out moral issues altogether, and that of changing a course, say in English, into an ethics course. The faculty feel that this third course can be followed, though it will not be easy to achieve the goals.

Junior Program

The Junior Program involves approximately 100 students each semester who meet one day a week in a general session, and two days a week in four separate discussion sections of 25 students apiece. Each discussion section is led by one of four participating faculty from four different disciplines. At the time of registration, the student specifies the discussion section of his or her choice and that becomes the course for which credit is given. Unlike the Freshman Program, each student is registered for only one course, although he or she is able to profit by the material being taken in the three other courses.

In the Junior Program the student is explicitly confronted with the experience of the problems associated with decision-making, both from a theoretical point of view and in terms of one or several of the great moral or social problems of our time. Where the Freshman Program is rather broad-based and sometimes very indirect in its approach to value questions, the Junior Program is quite direct and explicit. The purpose is to discuss the precise problems involved in decision-making in areas of ethical, moral and value choices and to exemplify these issues by consideration of one or several specific problems. It is hoped that the students will experience and appreciate the complexity of decision-making from the point of view of the identification and clarification of both facts and values and their mutual interrelation. It is expected that the interdisciplinary staff will provide the needed expertise in both information and analysis. Below are listed the themes and courses that were offered during the 1976-77 academic year.

Fall 1976
Theme: "World Resources and Human Liberation"
   Political Science—The Politics of Hunger—M. Fergus
   Theology—Liberation, Revolution, and Christianity—D. Moore
   Economics—Development and Organization of the Middle
      East—M. Parvin

Physics—Contemporary Problems: Science and Society—J. Shapiro.

Spring 1977
Theme: "Social Conflict and Human Freedom"
   Philosophy—A Search for Justice—C. Kelbley
   Sociology—Sociological Perspective on Poverty and Disarmament—J. Kelly
   Afro-American Studies—Racial and Ethnic Conflict in the American City—M. Naison
   Communications—Communications: Freedom and Control—J. Phelan

Evaluation Procedures

As indicated at the beginning of this chapter, the Values Program as herein described is still in its early stages. Hence there has not been sufficient time to give a full-scale account of the results of the evaluation. However, it is possible at this time to record the steps taken in developing the evaluation procedures. During the 1976 Summer Workshop, an Evaluation Committee was appointed. Its task was to develop a statement of mission, goals, and objectives of the Values Program and a plan for evaluation. The Committee tried to remain sensitive to the variety of perspectives among the faculty concerning these matters. After working through the summer, the Committee presented its recommendations to the program faculty and these were accepted with but minor modifications.

Mission, Goals, and Objectives

The concepts of mission, goals, and objectives were borrowed from management technology. The definition of these concepts is as follows:

   Mission: overall aim of the program, the common denominator.

   Goals: more specific than the mission, the more particular actions through which it is hoped the mission will be accomplished.

   Objectives: the specific measurable activities which will be used in achieving goals, the criteria for evaluation.

Mission

The mission of the Values Program is to promote a reflective awareness of the individual and social values which are manifested in human actions and to develop the critical skills with which to appraise those values, so that appropriation or rejection of those values may be conscious, deliberate, and informed.

Goals

To develop an integrated curriculum in which value issues can be examined in an interdisciplinary context.

To foster a spirit of community among students, among faculty, and between students and faculty.

To enhance the development of faculty as scholars and teachers.

To provide a framework in which Fordham's traditional concern for moral values is critically and creatively examined.

Evaluation

The primary purpose of the evaluation is to obtain a good deal of information, some anticipated, some unanticipated, which will feed back into the program to help the faculty to do better what they intend to do. The secondary purpose is to obtain information about the Values Program which can be related to similar efforts in American higher education, thus providing the benefit of the experience for teachers and students in other colleges and programs. To achieve these purposes, the following evaluation procedures will be followed:

1. During the first week of school, the faculty teaching in the fall semester will be asked to respond briefly in writing to three open-ended questions:
   a. What do you conceive the purpose of the Values Program to be?
   b. What do you expect your students to get out of the program?
   c. What do you expect to get out of the program?
2. During the first week of school, the faculty in each course of the fall semester will be asked to collect brief written responses from their students to three open-ended questions:

    a. What do you conceive the purpose of the Values Program to be?

    b. Why did you register for the Values Program?

    c. What do you expect to get out of the program?

3. During the first two weeks of class and once again at the close of the semester, a randomly selected and statistically representative sample of students will be asked to take a standardized 45 item survey. Approximately 34 of the 168 Freshmen and 20 of the 100 Juniors will be asked to assist in this effort. The test is the Allport/Vernon/Lindzey "Study of Values." It is a well-known and highly reputable attitude questionnaire designed to document change over time in six areas of value: theoretical, economic, aesthetic, social, political, and religious. The questionnaire will be administered outside of class time. While the information from it will be very helpful to Fordham, it is given with an eye to sharing information with a wider population. The six areas of value change seem well suited to the scope of the program.

4. The Kohlberg research material (e.g., the Heinz dilemmas) will be administered to a handful of students and this will be followed up with an in-depth interview to examine further the students' reasons for resolving the dilemmas as they did. The purpose of the interview is to attempt to detect in a qualitative way any changes in the students' level of moral reasoning according to the Kohlberg criteria. Improvement of the students' moral reasoning along the Kohlberg stages is not a deliberate objective of the program, but it will be interesting to see if it is occurring as an unanticipated phenomenon.

5. At the close of the fall semester, each faculty member teaching in the program that semester will be interviewed for one hour according to an open-ended interview schedule. Obviously the faculty member's semester-end appraisal of his or her experience in the program will be the focus of the interview. Seventeen questions have been prepared for this occasion. The faculty will not be presented with the questions ahead of time so as to assure spontaneity in the responses.

6. A small and random sample of students will also be interviewed at the end of the semester to gain insight into the students' evaluation of the program. Like the faculty interview, the questions (approximately 15) will be scheduled but the responses will be open-ended.

7. Based on the responses of the students in the written essay at the beginning of the semester regarding the reasons for their

selection of the program, a brief questionnaire will be developed by the Evaluation Committee during the course of the semester. This questionnaire, approximately 15 minutes long, will be on the true/false, multiple-choice order and will be given to all students in the fall semester. The faculty will be asked to administer this in class.

As can be seen, open-ended questions, some written but most in interview form and interpreted according to the purposes of the program, make up the primary method of data collection in the evaluation. The standardized, quantifiable methods have been kept to a bare minimum and chosen only after careful consideration of their value to the program and to a certain extent to the larger educational world. Most importantly, perhaps, this evaluation will rely on the ongoing self-evaluation of the faculty in the program who will be making constant observations of themselves, their students, and to some extent their faculty colleagues. Part and parcel of this observation is the mutual aid faculty can give one another by sharing insights within and between clusters and by mutual presence at one another's classes.

Though it will take several semesters before a judgment can be made regarding the success of the Values Program, several important and encouraging results emerged very early. The first result was the development of an intellectual and social community among the faculty during the two-week Workshop. Many faculty were really meeting one another for the first time, and genuine interests and friendships were formed. Twenty-seven faculty from almost every one of the seventeen undergraduate departments met to discuss, not this or that discipline, but the overall educational experience of the undergraduates. In the process they were educating themselves. Faculty in the same cluster or seminar were exchanging bibliographies so that a theologian was reading a book on sociology, or an historian an article on communications. A philosopher was learning for the first time what one of his colleagues who happens to be an art historian was doing in a particular course. An article could be written on this alone. But let it suffice to say that the faculty without exception found the Workshop to be a rewarding experience and they plan to involve more faculty in a similar experience.

A like result is being effected among the students. On any campus with a large enrollment and a fairly wide choice of courses and programs, students tend to become dispersed. Those who are together in one course rarely meet in any other course. In the

Values Program, however, the same students are together in several classes, especially in the Freshman Program. Students are getting to know one another on a first-name basis and friendships are being formed that hopefully will last throughout the four years of college and into the post-college years. Academically, the students find it extremely satisfying to have several of their courses integrated into a unified theme. This overcomes the fragmented nature that is frequently characteristic of the program of courses taken by a student each semester. The students also find stimulating the interchange and often sharp disagreement that take place among faculty and students where all opinions on a subject are given an open hearing.

In view of these preliminary results, it is tempting to say that the Values Program is "failure-proof." For there is every indication that these results will continue. In a more sober moment, however, one realizes that a further evaluation will be necessary to assess the program in depth in terms of its success as an experiment in moral education. While it is still hoped that it can meet this test, the experience so far gives promise that the program will prove to be well worth the time and effort put into it.

Moral Education at the Elementary School Level

Harry B. Kavanagh

In a previous chapter, Hersch and Paolitto described the cognitive-developmental approach to moral education (Piaget, Kohlberg and his associates). They focused especially on the implications of moral education research for teachers on the high school and junior high levels. By way of contrast, this chapter will focus more on the elementary and early childhood years and less on adolescence. The approach described will be less cognitive-developmentally oriented and more Freudian-oriented. It will not, however, follow the Freudian view that moral character is indelibly established in infancy. If this view were correct, moral education would be a futile activity. A more realistic approach seems to be that moral formation is a life-long process and every phase and stage brings challenges and opportunities for more mature morality.

This chapter will begin with some preconditions of morality which are deeply influenced in early childhood such as: personal identity, self-acceptance, moral models, conscience and competence. When these five preconditions of morality have been established, it will be argued that moral factors evolve as logical consequences. Five moral factors will be discussed: moral judgment, future orientation, moral personalism, moral tolerance and moral creativity.

Preconditions of Morality

According to Kay (1975), there are five questions asked by all children with the potential to be moral. These questions must be satisfactorily answered by each child before he can become a mature moral agent. Kay calls these questions the preconditions of morality and they are:

1. Who am I? or identification
2. What am I really like? or self-acceptance
3. How must I behave? or moral models
4. What is the right thing to do? or conscience
5. How am I doing? or competence

This is not an exhaustive list. Its accuracy is partly confirmed by Robert Ardrey (1967) who studied the animal origins of society. Among his conclusions was one that says even animals need to establish and maintain their identity, security and source of approval.

The preconditions do not rest on rationality but upon relationships. I argue that moral education must make a sustained effort to establish and develop these preconditions. Each precondition is examined below.

Identification

The fundamental human question, "Who am I?" can only be answered in a social context for our identity is established in social relationships. Long ago Aristotle defined man as a "social animal." Teilhard (1960) says that "union differentiates." These two words of Teilhard's contain the fundamental truth that a person's uniqueness emerges from his or her corporate life. In general, a child first establishes a "self" in a family. It is acquired by the child spontaneously, without direct training or reward, without anyone teaching, and without any intent of the child to learn. This subtle process is usually called identification and refers to the process that leads the child to think, feel and behave as though the characteristics of another person, usually the parent, belong to him (Mussen, Conger and Kagan, 1974).

Identification begins with the child's perception that he and the model are similar in some ways. Once the identification is formed it will be strengthened or weakened in the relationship with the model. Since identity is established in relationships, it is thereby intimately bound up with morality. As T. S. Eliot said, "There is no life that is not lived in community." Yet community life must be lived by autonomous individuals who act responsibly. Thus irresponsible individuality ought not to be confused with mature identity. A cell which goes its own way is cancerous.

Children identify mostly with people they love and admire. A child identifies with those he/she loves because he/she needs protection and security. He/she must, therefore, keep in with those who give protective love. Things do not always run smoothly in this process or work out for the best. Sometimes children admire undesirable characters, because they are strong and ruthless like the gangsters in films and on T.V. A boy may admire a father who is a big bully and so becomes a little bully himself. As the old saying goes "like father like son, like mother like daughter."

The tendency to identification does not pass with childhood, but continues throughout life. One of the forms it takes in early adolescence is hero worship, in which boys or girls admire some character, historical or fictitious, and model their lives on his or her standards. In later adolescence identification is frequently linked with ideals, that may be social, political, athletic, religious or scholastic. The adolescent says in his or her unconscious "I want to be like that person when I grow up." This innate tendency to impersonate, to live in the lives of other people is of great value in building personalities especially of children.

Some practical applications for parents and teachers

a. It is a good idea to help a child mix with a variety of children, adolescents and adults for the enrichment of personality. By this means a child develops a character and personality distinctly his or her own. He/she develops individuality. We have as many selves as there are people with whom we identify ourselves. It is undesirable for a child to live with one person alone, like a devoted mother, because he/she misses the opportunity of a variety of identifications with others which is the essence of individuality.

b. Some parents are neither lovable nor admirable and in such cases unless a child can find a teacher or kindly neighbor to identify with he/she may not turn out well. Sometimes a change from a bad home to a good home, in which there is love and affection, changes the child's character, because of the formation of new and healthier identification.

c. A child will accept the teaching and example of one with whom he/she identifies, and will reject the teaching of one he/she dislikes. A goal for the child is not merely good behavior but more especially to create the right dispositions towards morality, that is to say, to produce not merely a well behaved child but rather one who wishes to behave well.

d. A parent or teacher should not only help children to share their toys but to be generous in other ways as well, not merely to be polite but to be considerate of others also. Ways of thinking are even more important than ways of acting.

Self-Acceptance

In imitation a child takes over the action of others. For example, if you are planting the child wants to plant too, if you are eating the child wants to eat. If you smack him, he would like to smack you, but since you won't let him, he may smack the baby instead. In identification the child goes further and identifies his/her personality with that of another person. No longer does he say, "I'm brave like Daddy" but having incorporated his father's standards of behavior, says "I'm brave." There is a shift in the child from emphasis on another person's behavior to his/her own behavior now internalized. He/she moves from being told what to do, to telling self what to do. It seems to be by a perfectly natural process that a child develops standards of behavior and morality. If you never taught a child anything about right and wrong, he/she would develop moral or immoral standards by the process of identification.

By the time a child is four years old, he/she has an organized personality, with standards of judgment. Though not physically independent and capable of making its own way in the world, the child feels independent, dispenses with parents, tries to go its own way and sometimes get lost. When a policeman finds a lost child, he may say "Are you lost?" The child may answer "No, my Mommy is."

Once the child has developed a personality with standards of judgment, he/she asks "What am I really like?" The child usually learns that he or she is a mixture of good and evil. The discovery of this truth is frightening. Therefore, few children accept themselves as they really are. Here the use in the family of Rogers' empathic understanding and unconditioned unacceptance can help a child accept self as he or she really is. A good home is one in which a child can be "bad" and be corrected in an atmosphere of constant, unqualified love. This should also be true of classrooms, especially with young children. Kay (1975) maintains that unless self-acceptance is genuine, moral growth is impaired. Until a child can realistically accept himself as a person he cannot treat others as persons in their own right.

Kagan, Mussen, and Conger (1974) make some limited generalizations about the probable effects on children of different parental behaviors. Hostility on the part of parents tends to produce counterhostility and aggression. Parental refusal to allow the child to develop as an independent, self-reliant individual promotes infantile behavior, e.g., the boy remains tied to his mother's apron strings. The parent who is warm and accepting, encouraging autonomy, is usually regarded by child-rearing specialists as preferable. The child of such parents is likely to be active, outgoing, sociable, independent, friendly and lacking in hostility toward himself and others (Becker, 1965).

Some practical applications for parents and teachers

a. The child is more likely to accept himself or herself if parents and teachers show acceptance of the child through a policy of realistic praise for the child's efforts. There should be far more recognition of the child's efforts than criticism for errors. Errors can be corrected in a spirit of positive instruction rather than of blame. One can say "Here's a better way of doing that" rather than "Stop doing it that way."

b. Various authors have written of the child as a moral philosopher. The child shows signs of this bent when he/she asks the question "Why?" Instead of being impatient with these questions, adults should welcome them, especially when they pertain to reasons why he/she should or should not act in particular ways. Parents and teachers should accept the challenge of attempting to explain the basis for moral behaviors to children. Obviously they should adapt their explanations to the age and development of the children they are dealing with.

c. Parents and teachers should provide materials and opportunities for children to direct their energies in constructive directions. For instance, they could take up hobbies, learn to play a musical instrument, learn to cook, have a share in household chores or schoolroom chores. Each of these activities involves the child's personally completing a task and feeling a sense of accomplishment for doing it well. When the task is well done it is important that adults give proper praise for the achievements. Thereby the child's self-acceptance is facilitated.

d. Parents and teachers should recognize the importance that games can play in the social and moral development of the child. Opportunities for the child to play in large groups, in small groups and alone should be provided as each type of play aids in social development. The child's knowledge of the rules of the game and growth in reasoning about the rules are important for moral development.

Moral Models

As the child goes through the process of identification and accepting self, he/she asks the next crucial question, "How must I behave?" It is at this point he or she needs moral models to imitate. According to Baldwin (1956), one of the strongest and most deeply rooted factors which help a young child to adapt to life is imitation. The child is not taught to imitate but does so naturally, as do young animals, e.g., a young rabbit is not afraid of humans and runs away only in imitation of its mother. Parents are usually the first models but this is not exclusively a parental function. Siblings also can be models. As the child's social environment expands, other figures emerge, such as peers, teachers and other adults.

There has been much research to show, even with adults, that a model can elicit moral or immoral behavior (Bandura and Walters, 1963). After a child has observed other people (models) who obtain positive consequences for behavior, he or she tends to act more readily in a similar manner. If a child sees other children receive praise for being helpful at play, his or her tendency to behave in a similar manner increases. Conversely, when models are punished for their behavior, observing children tend to become more inhibited about displaying similar behavior (Bandura, Ross and Ross, 1963).

Modeling may have powerful effects on behavior, but not all models are equally effective for all children. The attributes of the observer (Bandura and Walters, 1963) and the model, as well as the model's relationship with the child will affect the likelihood that the modeled behavior will be influential or not (Mischel and Liebert, 1967). Children tend to adopt the standards of models who are rewarding and powerful, but tend to reject the same standards when they are modeled by persons low in these attributes (Mischel and Gerusc, 1966). These experimental findings are congruent with studies reporting correlations between the affection of parents and prosocial behavior of their children (Hoffman and Saltzstein, 1967) and suggest that parental affection and moral modeling tends to be conducive to children's moral behavior. Just as aggression feeds on aggression, so does future moral development to a considerable degree depend on past moral development.

Practical applications for parents and teachers

a. Since a child learns through imitation he/she finds it easier to do something when shown how to do it than being told how to do it. A child will imitate even when it can't understand verbal explanations. Because of this fact parents and teachers will be concerned about the "good example" which they and others present to children.

b. Inconsistencies between adults' instructions and behaviors are readily detected by children. Adults may instruct children to obey traffic lights and yet cross the street against the red light. They may instruct children to be honest and not to cheat and yet boast of "killing" a summons or not paying a legitimate tax. Young people will seek to imitate the behavior and not the instructions of adults. Reflection upon this fact could cause adults to improve their personal behavior.

c. Parents and teachers model both behaviors and attitudes. Attitudes of self-acceptance and acceptance of others are indicated not only by what is said but by such things as choice of TV programs, favorite athletes and entertainers, magazines, art and photographs displayed in the home and in school. Teachers and parents will be concerned that these more indirect modeling activities show respect for all ethnic, cultural and religious heritages.

Conscience

A child's models may exhibit a great variety of behaviors from right to left and from a high stage of development to a low one. Thus a child must ask "But what is the right thing for me to do?" Some say, "Let your conscience be your guide." This response is deceptively simple. When we look back through history we find people who murdered, pillaged and tortured others at the behest of conscience.

According to Wright (1971), conscience, from a psychological point of view, is a faculty of the mind which enables an individual to discriminate right from wrong; to generate an impulse to act in the right way and to avoid acting in the wrong way; to observe and record the individual's actual behavior; and to blame or approve him after he has acted. Since it is a faculty of the mind, it is assumed all people have some kind of consciences. The question is often asked as to whether this moral sense is innate or not. Psychological evidence suggests that the moral sense as such is not innate but the ingredients which go into the formation of a moral conscience are innate, namely the processes of imitation and identification.

A child's development of conscience is very much influenced by parental values and the nature of the parent-child relationships. A parent whose own conscience is defective can hardly serve as a good model for conscience development in a child. According to Mussen,

Conger and Kagan (1974), it would appear that optimal conscience development in the child is facilitated (1) if the parents' own moral standards are mature and reasonable, (2) if adoption of the parents' standards by the child is based on positive identification and modeling.

If the child's development of conscience is impaired, either because of deficiency in the parents' standards or because disturbed relationships militated against identifying positively with parental values, or both, he or she may become delinquent or otherwise lacking in social responsibility. Rather than being guided by internalized moral values he or she may be guided by external considerations of probable reward and punishment.

Some Practical Applications for Parents and Teachers

a. A child may ask "What is the right thing for me to do?" From a social point of view the answer is that which is in conformity with social customs and doesn't break the public law.

From a religious moral point of view, right may be said to be following the major laws and perhaps less important rules of one's religion.

b. In view of their importance in the development of the child's conscience, parents and teachers should not hesitate to discuss the range of motivations for moral behavior (ego-centered, social, principled, religious). Thus the young person can find and accept his present dominant level and yet become aware of other possibilities. Parents and teachers can seek illustrations of behavior and motivation for the behavior that approximates the age and development of the child. The illustrations can be literary, historical or culled from current events. Nagging and excessive sibling comparison should be avoided.

c. There is a clear relationship between moral modeling (discussed above) and the growth of conscience. Parents and teachers will be sensitive to the importance of their moral consistency and their universal quest for justice in their personal behavior. Thereby they will earn the esteem of the young and the right to help them distinguish right from wrong.

d. Parents and teachers should be cautious about expecting the child's conscience to be developed beyond his years and reasoning capacity. For instance, it is unrealistic to appeal to principled motivation to the young child. In addition, parents and teachers should be patient with the young person's efforts at impulse control; the effort toward control and to follow conscience should be acknowledged and encouraged.

Competence

After the child has acquired an identity, accepted himself as he is, modeled himself on an ideal person and developed an internalized control, he wants to know, "How am I doing?" Everyone knows from experience "nothing succeeds like success." Love alone is no longer enough, the child also must experience some kind of success and the praise which accompanies it. Any kind of ridicule, sarcasm and personal belittling of children, common in some homes and schools, hinders the establishment of this precondition.

According to White (1966), the concept of self is partly determined by the way others treat one, but the core of this self-feeling consists in what one feels one is able to do. In a society as achievement-minded as ours, a person's worth is established in large measure by what he can do. It is only in textbooks that people are accepted for their own sake, independently of what they can do. Even with the young the ability to do something well gives a child confidence, self-respect and acceptance by other children, teachers, counselors and parents.

A strong argument could be made to help every child acquire some unique competence, some skills that would help him assert himself as a unique person. The necessity of being a distinct individual in one's own right within a social framework is described by Erikson (1963) who says that a necessary nucleus for a sense of identity is a progressive mastery of useful actions leading to a sense of competence:

> Ego identity gains real strength only from wholehearted and consistent recognition of real accomplishment, and this recognition must be on the part of the child, for he cannot be fooled by empty praise and condescending encouragement. (p. 277)

According to Erikson, it is especially important for the child to see his accomplishments as being relevant to adult social reality. The child's accomplishments must have meaning in his culture. The child needs a relationship, as soon as possible, with the larger world. Erikson (1968) further remarks that:

> The real danger is that throughout the long years of going to school a child will never acquire the enjoyment of work and pride in doing at least one kind of thing really well. (p. 125)

Every child, however inadequate, should enjoy the dignity of some personal success. On the other hand, psychological wounds of any kind, so often inflicted without any realization of the profound damage, must inevitably affect individual morality. Hemming (1957) describes the dark side of the picture. He notes that a child's confidence can be undermined by too much criticism which makes him feel worthless.

Practical applications for parents and teachers

a. While some children, the rare geniuses, achieve great skill or other accomplishments at a very early age, most children demonstrate their first meaningful accomplishments between the years 7 and 11. These accomplishments which give them a sense of competency are shown primarily in school work and in athletics.

b. Teachers and parents should try to foster children's accomplishment at school by sparking their interest and motivation. Learning should be made attractive and knowledge should be regarded as a good area for accomplishment. Those children who achieve well at school should be praised. Special efforts should be exerted with the non-achievers to have them learn what they can, especially the knowledge and skills that are fundamental to today's living.

c. Parents should foster achievement in other areas in which the child shows an interest. Many children, boys and girls, seek to distinguish themselves in athletics and their participation in Little Leagues should be encouraged unless coaches push the children excessively.

d. Competency should also be fostered in the social area. Young people should be encouraged, not forced, to mingle with members of both sexes. Parents should encourage a sense of ready communication between themselves and their children. The discussion of family problems in the family conference should foster this easy communication between the generations. Children who feel that they can communicate with peers of both sexes and with members of an older generation have a sense of personal competence which helps them in their psychological and moral growth.

Summary

A sense of identity is necessary before an individual can become autonomous. Self-acceptance aids one to make valid moral judgments. Moral models facilitate the young child's way of behaving and helps to guide early conduct. A mature and informed conscience provides the inward validation of such judgments. Competence causes all the elements to cohere and are usually confirmed by reward and reinforcement. These "conditions" take place mostly in the home. Hence child-rearing techniques and the general quality of home life are crucial to later moral development.

Moral Factors

As the child's social environment expands from the family to the school and larger society, he or she is subjected to ever-widening influences—peers, teachers, books, television. Yet the most significant factor in determining the kind of person he or she will become is the home and the kind of relationships he or she has with parents (Freud, 1933). The second most important factor in determining the future person is the social milieu in which he or she develops (Erikson, 1950). Unless standards of right and wrong are learned in the home and the social milieu, the child, and later the adolescent and adult is apt to yield to asocial temptations or to his own urges for uncontrolled aggression, sex, and regressive behavior.

Mature conscience development requires cognitive maturation to make moral judgments. While developing, the child internalizes important concepts in the home and in society such as future—orientation, consequences of right and wrong, values, ideals, the feelings of others and the logical necessity for people to cooperate with one another in the interests of all (Kohlberg, 1963). In the following section six moral factors are discussed. They are chosen as among the most important elements that pertain to moral growth. They are: moral judgment, future orientation, moral personalism, moral tolerance, moral creativity and empathy.

Moral Judgment

Moral judgment is probably the only truly moral characteristic of behavior in that it is cognitive and hence the only uniquely human element. It is a cognitive process that develops through invariant sequential stages and levels. In the very young child it is absolute, then it becomes relative and finally with some people it becomes principled. According to Piaget (1932), the child begins life with a state of mind which causes him to merge with the environment as if he and the environment were one. The earliest forms of stimulation help him to separate himself from the environment conceptually and think of himself as a separate entity. As time passes and as he encounters the environment through a variety of situations he tends to be a realist. He is very much concerned with one adult, namely, his or her caretaker and to a lesser extent with other adults. In his world adults are all powerful. He sees them as the sources of authority and the objects of dependency. As far as he is concerned, they are always right and they are to be obeyed regardless of all other considerations. He, therefore, sees all rules as being absolute, inflexible, final and beyond his control. Like all other rules, he sees moral rules as fixed rather than as instruments of human purpose and values. Later as a realist, the child lives in a world which is controlled for him in the nature of an absolute dictatorship and in which he must serve unquestioningly. The locus ôf control is external; there is a "unilateral respect" for adults.

Piaget conceptualized a gradual shift in the child's reasoning as interaction between the child and other children increased. In the games he played, conflicts and disagreements were resolved but only as a result of cooperation and compromise. Seeing another's point of view and viewing situations from angles other than his own, he begins to query the absolute standards he formerly observed. He changes from being a realist to being a relativist.

As a relativist he is prepared to share in rule-making. Instead of living in an absolute dictatorship he is now living in a democracy. Rules are not fixed and unchangeable. On the contrary, rules are for people and people can change rules. Whereas formerly he judged human behavior in terms of a result or outcome he now takes into consideration not only the consequence but also the intention of an individual. In a word, he weighs all considerations rather than just one consideration. When "the whole jar spilled" the damage would be taken into consideration but also the conditions or circumstances that caused it to happen.

In terms of their psychological functioning these two moralities (moral realism and moral relativism) are in Piaget's view, quite different. Though they can be conceived as distinct, the moral thinking of a child is a mixture of the two. Indeed, many of the traces of moral realism can be detected in the thinking of adults.

It is important to remember that Piaget's study of moral judgment occurred relatively early in his career and appeared in a seminal monograph, *The Moral Judgment of the Child* (1932). Consequently, important outcomes from Piaget's later investigations could not have been taken into consideration in developing a theory of child morality. For example, the sequential nature of the stages might not have been fully conceptualized by Piaget at this particular point. Similarly, the role of peers as change agents in moral reasoning might not have been as clearly conceptualized at this point as it was later on. In general, the data on which Piaget relied may have been thin by necessity, thus limiting a detailed explanation of the processes by which children develop moral concepts.

Most probably the work of Kohlberg (explained in the previous chapter) has compensated for the deficit in Piaget. Kohlberg has carefully taken relevant features of Piaget's later thinking and applied them to the area of moral judgment. In doing so, Kohlberg has expanded and in some instances reformulated the original statements of Piaget. One of the more important additions of Kohlberg is the area of assessment of moral judgment through the use of hypothetical dilemmas. This in turn opened the way for further research and further expansion of existing theory, some of which we read in this book.

The implications of the theory and research initiated by Kohlberg to moral education in the school are important. Since mature morality consists in applying moral standards to concrete situations, it is evident that each person should decide upon norms or standards for behavior. These norms should develop with maturity. If children are fixated at the authoritarian level of moral judgment, they will always have to live in a state of dependence on authority for moral decisions. Teachers must attempt to help children develop moral judgments to a mature level. They must help children develop that inner discipline which does not leave them at the mercy of impulses and immediate gratifications. The "now" generation seems to have been shortchanged in this regard by parents and teachers. Teachers could provide more opportunities in classrooms for moral sensitivity and empathic role taking. Finally, children must be helped implement their moral decisions so that they don't just become smart moral thinkers who can reason one way and behave another.

Some Practical Applications for Teachers and Parents

a. Most elementary school children will be at the preconventional level of Kohlberg's hierarchy. Teachers should begin their moral education program by assessing the current stage of each of their students. Thereby teachers can avoid the use of too high a level of moral reasoning which is incomprehensible to the child and consequently ignored. Likewise teachers can avoid use of too low a level of moral reasoning.

b. Teachers can present students with dilemmas emphasizing moral reasoning one stage above his/her reasoning level. When doing this, the teacher should point out to the students how such thinking (higher stage) produces a more adequate solution. The emphasis should be on growth in moral judgment, not merely on clarification of the child's current stage.

c. Teachers should provide students time to reflect in a meditative manner on their dilemma solutions. They could, for example, keep personal journals (if they can write) on their solutions. The teacher could then identify the students' thought processes from their journals. Later the teacher could meet with each child and discuss the reasoning indicated in the writing. Encouragement and stimulation of the child will characterize the meeting, though inconsistencies and inadequacies of reasoning will be pointed out.

d. Parents should be aware of and involved in the process of stimulation of moral judgment as described above. An orientation program emphasizing the goals of the program should be planned and presented. Suggestions regarding cooperation at home should be presented.

Future Orientation

Valid moral judgments will always involve the possibility that any deferred benefits may outweigh immediate gratifications. The ability to defer one's desire for gratification has many moral ramifications. Our society stresses present deprivation for future gratification, though it could be argued that the counter-culture concept is displacing the traditional deferred-gratification pattern in favor of a present-gratification pattern. The "I-want-it-now" mentality has moral implications, ranging from temper tantrums and theft to quickie wealth, sex and power. This mentality causes some children to choose things that are immediately rewarding but ultimately defeating. In contrast, there are other children who are able to consider future consequences of conduct and as a result can defer gratification of an impulse, in order to obtain a more adequate satisfaction in the future. Obviously, the deeply religious-minded are future-oriented in that they decide upon behavior in the light of their belief in an afterlife and in the conviction that ultimately good deeds are rewarded and evil deeds are punished.

Future orientation is part of socialization, which takes place especially between ages seven and twelve, when children like playing together in groups and are no longer egocentric. This stage is sometimes called the primitive man phase because it represents a period in evolution when the savage was at his prime, when he successfully struggled with the forces of nature and adjusted them for his own purpose. Children at this stage utter wild war whoops; plot among themselves, go hunting and fishing, are untidy and steal when inclined to do so. They tend to regard other groups including adults as hostile and therefore fair game.

One might say that stealing and cheating is almost a natural characteristic of this stage. Mischel and Gilligan (1962) did research to check the relationship between children who could delay gratification and those who could not. Children could get prizes for cheating. They could get better prizes later, if they could delay gratification, namely, by not cheating. Those who got the best prizes and were able to delay gratification, cheated much less than those who preferred immediate rewards.

Berkowitz (1964) extended this research beyond the school situation when he suggested that a history of protracted failure and frustration would inevitably cause an individual to lose all hope of ever succeeding. Consequently, a person anticipating further failure and frustration is more likely to take what he can when he can.

The development of impulsivity and its attendant practice of acquiring immediate gratification is learned in the home and often is not corrected in the elementary school as it should be. It frequently occurs in lower socio-economic homes where both parents have to work, and the children are turned loose in the streets. The powerful appetites of the children are unchecked, like those of primitive mankind. Such children are at the mercy of their own impulses. As they grow up, drinking, drugs, violence or sex may become their favorite recreation as was pointed out by Claude Brown (1965). Children growing up in such an environment are unlikely to acquire the habit of deferred gratification or develop a life-style in which moral development plays an important part. It is more likely to be "survival of the fittest" and "might makes right."

The relevance of deferred gratification to morality is such that crimes may result when the young person rejects the idea of deferred gratification. A delinquent may be one who desires the socially approved rewards but rather than study, work or save to get them, turns to crime to facilitate immediate gratification. Charis Frankenburg (1961) wrote a book upon this foundation, that immediate gratification progresses from an over-indulged infancy to a criminal adulthood. In order to stress the point, she subtitles her book, "*Spoilt Baby into Angry Young Man.*" She argues, when an infant cries, a pacifier is put in his or her mouth for gratification. When a child cries, a lollipop is provided, when the adolescent has a strong feeling, a cigarette replaces the pacifier and the lollipop. The "I-want-it-now" mentality, she argues, is the root cause of the delinquent cases she tried as a magistrate in Oxford, England.

Some Practical Applications for Teachers and Parents

a. The family and school policy regarding money and tokens (for rewards) should have the idea of future orientation in mind. The benefits of saving for a superior purchase or exchange should be emphasized. Children should be encouraged to make these special purchases themselves rather than having someone else do it for them. Families should consider the advantages of a regular, realistic allowance, supplemented by moderate paid work, as a basis for planning for the needs of the coming week or weeks.

b. Parents and teachers should adopt a consistent policy in reaction to disapproved behavior. One approach involves negative reinforcement, i.e., the child does not receive any reaction to the behavior. Another approach is that of "natural consequences," i.e., a child makes a demand of a parent because he says he's sick and so he's immediately put to bed. In instances such as these the child learns a sense of responsibility because of the immediate future results of his behavior. The connection between their behavior and future results often must be pointed out to children.

c. Certain types of play pit children against the forces of nature instead of other humans and bring out cooperation, comradeship, leadership, more than do conventional games. Such play includes sailing, swimming, mountain climbing, hiking, camping, jogging. In general, they require and encourage a degree of self-discipline and an orientation toward future self-development based upon the hope of improved achievement later on.

d. Parents and teachers can encourage a sense of future-orientation among the young by frankly discussing their own experiences regarding deferral of gratification, such as a willingness or unwillingness to work hard before obtaining medium or high level employment. In addition, they should point to the long years of preparation which outstanding models undergo. Such models include great athletes, political figures, inventors, and the great moral leaders of our time and of the past.

Moral Personalism

Moral personalism in this context refers to the degree to which parents and teachers regard children as persons or the degree to which any individual is capable of treating others as persons. It is only after a child has been loved and respected that he or she can love or respect others. A fundamental law of social interaction is to treat others as we ourselves have been treated (Kay, 1975). We tend to do to children what was done to us, especially in the home and in the classroom. Moral education in the classroom is very much learned in relationships. These relationships may be between teacher and student or student and student. Neither in the classroom, the home nor society is anyone 'an island unto self'. Since we live in relationships, morality becomes necessary. Morality only exists between persons in relationships. If people are treated as things, there can be no morality. Mounier (1952) argued that when we treat people as objects we despair of them, and when we despair of them we evacuate their lives of meaning, purpose, hope and potential. "To despair of anyone is to make him desperate." Along the same lines, Maslow (1970) found that the mature self-actualizing person always acknowledged the worth of others by according them the personal respect they deserved. For this, he says, "acknowledges another person as an independent entity and as a separate and autonomous individual" (p. 196). Teilhard (1960) with his cosmic perspective makes the same point by arguing that when people abuse human relationships "they fritter away, by neglect or lust, the universe's reserves for personalization" (p. 75).

In light of the above, a great moral problem of our time must be the fact that people are no longer regarded as human persons but services. It is a prostitution of an individual to think of him or her in such a manner. This is true not only of individuals but of whole societies through industrialization. People become depersonalized, alienated, less human and less moral. Insofar as the school reflects the society in which it exists and prepares children for a capitalistic society, it also may contribute to depersonalization. It frequently stresses systems for doing things and not the quality of teachers and students. As Kant pointed out, we should treat each other as ends rather than means to an end. In many institutions, the personal element has been sacrificed through increased use of computers, bureaucracy, depersonalized administrators and impersonal systems. Such institutions are not conducive to morality. It is very important for schools, especially elementary schools, to regard children as persons, to emphasize human relationships and personal values. Even though the school may reflect the society in which it exists, it must also help to reform it. It is only when children are treated as persons that they can treat others as persons in their own right.

Thoughtful parents and teachers will help children to appreciate what is special about humans that makes each human person endowed with a great dignity, regardless of actual achievements. The fact that humans are superior to animals in many ways should be developed: that they can distinguish right from wrong, have the ability to solve difficult problems, have great literatures, have a free will (as illustrated by many individuals' resistance to tyranny). Religious parents will discuss the soul and afterlife as special factors of humanity. All these considerations will help the child to evaluate highly all other humans and to avoid considering them as services or as means. The child will be more likely to take into account the thinking, the feelings and the welfare of others, and is not likely to accept as model the "con" man, the clever fraud, whose fortune is made through abusing human relationships and using others as means for personal gain.

Some Practical Applications for Teachers and Parents

a. Teachers and parents with a sense of moral personalism will habitually act toward children and others with deep respect, fairness, consistency, consideration for others' feelings. They will avoid such behaviors as sarcasm, belittling, self-aggrandizement at others' expense.

b. Teachers and parents demonstrate their moral personalism not only by empathic listening and attending behavior but also by their critical assessment of ideas and expectation of careful reasoning on the part of the young. They should show their respect by probing for the reasoning or basis for children's ideas.

c. Respect for children is shown by parents and teachers when they reveal their reasons for rules in the home and in school. This kind of openness helps induct the young into adult society and into a sense of responsibility for their behavior. A result of this kind of openness with children may be a modification of the rules after parents and teachers have heard evaluation and criticism from children.

d. A critical test of teachers' and parents' genuine sense of the personhood of the young is their reaction to irrational and mischievous behavior. In these situations adults can appeal to the self-respect of the young persons, and try to model rationality and a sense of empathy.

Moral Tolerance

Bronfenbrenner (1960) concluded that Piaget's two stage morality, moral realism or restraint and moral relativism or cooperation, reflected the fact that dominant authoritarian parents led children to adopt a morality of adult restraint in infancy. Children with a high degree of restraint in their personalities are basically authoritarian. They are most secure and happiest when the conduct, the ideas, and the people around them are always the same. They want to subscribe to a specific authority always and in this sense are conformists. They cannot tolerate new ideas and new modes of behavior. They only see black and white; grey is a color of threat. Such children can easily grow up to accommodate to the monotonous work of business, industry, the military and indeed many of our educational institutions. But this limited viewpoint and behavior breeds intolerance, which is inimical to morality development in children because it prevents them from abstracting moral principles from a variety of concrete experiences.

A tolerant child is more accepting of change in his or her social environment. As such a child grows up he tends to solve problems by looking for principles rather than formal, legal prescriptions. In looking for moral principles, he will feel neither inadequate nor insecure, though personal experiences may not have provided any clear guidance. Thus the more tolerant child will tend more towards the development of inner control and autonomy. The tolerant child will not depend on authoritatively imposed directives for moral decision making.

It seems that the structured-democratic home or classroom, rather than the heavily authoritarian one succeeds best in allowing tolerance in children to develop. Sugarman (1970) writes about Daytop Village, a therapeutic community for drug addicts: "There must be some clear authority structure so that residents know whose orders they are required to follow" (p. 80). The authority structure must be used to prepare children for the day when they can travel alone in life. Erikson (1963) referring to the need for the child to exercise autonomy within a stable structure says: "This is the infantile source of later attempts in adult life to govern by the letter rather than the spirit" (p. 244).

In conclusion, a parent or a teacher must enable children to attain freedom of inquiry and discussion so that they can probe behind the regulations governing behavior to the underlying principles. The socio-economic backgrounds of parents and teachers seem to profoundly influence their behavior in this matter. Parents and teachers from low socio-economic backgrounds tend to tolerate less from their children and place more emphasis on the need for authority and obedience.

Some Practical Applications for Teachers and Parents

a. In the classroom and at home children should be encouraged to discuss problems that pertain to their behaviors such as learning problems, fighting, name-calling, talking out of turn. The purpose of the discussion is to learn the basic motivation of the behavior and alternate methods of achieving the desired goals. This kind of discussion should help children become aware of different ways of expressing self. Children would be less demanding of a uniform method of behaving.

b. The method of "brainstorming" can be helpful in helping children become more tolerant of different positions. In this method a problem is proposed and the first step is that of encouraging everyone present to propose a solution and no criticism is allowed. Everyone sees the positive side of the proposals. This kind of exercise can broaden the perspective of children as they become aware of ideas that they had never entertained favorably before. Obviously, in the long run each of the ideas must be critically examined for the best possible solution.

c. Parents and teachers should encourage children to read about or view entertainment programs that demonstrate customs and behaviors of other nations, other groups in society, other cultural backgrounds. This kind of exposure should help the young person to be better aware of his own heritage and to appreciate the values and strengths of others. Thereby the possibility of future bias toward others will be undermined, and the likelihood of a broad view towards those who are "different" will be increased.

d. Parents and teachers will discuss with children the nature of authority in the home, in the school and in society. They will help children see that the purpose of authority in the home and in the school is to gradually help the young to reach autonomy, self-governance. In the greater society, authority is directed toward carrying out the will of the government, which is hopefully the will of the people. At any rate, children should see that their obedience to authority is reasonable, has a time-limitation, and is to be ultimately phased out and replaced by the individual's self-determination. Yet obedience to other authority, e.g., to government and to one's Maker, perdures and is an acceptable function of a reasonable person.

Moral Creativity

Moral creativity in this context does not mean we can act as we like. It means we act on moral principles but always with openness that is guided by clarity and reason with a certain personal uniqueness. Torrance (1962) maintains that creative children are characterized by "searching for rewards and searching for uniqueness" (p. 124). In a crowded, technologically oriented urbanized society like ours, personal uniqueness may be rare and difficult. Barron (1963) studied creative individuals and noted that they refused to surrender their originality to the demands of society. Five years after the original study such children were also characterized by flexibility of personality and dynamism of thought. Getzels and Jackson (1962) conclude that when a child "chooses the ethical rather than the expedient alternative and holds to personal ideals transcending such qualities as appearance and social acceptability, he is displaying creativity of mind" (p. 135). A child who displays creative originality, seems to be more tolerant and receptive to new experiences and tends towards more autonomy in personal expression.

Creativity also seems to correlate highly with divergent thinking in children as opposed to convergent thinking. Researchers sometimes divide children into two groups—convergers and divergers. Convergers follow traditional ideas. Divergers spread outwards in a creative search for new ideas and answers. According to Hudson (1968), convergers tend to hold authoritarian attitudes, disapprove of those who are too independent, and strongly approved of obedience. Hence the relevance of creativity in a discussion on moral development. Maslow (1970) also found that self-actualizing people were very high on autonomy, responsibility, moral maturity, but their prime characteristic was creativity. He found that their codes of ethics are individual rather than conventional. The unthinking observer might sometimes believe them to be unethical, since they can break down not only conventions but laws when the situation seems to demand it. However, Maslow concluded that they are the most ethical of people even though their ethics is not the same as that of the people around them (p. 158).

Creativity is not inborn. The creative person can be taught. Teachers in the classroom can teach pupils to think in uncommon ways, to develop divergent solutions to problems. The greatest problem is to break the set in thinking or to break out of "functional fixedness." Teachers should provide some time in the curriculum for alternative learning experiences. Obviously, children will not learn creativity through exhortation.

Mature or high level morality is only possible when the agent is an autonomous, dynamic, creative person. A mature, moral person faces moral problems, not only as a responsible person, but as one who recognizes that there may be many creative, moral solutions.

Some Practical Applications for Teachers and Parents

a. Teachers in particular should try to identify children who are creative and divergent thinkers. Tests for this purpose can be found in Torrance (1970). These talents are not necessarily correlated to measured mental abilities. Parents of children with such assets should be helped to understand them as many such talents have been effectively dissipated through parents' and teachers' lack of appreciation and belittling of these special children.

b. Teachers and parents should recognize that creativity can assert itself in many different ways, in literature, in music, in mechanics, theology, philosophy, as well as in moral and ethical solutions to problems.

c. It is possible that teachers and parents may be convergent thinkers and tend to believe that all original thinking about moral issues was completed long ago. It is important that they be open to new possible solutions to moral problems such as injustice, unequal distribution of wealth, etc. Moral creativity among young people should be encouraged. Their personal, individualized response to the moral problems of the world should be treasured, not repressed.

d. The history of successful creative individuals show that they need a sponsor, a patron or a refuge. Parents and teachers should regard it as a special privilege to assist the creative moral person. Perhaps the young person is a new Pope John XXIII, a Mother Teresa, a Dr. Schweitzer.

Empathy

Empathy has been described as the ability to project oneself into the place of another, to "walk in another's moccasins." Since moral development involves relationships between people, it is clear that the sense of empathy is important as a preparation for higher levels of moral activity such as altruism.

In an excellent contribution, Hoffman (1976) points out that research on empathy has been devoted almost exclusively to awareness of the feelings of others. Yet true empathy requires a strong cognitive aspect wherein the person has a deep awareness of the thoughts and thinking process of the other.

The question arises as to the age in which one can empathize with another. Hoffman (1976) presents laboratory data but also offers anecdotal material to indicate that the very young demonstrate this ability. He tells the story of Marcy, aged 20 months. Marcy asked her sister for a toy and was refused. At this Marcy went to the sister's rocking horse (which was so special no one was allowed to touch it) and stroked it, shouting "Nice horsey! Nice horsey!" Predictably, this procedure produced a violent reaction from the sister who dropped the toy she was holding to rush to the rocking horse. Marcy got the dropped toy and demonstrated an awareness of her sister's psychology.

The basic origin of one's ability to empathize may be associated with one's earliest feelings of pain or tension. The young person recalls the feeling of hurt when he falls and scrapes his knee or when he has a stomach ache or receives a slap. When he sees another child with these same kinds of problems, especially if the child is of about his own age, a sense of sharing dominates the child's reaction. Later on as the child's range of emotions increases, the likelihood of empathizing with the emotions of those of other ages in a wide variety of emotional states increases.

Does every human person have the potential for empathy? Hoffman (1976) declares that the answer is Yes, "assuming he is sufficiently secure emotionally to be open to the needs of others" (p. 142). Of course, the child's family and social environment will have a lot to do with the deepening and broadening of the feeling for-and-with others. Parents, teachers and other important figures in the child's life can assist the young to grow in empathy not only by demonstrating altruism toward others but by sharing their feeling and thinking processes regarding those whom they seek to help.

Some Practical Applications for Parents and Teachers

1. As indicated above, adults who have developed a sense of empathy and who wish young people to grow in the same way, should be open in declaring their positive feelings towards others. Individuals who view others in a hostile, negative light often speak their mind. The authentic self-expression of positive empathizers will help the young toward imitation.

2. Teachers particularly should look to the school curriculum for materials that help the young have a sense of empathy. The social sciences and works of literature should be an abundant source for an awareness of the feelings and thinking of others. Entertainment programs also often contain similar materials but their value is often lost if the potential for empathy is not reinforced through discussion or other exercises.

3. Discussions of current events can be a treasure trove for parents and teachers in the development of empathy. When a tragedy of some kind occurs, there should be an attempt to probe the feelings of those involved, especially the victims and survivors.

When a crime is committed against a person, an often neglected topic is the emotional impact on the victims of the crime. This awareness could be a step toward alerting future adult citizens against their committing crime and taking steps against criminals.

4. Parents and teachers can help the young more directly by encouraging their facing the usual run of life experiences and not sheltering them from them. Thereby they will experience the feelings and thinking that will foster empathic growth. In addition, young people should be assisted to realize how their actual or contemplated behaviors will affect the feeling and thinking of other persons. Of course, such a direction toward empathy would not be offered as a norm for behavior but as an important ingredient of it. Growth in the ability to view behavior from another's perspective should enable young people to participate more fully, more humanly, in family, school and peer communities.

Conclusion

The moral factors (moral judgment, future orientation, moral tolerance, moral personalism, moral creativity, and empathy) develop out of the preconditions of identification, self-acceptance, moral models, conscience and competence. All the elements in these preconditions and factors are primarily affective and interpersonal. All of them can be aligned with the cognitive development of children and therefore incorporated in varying degrees in school curriculum. Parents and schools must deliberately attempt to develop the moral judgments of children to maturity. They must develop in children self-discipline so that they are not left at the mercy of their whims and impulses. Children must learn to see people as persons and not mere service instruments in a materialistic society. Children ought to be helped implement their moral decisions. That is, they must not only be given the opportunity of moral knowing but also of acting with an awareness of the feelings and thinking of others.

Parents and teachers who help mold the moral growth of the young should regard this work as a great opportunity and a great challenge. If they accept the suggestions offered above they will add some dimensions from psychological research to their predominant love and concern.

Moral and Cognitive Development for Teachers: A Neglected Arena*

Norman A. Sprinthall and Joseph E. Bernier

Introduction

A few years ago George A. Miller, then president of the American Psychological Association, urged psychologists to "give psychology away to the people" (Miller, 1969). Miller felt that with the shortage of trained psychologists people would have to be their own psychologists and make their own self-conscious applications of principles of psychology. It was his premise that by this process of the practice of psychology that people would change their conception of themselves and what they can do. Miller saw particular institutions—hospitals, prisons, schools, industries—as promising sites for this innovation.

For several reasons the public schools seemed a most appropriate setting in which to give psychology away to the students—in order that they may live more effective lives. First there has been a growing concern over the negative effects of schooling. A host of writers and researchers have documented these results from a variety of perspectives. These studies, are perhaps best summed up by Sprinthall who after reviewing the effects of schooling concluded:

Obviously we need to change the learning experience for school children. The effects are not benign, nor is schooling simply a baby-sitting

*The study described was partially funded by the Bureau of Educationally Handicapped, USOE, Washington, D.C., Grant #G00-75-00517.

placebo. The impacts seem to be a negative personal-psychological education for most pupils, a boring tiresome, mindless experience. (Sprinthall, 1974, p. 94.)

Secondly, previous attempts by schools to reverse these negative effects and promote positive psychological or personal growth have not been particularly successful. Often this is so because no real deliberate attempt is ever made to have learners think and respond to inner experiences that would help them relate more effectively with themselves and others. Most school experiences are directed toward having students think and respond to such outer areas as science, history, math, etc. Many falsely assumed that positive personal growth would emerge as a by-product of the "new" math, social studies, science, and English. In fact, it may well be that in some instances, mastery of cognitive tasks may lead to negative values or attitudes (Krathwohl, Bloom, and Masia, 1964). Even in those instances where educators have shown enough concern about the emotional and social development of children to consider personal growth a legitimate educational objective, the results have at best been sporadic. Most of the time only lip service is given to these personal growth objectives because educators didn't know what to do about them since very little time, energy, and money has been devoted to systematically develop personal growth programs.

It is obvious that there is a need for the development of curricula and new educational interventions that will promote healthy psychological growth. However, it is also apparent that the process of reforming curriculum materials cannot succeed without systematic attention toward the problems of teacher education or even the re-education of teachers. The rationale, need, and review of new directions for moral and psychological education for pupils has been presented in extensive form and will not be repeated here (Sprinthall 1976). Rather we will focus on the teacher education question. It will accomplish little to create materials which are either ostensibly "teacher-proof" or even worse to simply ignore the question of teacher education, and hope that it will simply go away. As Geoghegan has acutely commented on this point in regard to developmental curriculum materials for schools, we can't simply turn over materials and programs either to the inexperienced or the amateur (Geoghegan, 1976). To understand the scope of the teacher training question we will present a brief review of the current state of the art vis à vis teacher education.

Teacher Education, The State of the Art

Research in teaching, teacher effectiveness, and the preparation of teachers has had a long history. The literature is extensive and almost unmanageable. Three major literature reviews (Getzels and Jackson; Cyphert and Spaights; and Biddle and Ellena) published in 1964 provide us with a status report, bringing one phase of the research to an end. At that time, the investigators (Getzels and Jackson, 1964, and Cyphert and Spaights, 1964) characterized the research on teacher personality, effectiveness and training as confusing, often of poor quality, largely atheoretical, and not showing clear and consistent developmental trends. Biddle and Ellena's (1964) almost classic statement serves as a comprehensive summary: "(after 40 years of research) we do not know how to define, prepare for or measure teacher competence."

Cyphert (1972) points out that one of the major problems plaguing research in teacher education has been that, while scholars and researchers in this area have been asking one set of questions, the teacher education practitioners have been asking a different set of questions. Researchers study the dynamics of teaching, yet teacher educators ask what characteristics, attitudes, and facts make up effective teachers. But it's not so much that teacher educators have been unconcerned with effective classroom practices as it is that they have been using models which fail to provide an adequate link between teacher personality and classroom behavior. Biddle (1964) sees this as a failure to bridge the competence (teacher personality, attitudes, and values) versus performance (behaving in a given situation) gap.

Glaser (1976) in a similar vein has noted that one of the major difficulties has been the failure to link theory and practice. In a sense psychologists and educators have been like ships passing in the night. Dewey, long ago, exhorted these two groups to work toward a "linking science" between psychology and teaching: "It is the participation by the practical man (sic) in the theory through the agency of the linking science that determines at once the effectiveness of the work done, and the moral freedom and personal development of the one engaged in it" (Dewey, 1900, p. 111).

William James always maintained that the separation of theory and practice would lead to disaster. We couldn't simply assume that psychological knowledge about children was all that was requisite for effective teaching. "To know psychology, therefore, is absolutely no guarantee that we shall be good teachers—the science of logic never made a man reason rightly, and the science of ethics never made the man behave rightly" (James, 1889, p. 24).

James, instead, suggested (using nineteenth century rhetoric) that effective teaching involved a process application by what we would now call a developmentally mature adult. "An intermediary inventive mind . . . originality . . . tact . . . ingenuity for the concrete situation . . . meeting and pursuing the pupil" (James, 1889, p. 24).

Unfortunately for the field of teacher education little has been accomplished in the intervening 70 years to view the problem of teacher education from a developmental perspective, or indeed from any consistent framework which would begin to bridge the dichotomies of education and psychology or practice and theory. Ryan, especially, has been quite pointed in his critique. Teacher educators in this country too often attempt the impossible, they prepare pre-service and in-service teachers, "For the very active role of teacher by treating them as passive agents" (Ryan, 1970, p. 187). The bulk of teacher education is in the form of classical education, taking notes, memorizing, writing papers and paper and pencil exams.

Ryan notes, "While this may be an efficient way to learn economic theory, the structure of a sonnet, and the concept of a light year, it is not a very effective way to prepare someone to teach" (Ryan 1970, p. 187).

After completing an extensive review of the inadequacy of teacher preparation John Goodlad, regarded as the dean of this country's educational establishment, commented despairingly, "There is no point in continuing to tinker with teacher education programs. They must be revamped from top to bottom" (Goodlad and Klien, 1974, p. 105).

In an over-simplified way then we may conclude that both an adequate conception of the goals of teacher education is lacking as well as a system of instruction to achieve those goals. The universities tend to view teacher education as a question of subject-matter discipline—the elementary and secondary school teacher as a mini-scholar, a smaller version or perhaps even an homunculus of a university professor. Practical classroom management techniques are essentially regarded just so, and of lesser importance. This dualism acts to increase the separation of function within the teacher and equally unfortunately projects negative impacts upon the pupils.

Life in Classrooms: Teaching as It Is

At this point it is important to underscore the reality of lives in the classrooms.

In the late nineteenth century, a visitor to the public schools of the day concluded that most of the activity in classrooms consisted of what he called a game of recitation. The pupils and the teacher seemed to follow a systematic question and answer exercise. The teacher would ask a series of short factual questions with the rapidity of a machine gunner—"Now class, pay attention . . . Tell me, who discovered America? _____, What year? _____, How many ships were there? _____, What were their names? _____, How long was the voyage? _____, etc." Each question was followed by a brief pause and then students with hands raised were called on, again with the speed of light until one student said the correct answer. At this point the teacher would fire the next question and skip around the class calling on pupils with hands raised appropriately until the next right answer was called out. The observer in the 19th century classroom noted that the interaction between teacher and pupil seemed exclusively mechanical. The process seemed to emphasize rote learning, repeating back facts memorized from the teacher and the textbook. Inquiry was unknown. "In several instances when a pupil stopped for a moment's reflection, the teacher remarked abruptly, 'Don't stop to think, but tell me what you know' " (Rice, 1893).

These impressions of what we might call "Trivia in the Classroom" were given further credence by other observers. An English educator in 1908 noted the "time-honoured" tradition in American classrooms of question-answer recitation in distinct contrast to the lecture method employed on the continent of Europe. A systematic study of classroom interaction further substantiated the question-answer method as the predominant approach to teaching in this country. Using stenographic notes of actual classroom discussions (this was in the days before tape recorders and other mechanical means of recording teacher-pupil classroom "talk"), a researcher found that over 80 percent of all classroom talk consisted of asking and answering brief fact questions—questions that called for a good rote memory and an ability to phrase the answer in the terms that the teacher used. The rate of questioning was between one to four questions *per minute*—thus much like today's popular T.V. quiz games in that each pupil (or contestant) is given a few seconds to come up with the right answer. If he doesn't have the answer at the tip of his tongue, he loses his turn and the teacher (or master of ceremonies) moves on to the next pupil. The researcher noted that it might be unimportant if in 1912 she found one teacher who fired questions at pupils in staccato-like fashion, however: "The fact that *one hundred* different classrooms reveal the same methods in vogue is quite a different matter. The fact that one history teacher attempts to realize his educational aims through the process of 'hearing' the textbook, day after day, is unfortunate but pardonable; that history, science, mathematics, foreign language and English teachers, collectively are following in the same groove, is a matter for theorists and practitioners to reckon with" (Stevens, 1912).

In the 1960's, fully one-half century after the above observations, educational researchers studying the classroom interactions between teachers and pupils made the following comments. (1) The teachers tend to do about 70% of all the talking in the classroom. (2) Most of this talk is in the form of asking questions. (3) Between *80% to 88%* of all teacher questions call for *rote memory* responses by the pupils. (4) The teachers generally ask questions on a cycle of about 2 per minute. (5) Pupil talk was almost exclusively a short response to the teacher's question. (6) Inquiring or suggesting other reasons or questions by pupils was virtually non-existent (Bellack, 1966).

Unfortunately even the most recent studies in the 1970's reach the same depressing conclusion. Gump has noted that recitation is still the single most common teacher act (1975). Goodlad and Klien reported in their 1974 study, "at all grade levels . . . the teacher asked questions and the children responded usually in a few words and phrases and usually correctly . . . It is fair to say that teacher to child interaction was the mode in all but about 5 percent of the classes" (Goodlad and Klien, 1974, p. 51).

Impact of Teacher Training

The current decade, then, finds us still confronting the same questions and the same needs for teacher education. We have been spectacularly unsuccessful in responding to George Miller's call for psychology to contribute in positive ways to the human condition. Shutes has suggested after examining current theory and practice for teacher education that the field will continue to wander aimlessly until both theory and practice are connected to form a consistent framework. "Without theory, both research and practice are fragmented, capricious, guided at best by folk-wisdom and unevaluated experience, and noncumulative in building a growing body of reliable, replicable information . . . It is past time for teacher education to be placed on a theoretical basis" (Shutes, 1975, p. 85).

It is an oversimplification yet reasonably accurate to say that the research has too often examined one single variable at a time. An overall conception has been noticeably absent. While researchers fiddle, the schools burn.

Perhaps the penultimate irony is that the process of teacher education itself has been found iatrogenic. In other words, the process itself has been documented as negative. Teachers in training become more authoritarian, more hostile and less empathic toward children as a result of their experiences. Studies such as those by Gewinner (1968), Iannacone (1963), Matthews (1967) and Osman (1959) indicate that negative changes in both attitudes and behaviors are almost universal phenomena when the study is conducted over the actual time period of the student teaching experience. The seminal study of Mosher (Mosher and Sprinthall, 1971) is the outstanding exception, probably a result of the unique intensive individual counseling provided the student teachers.

From almost any perspective, then, there is substantial need for educational reform, including new learning experiences of pupils. Any significant reform must include a focus on the teacher education question. And it is our contention that such a focus must include work toward a conceptual framework that comprehends *theory for practice* in teacher education.

Some Promising Trends: A Developmental Conception

Starting with the pioneering work of O. J. Harvey including more recently the work of David Hunt and Bruce Joyce, we can discern a significant trend toward practice and theory for teaching and teacher education. These researchers can also be linked with some emerging trends in cognitive-developmental theory from Kohlberg and Loevinger. Such a framework rests on a series of logical assumptions as well as an emerging data base.

In the cognitive-development view the quality of how a person functions is essentially determined by the complexity of one's own cognitive structure. Piaget uses the phrase "schema" to describe the cognitive system that a person employs to make meaning from experience. O. J. Harvey employs the phrase "conceptual system," Hunt and Joyce denote the concept as "conceptual level" (CL), while Kohlberg terms the process "Moral Judgment Stage" and Loevinger defines it as "Ego Developmental Stage." Even though none of these concepts are synonymous, there is considerable theoretical overlap. All assume that an individual's actions are governed by an internal mediating cognitive process. The quality of such mediation will vary by age and stage of development. Also at higher stages an individual will function more complexly, abstractly, comprehensively and empathically. Such a broad conception also presumes that development is not value-free nor relative. The higher more complex stages of thinking and valuing are not separate and represent complementary educational goals.

With regard to the teaching function, Harvey has been able to define four stages of conceptual functioning through his Conceptual Systems Test (1966).

Several studies have sought to establish the relationship between conceptual systems (CST) and teaching style. For example, Murphy and Brown (1970) administered the Conceptual Systems Test to 136 student teachers. These same teachers audio-taped three lessons, from which three 20 minute segments were randomly chosen and coded for handling information and applying sanctions. Qualitative differences in teaching styles were apparent and seemed to be associated with CST. It was found that the amount of information handled by helping students to think divergently, theorize and engage in self-expression increased with each teacher stage, while asking rote questions decreased with CL. Similarly, with increasing teacher abstractness, sanctioning of search behavior and less reinforcement of attainment behavior was seen.

Several other studies have yielded results consistent with the above. In two studies, Hunt and Joyce (1967) found significant positive correlations between indices of reflective teaching (use of the learner's frame of reference to plan, initiate and evaluate performance) and conceptual level. In another study, Harvey, et al. (1966) rated kindergarten and first grade teachers on 26 dimensions yielding two major factors—Fostering Exploration (FE) and Dictatorialness (D). It was found that system 4 teachers (most abstract, informationally independent) scored highest on FE and lowest on D, while the reverse was true for system 1 teachers. Two years later these findings were replicated and supplemented with data pertinent to the direct effects of teacher CL on student functioning. Rating kindergarten and first grade teachers on 30 dimensions, it was found that students of system 4 teachers were more cooperative, active and involved in their work, higher in achievement, more helpful and less dependent, and operated at higher cognitive levels (Harvey, et al., 1968). Joyce and Weil (1973) found that a teacher's ability to radiate a variety of educational environments was correlated with CL. They found that other value and attitude inventories failed to correlate with performance and acquisition of specific teaching models. Higher conceptual level teachers were more flexible in their classrooms, able to function in a wider variety of the Flanders Interaction Categories. These findings established a critical bridge between theory and practice. Classroom performance is logically and empirically connected to the developmental level of the teachers. The more usual tests of static traits and teacher attitudes failed to show consistent predictive relationships to actual teacher performance.

Finally, in a counselor analogue study, Goldberg (1974) found that counselor trainees with more abstract CL were more likely to accept their client's feelings and ideas, use encouragement and praise, respond to affect, deal with core rather than peripheral material, and use open-ended questions. This study demonstrates the versatility of the CL model and is important for teaching because the rating scales in the Goldberg study are similar to the Flanders Interaction Analysis, an instrument commonly used in teacher effectiveness research (Flanders, 1970).

Goals for Teacher Education: Promoting Cognitive/Moral Development

The studies, taken as a whole, suggest that teachers at more complex developmental levels perform the teaching act with greater comprehensiveness and empathy. Also, their pupils evidence higher levels of thinking, self-exploration, co-operation, independence, and involvement in school activities.

The cognitive-developmental model mentioned in connection with O. J. Harvey and others, thus seems to represent an adequate new framework for conceptualizing teacher education research and practice on two counts. First, it is an alternative conception of personality which has begun to bridge the competence-performance gap. In short, developmental research and theory suggests that teachers at higher stages show greater cognitive and behavioral flexibility. They may be more "trainable" and show a richer and more varied repertoire of teaching skills, being very much aware of individual differences in themselves and others and eclectic in structuring learning environments. Higher developmental level teachers seem better able to individualize instruction and to take into account the variety of pupil differences.

At the same time research also indicates that such behavioral skills as implied by complex developmental stage cannot be learned through a rote-like process. In fact a major problem confronting teacher education has always been the definition of educational objects and goals as well as methods. What is or should be the dependent variable or the major outcome of a teacher education program? The research reviewed earlier indicated that conceptualizing teacher education goals in static personality traits like friendliness, warmth, etc., has led to few positive outcomes. At the other extreme programs designed simply to teach skills directly to teachers fail to generalize or transfer. The recent programs of teacher micro-teaching have not succeeded largely because of their robot-like emphasis. Teachers are asked to master a series of discrete separate skills which tend to wash-out when they return to the classroom.

In his excellent review, MacDonald (1973), one of the originators of micro-teaching, states that many of the claims made attesting to the effectiveness of micro-teaching and micro-counseling have little substance. He notes that its present popular use is far removed from its original intent to serve in studying the effects of modeling and reinforcement in shaping desirable, concrete teaching behavior. In effect, micro-teaching has lost its behavioral paradigm and has become a video "practice-playback" technology. Research on the generalizability of such "skills only" training programs as typified by Carkhuff's human resource development approach and Ivey's micro-teaching procedure has generally been equivocal.

In one study, using a Carkhuff-type training paradigm, Collingswood (1971) followed up his participants for 5 months and found a significant drop in skills after one month, which was maintained until a re-training period. Gormally et al. (1975) found that undergraduates who received 40 hours of empathy training showed decreases in empathy level at a 6 month follow-up. However, the graduate counselors who participated maintained their gains presumably because they continued to practice and were reinforced for their performance. Using Ivey's micro-counseling model, Hasse, DiMattia, and Guttman (1972) found that after one year the occurrence of every skill (excluding eye-contact) had dropped off significantly. Finally, comparing a communication skills training group, t-group, and self-directed learning group, McAuliffe (1974) found that both the skills training and encounter groups evidenced significant drops in communications skills at the follow-up. These studies serve to illustrate the "wash-out" effect which often plagues the brief and somewhat episodic communication skills training laboratories.

We suggest, then, that the process of teacher education may now be viewed in developmental terms. The outcomes of educational/training program can be conceptualized as promoting developmental growth on the part of the teachers. We can view teacher education in broader terms than instruction for pedagogical skills. Also we can suggest objectives that are not simply static personality traits like friendliness or warmth.

There are advantages to moving in this direction. In considering psychological/moral development a legitimate and necessary aim of teacher education, we are confronting the larger "values" question and are, in effect, attempting a change in the structure of professional teacher training. Here developmental ends could be used to link the various training strategies that are presently in operation but remain unconnected.

Also, the model is very much in tune with the current educational imperative to promote pupil growth and individualize instruction. As already indicated, higher level teachers are more sensitive to individual differences between people and are better able to learn and systematically employ a wide variety of teaching strategies (Joyce and Weil). This enables them to respond to the special needs of their students. In other words, we can define educational goals for teacher education in developmental terms. The dependent variables or outcomes are the developmental cognitive/moral stages and the associated behavioral skills of the teachers. The value base clearly denotes that teachers who are "further along" or at higher developmental stages are more adequate as professional teachers, more competent in the classroom, have access to a greater repertoire of teaching styles, are more cognitively flexible, can vary the level of questions asked, and can identify and resonate to a wide variety of pupil feelings and emotions. Thus we are suggesting that growth and development toward more complex cognitive/moral stages *ought* to become programmatic objectives not only for the benefit of the teachers themselves but also and ultimately for the pupils in their charge.

Developmental Goals: Increasing the
Accommodative Capacity of Regular Classrooms

Further emphasis toward the conception can be found in the recent emphasis on mainstreaming previously designated retarded pupils into regular classrooms. As a result of extending the Brown vs. the Board of Education principle that separate educational facilities are inherently *not* equal, many recent court decisions have ruled that previously segregated special classes must be phased out. Such action will increase the array of individual differences in regular classes, call for teachers with increased flexibility, greater human responsiveness, a more substantial repertoire of teaching styles—in short all of the attributes of higher developmental levels. To increase the accommodative capacity of regular classes is a present pressing educational need increasing the urgency of more effective teacher education.*

A Program for Teacher Development: An Initial Study

Given the logic and evidence already outlined we decided to create an initial study designed to directly impact the cognitive/moral developmental level of classroom teachers. Thus the purpose of the present study was to create and pilot a curriculum designed to promote positive movement in the developmental stages of personal and social growth with adult teachers. It represents an adaptation and upward extension of the Mosher-Sprinthall (1971) deliberate psychological education model, which has been previously tried with adolescents and serves as a first attempt at employing the procedures with a post-college population. The intervention squarely confronts issues pertaining to the reality of developmental stages in adulthood and the possibility of stimulating adult growth, areas of new and generic significance.**

Goals: Developmental Growth

The curriculum project was aimed largely at practicing elementary and secondary teachers. As such, it provides an alternative model for conceptualizing in-service training and staff development. Here personal and professional development interact and become alternate sides of the same coin. Thus, personal development is seen

---

*Last year 25,000 pupils were mainstreamed in one state alone, a note to indicate the rapid pace of educational change that can result from legal activity. See also Chapter 23, "Educating Retarded Children in Mainstream Classes," R. C. and N. A. Sprinthall, *Educational Psychology: A Developmental Approach*. (2nd Ed.) (Reading, Mass.: Addison-Wesley, 1977).

**Classical developmental theory has generally assumed that stage growth ceases at about 18 years and that further changes during adulthood are quantitative, not qualitative, an assumption currently being challenged.

as a legitimate and necessary component of a professional training program. It is also well to recall that cognitive-developmental theory is comprehensive in that aspects of growth are not separate. Thus conceptual development, psychological development and moral development are connected parts, not isolated distinct variables. Kohlberg and Piaget have already commented on futility of treating intellectual, affective and moral growth as if such factors were segregated and orthogonal.

Rationale for the Curriculum for Teachers

Previous theory and practice had indicated that a series of necessary educational conditions are requisite to promote cognitive-moral growth.

The curriculum was implemented in an attempt to maximize several "sources of gain" believed by Kohlberg and others to be instrumental for adult cognitive-structured development. An environment was created that enabled the teachers to assume a position of *responsibility* in an atmosphere of shared leadership of *collegial relationships* where one must *take the perspective* of others in making *choices* and also regularly *examine* these decisions and relationships.

These sources of gain (responsibility, perspective-taking, etc.) are generic to all Deliberate Psychological Education classes as currently practiced. Through the summer laboratory and supervised practica in the fall term the teachers were offered training and experiences in perspective-taking (via active-listening) and were placed in positions of leadership and responsibility for others by serving first as peer counselors and later as teachers in their own classrooms. In other words a broader role-taking perspective was created. During the didactic, laboratory, and supervision sessions, an emphasis on open communication and colleagueship enhanced these role-taking opportunities. Sometimes this process is termed training teachers through an "inside-out" model, that is the learning activities involve real rather than simulated experiences. The learning atmospheres are set in such a manner that the participant experiences firsthand the process he or she is expected to implement in his/her own classroom.

All this amounts to a significant role change for many teachers. It was hoped to encourage them to shift from the traditional mediator or direct "transmitter of knowledge" role to the consultant, supervisor, and resource person position. It was also hoped that this shift would be significant and powerful enough to "jam" or "stretch" the teachers' thinking about themselves and thus result in cognitive-structural change.

In order for this development to occur, the curriculum involved a deliberate blending of real experience *and* thought, of doing *and* thinking, of process *and* content, and of action *and* personal reflection. Thus the curriculum combined a practicum experience intended to create some degree of cognitive disequilibrium with a seminar in which the participants reflected on the impact and meaning of the experience for themselves personally. The seminar or supervisory sessions helped participants to reflect on their own thoughts, feelings, choices and actions and thereby generally restructure their way of thinking about themselves and the world. The supervisors enabled the teachers to take a close look at the processes by which they resolve "self-other dilemmas" in real life situations.

Specific Curriculum Procedures

The program involved two main segments: 1) an intensive six-week summer workshop on campus and 2) a supervised practicum in the fall semester for the teachers returning to their regular classroom assignments. The summer component met four mornings per week for three hour class sessions over the course of six weeks. Each class was divided into large and small group sessions. The large group relied heavily on didactic learning in the form of lectures and discussions of how principles and techniques borrowed from human development, behavior modification, and group dynamics related to educational practice, individualizing instruction and mainstream education. Eighteen teachers were enrolled mostly from a nearby large urban public school system.

Learning Skills

Small group meetings were organized around learning and practicing counseling skills, indirect teaching skills, behavioral self-management procedures, and group facilitation skills. Cognitive-developmentalists believe that effective skills learning in these areas provides a means to participants whereby they may experience the world differently and broaden their experience tables, thus resulting in a higher level of psychological maturity.

Essentially the workshop instructed the teachers in three basic skills which, when integrated, would hopefully promote higher and more complex functioning: counseling skills, supervision skills, and individualizing instruction. 1) *Teaching Counseling Skills* involved specific role-taking training in so-called "active-listening" and empathy responses. The objectives included, to accurately identify feelings and content in counseling relationships, to accurately "read" non-verbal behavior in self and others, to send and receive "I" messages and to process observe dyadic small groups. 2) *Teaching Supervision Skills* to the teachers involved developing competencies in all of the Flanders Interaction categories especially the four components of indirect-teaching. In our view effective supervision involves these responding activities. Also since we planned to ask the teachers to supervise some of their pupils in cross-age and peer tutoring when they returned to their own classes in the fall, we felt it crucial for them to learn and practice effective supervision skills. 3) *Individualizing Instruction* involved teaching the teachers some of the so-called behavioral skills management techniques or "precise-teaching." Carefully defined educational objectives were set by teacher and pupil, rewards were defined, charts were created to monitor progress, etc.; these were all aspects of the procedures. The goal however was *not* to teach all the teachers how to keep charts for all their pupils, but rather to instruct the pupils to manage the system themselves.

Learning Concepts

While the teachers were learning these three skills during the summer workshop they were also receiving instruction in theory. In other words the workshop involved skill training plus theory. We emphasized the need to understand pupils and self from a developmental perspective. Concepts and definitions of stages of development during childhood and adolescence were presented through lectures, simulations, films and readings. Stages from Kohlberg, Piaget, Erikson, and Harvey, Hunt and Schroeder were discussed. Aspects of developmental interaction theory were considered with case studies and readings. In a sense the goal of these "didactic" experiences was to create theory for the role of teacher as an applied behavioral scientist in the classroom. We were attempting to consciously provide them with a complex set of constructs to understand how children think and feel at different stages. Children and teenagers, in this view are not midget-sized adults but rather have unique and qualitatively distinct systems for processing thought and action.

In addition to this developmental component a unit on individualizing instruction included a description of behavioral contracting, the use of charting and precise teaching, especially for school pupils recently "mainstreamed." This high structured approach for teaching was emphasized as particularly appropriate for pupils at relatively low conceptual levels of development, and for most pupils during periods of transition from stage to stage and/or during times of high anxiety.*

The actual sequence for large and small group instruction is outlined in Chart 1.

Chart 1
An Outline of Summer Workshop Topics

	Large Group Session *8:30–10:00 A.M.*	Small Group Session *10:30–12:00 P.M.*
June 17	Introductions and Testing: Communication Video Tape.	Introductions.
June 18	Complete Pre-Tests	Develop General Communication Skills and Build Group Maintenance.
June 19	Dewey and the Concept of Development (Read Sprinthall, et al., 1975, Chap. 2)	Begin practicing active-listening/Indirect teaching and group process skills.
June 23	Cognitive Development (Read Sprinthall, Chap. 6).	Practice active-listening/Indirect teaching and group process skills.
June 24	Cognitive Development (Con't.)	Practice active-listening/Indirect teaching and group process skills.
June 25	Personal Development (Read Sprinthall, Chap. 7).	Practice active-listening/Indirect teaching and group process skills. (Read Wittmer & Myrick; also Becvar, R.)

*Hunt and Sullivan (1974) have shown that the need for high structured, concrete, explicit teaching with short cycle feedback is appropriate not only for so-called slow learners but also for "intelligent" but low conceptual level pupils.

	Large Group Session *8:30–10:00 A.M.*	Small Group Session *10:30–12:00 P.M.*
June 26	Moral Development	Practice active-listening/Indirect teaching and group process skills. Practice in Video Lab in alternating sequence.
June 30	Read Sprinthall, Chaps. 8 and 9.	Practice active-listening/Indirect teaching and group process skills. Practice in Video Lab in alternating sequence.
July 1	Action Learning. Role taking. Deliberate psychological education: examples (Read Sprinthall, Chaps. 14, 20)	Practice active-listening/Indirect teaching and group process skills. Practice in Video Lab in alternating sequence.
July 2–10	Techniques for individualizing instruction: Behavior modification and precise personal management	Learn and practice behavioral self-management procedures. (Read Foster, 1974.)
July 14–17	Group Leadership Techniques. Review and planning.	Behavioral skills, goals, and plans.
July 21–31	Individual conferences. Writing psychological education curricula.	(No small group sessions.)

Break

Post Summer Workshop

September to October, 1975	Small Group Supervisory Sessions (3 Hour Sessions, Twice a Month)
and	
January to February, 1976	Field-based practica: Implementation of curriculum in peer counseling, cross-age teaching, precise personal management, etc.
	Supervision of facilitative teaching via video analysis and continued practice of communication, group process, and self-management skills.

The Fall Practicum: Applying Theory and Practice

During the fall term the teachers returned to their own class-rooms and continued to meet twice per month for a two-hour supervised practicum in small groups (5 to 8 teachers) with the project staff. Since the Deliberate Psychological Education programs had in general found that it was important to "learn by doing" reminiscent of Dewey's dictum, the fall program was focused on providing support for the teachers to try the skills of counseling, supervision, and individualizing instruction in their own classes. The balance of real experience and examination through the on-going supervision was hoped to become the vehicle for transfer and internalization. Also as we noted at the onset we were following George Miller's dictum to give the "secrets" of psychology away to the public. By helping teachers learn to teach counseling skills to their own pupils, to teach their own pupils how to teach, and to chart their own individual progress, we were seeking to change the teachers' role to one of more complexity.* At the same time we were attempting to help teachers shift some of the responsibility for learning directly to the pupils. The passivity of the current pupil role acts as a deterrent to personal development.

During the fall semester, then, the participants were asked to try out their new skills in their regular classrooms by implementing a psychological education project. For example, one might attempt to teach either peer counseling, cross-age tutoring, behavioral self-management, or magic circle to their students. The teachers themselves met in the small group twice each month for continued supervision to critique audio and video tapes of each other in the natural setting. Here the workshop directly attempted to implement the focus on the program, namely that the teachers could learn and implement the skills, review their own progress and learn to supervise each other in a collegial atmosphere.

Results: Good News and Bad News

To measure the impact of the summer and fall workshop we used three general domains: 1) assessment of skill development, 2) assessment of general cognitive/moral development and, 3) assessment of personal/clinical self report experiences by the participants.

---

*It is probably important to note that although the teaching role as conceived is more complex than the traditional, it is not necessarily more difficult. In fact we feel that the present "Toscanni-in-the-class" role is not only difficult but almost impossible.

Instrumentation

As noted elsewhere (Mosher and Sprinthall, 1971), we are still in need of a single comprehensive theory of adult development. Until recently, those who conduct research on developmental stages have worked independently and idiosyncratically and generally with different populations in different settings. Obviously, no single instrument presently available would satisfy validation questions. Thus, this study employed a series of proximate measures, encompassing both "hard" and "soft" instruments, which allowed multiple perspectives on the teachers' psychological development. Here we are attempting to strike a critical balance between Paul Meehl's "simple-minded" and "muddle-headed" approaches in evaluating the intervention. The following sections provide an overview of the assessment procedures.

Standardized assessments were made both pre and post.* Pretests were administered in June during the first week of the workshop, while posttests were completed by mail at the end of the fall semester.

Skills

To tap the teachers' performance in communications skills, a central aspect of the counseling and supervision training, a Reflection of Feelings (RF) Scale was employed.

The scale, developed by Thompson (1976) is a means of assessing the degree to which a person accurately identifies and reflects the feelings expressed by a "client." The RF scale is a five point rating instrument which, when applied to segments of client-counselor interaction, yields an index of one's listening or perspective-taking skills similar to those instruments developed by Carkhuff (1969) and Gazda (1973). One advantage that the Thompson scale has over these other measures is that it provides clearly defined and discrete categories of responses which are ordinarily arranged but can be assigned interval weights of either 1.0, 1.5, 2.0, 2.5, and 3.0. Generally speaking, 1.0 is defined as a failure to acknowledge a speaker's feelings. A minimal acknowledgement of feelings but no reflection is rated as 1.5. An inaccurate, general, yet incomplete reflection is considered a 2.0. Noticeably but not totally accurate reflections are weighted 2.5. "Interchangeable responses," that is those reflections which capture all the major feelings expressed by a speaker, are rated as 3.0.

*For complete details of the research design see Bernier (1976).

Table 1
Accurate Reflection of Feelings Scale Scores
(N=18 Teachers)

Pretest	Posttest	
2.02	2.46	$t = 5.71$
sd .35	.21	$p < .0001$ (2 tail)

A rating of 2 indicates an incomplete and generally inaccurate reflection of feeling.

A rating of 2.5 indicates a generally accurate response to most but not all of the feelings expressed by the "coached-client."

The teachers were presented with seven video "coached client" responses on a pretest/posttest basis. Their answers were scored blind by two independent judges trained in protocol scoring.*

The results indicate that the teachers did learn the communications skills during the summer workshop and that their level of performance did not drop significantly after they returned to their own classrooms. In other words the skill acquisition in accurately identifying and appropriately responding to emotions improved dramatically and remained at an effective level over a six month period. When compared to the studies previously noted documenting the usual wash-out effect of general communications training programs, these results are encouraging. Since there is ample evidence from the almost innumerable studies of Carkhuff (1969) that communication accuracy does not improve over 6 to 12 month time periods, we did not test a separate control group on the skill for comparison purposes. Overall the shift in communication functioning was substantial. The pretest scores indicated that most of the participants started the workshop at very modest levels, manifesting quite minimal ability to recognize emotions and accurately respond to feelings in others. These initial scores were congruent with both the teachers' own comments and the observations of the staff. They did experience difficulty at the outset in learning and applying this fundamental communications skills. Also their improvement during the workshop and their ability to employ this "set" in their own classes was noted. The posttest scores thus were also congruent with the teachers' self reports as well as with staff observations during fall semester.

Tests of Cognitive/Moral Development

In addition to the skill assessment we attempted to measure the teachers' level of psychological-cognitive-moral development on a

---

*In interclass correlation (Ebel, 1951) was the measure of inter-rater reliability with a r of +.86. The interrater agreement was, r + .88 for exact "hits" in scoring.

pretest/posttest basis. Since a major objective, or dependent variable, of the program was to impact the cognitive "system" of each participant, or as it's sometimes called, a cognitive—"structured" change, we employed two measures designed to tap functioning in this area: (a) The Rest Defining Issues Test (an objective measure of Kohlbergian Moral Stages) and (b) The Loevinger Test of Ego Development (an incomplete sentence test measuring ego stages of development).

The teachers were given the six-moral-dilemma version of the Rest instrument. The results indicate that their scores on amount of "principled thought" increased significantly over the six month time period (from 56.8 to 65.8). This difference was significant according to statistical analysis. This means that the teachers' level of conceptual ability in moral reasoning was positively effected by the workshop. The Rest instrument has been shown to be fake-proof and reliable over time. Thus the improvement in P-Score (Principled Thought) could not be attributed to either the practice effect or "natural" growth over time. Information on base rate or comparison groups indicates that usually adult scores do not change over a six-month period. In fact, levels of moral judgment in general seem highly stable in the adult population such that significant change over a 6 to 12 month time period probably cannot be attributed to natural history. Also as noted, research has indicated that subjects cannot be "taught to say" the right answer on the test so that a response set improvement could not account for the score increase.*

Table 2		
Rest's Defining Issues Test		
(A Measure of Principled Moral Reasoning)		
N = 18 Teachers (7M + 11F)		
Pretest Score (June 1975)		Posttest Score (Jan.-Feb. 1976)
P = 56.8		P = 65.8
		Correlated t = P < .01
Age *Mean:* 33.6	*Teaching* *Experience* 8.6	*Level* Elem. 7 Secondary 8 K-12 3

*See the Rest Manual as well as a series of stability and fakability studies conducted by Rest and his associates. See also Rest's article in Hennessy (1976).

A separate analysis of a small (N=7) comparison group of classroom teachers from a different section of the country indicated (once again) that there is no change in level of "Principled Thinking" over the time period in question.

The overall level of principled thought (P-Score) at the end of the workshop was similar to scores obtained by graduate students in moral and political philosophy. This means that the teachers demonstrated a significant increase in their ability to reason concerning human dilemmas at high ethical and abstract levels.

On the Loevinger Test of general ego development the results were not as encouraging. In fact, over the time period of the workshop there was no significant change as measured by this 36 item sentence completion test. The pretest scores identified the teachers at Loevinger's Stage 3/4. The posttest indicated no change.

Table 3
Loevinger's Test of Ego Development
(A General Measure of Personal Stage Functioning)

N = 18 Teachers

Pretest	Posttest	t=
Stage 3/4	Stage 3/4	Non-sig.
Mean = 6.0	*Mean* = 5.8	
sd = .7	*sd* = 1.2	

Since the Loevinger test purports to measure the most basic "master trait" in developmental terms (Loevinger and Wessler, 1970) we may conclude that the workshop did not impact the most general level of developmental functioning. Loevinger considers that stage 3/4 is a highly stable adult stage. According to the definition, an individual at this stage manifests an initial appreciation for individual differences, and shows movement from other-directedness to inner directed and self-evaluated standards.

Self-Report and Clinical Observations

Although it is virtually impossible to codify such data gathered from the teachers' own journals, written responses to our open-ended questions and our observations, there are some subjective impressions of significance. In general, there was a strong subjective

*The slight decrease apparently a common testing effect according to Redmore and Waldman, 1975.

judgment that the fall semester supervised practicum was not sufficient to really aid teachers in the implementation of the workshop objectives in their own classes. Most (roughly 80%) of the teachers felt that the intensive summer workshop had been extremely rewarding and personally stretching. The presentation of theories and the laboratory (small group) experiences were rated very positively. Unobtrusive measures such as attendance, participation, "corridor", comments, and free comments in their journals; all were supportive. Also at least 75% of the participants, without solicitation on our part, recommended the program to their colleagues for the following summer.

At the same time, there was some feeling of let-down at the end of the summer. Although most of the participants were from the large local and urban school system, they were from many different schools. This meant there was little building-level support when they returned and colleagueship was limited to the bi-weekly meetings.* Since we were asking the teachers to risk a great deal, namely to try out the new techniques of counseling, supervision and precise teaching in their own classes, the failure to provide more on-site and "clustered" grouping was a clear error. We did not sufficiently take into account what had been written concerning the loneliness of teaching, the low visibility and the isolation of self-containment (Miles, 1967). Because the teachers were scattered across so many buildings we could not provide on-site colleague supervision, videotaping of new technique trials and the group support so necessary for new risk taking. In a sense this failure may have also accounted for the lack of significant change on the Loevinger test. If we can view the three sets of objective instruments as measuring different levels of complexity from surface skills to depth personality stages, we can consider that the results support such a conclusion. The teachers learned the skills of communication and these generalized. Their level of reasoning on complex moral issues also improved. Test theory would suggest, however, that both these sets of measures assess recognition process while the Loevinger requires more "psychological work." As a semi-projective test the Loevinger purports to tap *not* comprehension and preference but rather spontaneous cognitive processing. Thus it may be that the workshop failure to significantly follow-up the summer program with an intensive (both supportive and demanding) full on-site practicum was the basis for the lack of impact at the most general level of developmental

*We have remedied that in a second workshop. We recruited teachers in clusters and have retained those intact groups for the summer and fall seminars.

functioning. In general, our other studies with school pupils all indicate the need for an effective balance between experience and
reflection and significant on-going supervision (Sprinthall, 1976).

Summary

It is obviously unnecessary to over-play either the positive or
negative outcomes from this study. This was a first attempt to create
a teacher education program aimed directly at the cognitive/moral
developmental level of the teachers. Previous studies had indicated
the futility of following either the skills-only approach, or the search
for single static personality trait variables. Rather, the conceptual
framework for the study was derived from a series of promising
trends based on a cognitive-developmental view of human growth.
We were attempting through this theory to have our cake and eat it
too in the sense that we sought to effect *behavior* and *psychological
cognitive* variables. We do feel that it is necessary to focus on behavior skills and mediating constructs such as developmental stages
when we are examining such a complex area of human functioning
as teaching. Effective teaching behavior is a high order, complex
human function. To reduce it to a simple skills-only Skinnerian S-R
pattern is an absurdity. We can only echo Gordon Allport's words
that such a conception of human being is "thread-bare if not piti-
able." Likewise we do not feel that teaching should be viewed only
as an inner process or an abstract mentalistic and theoretical conception. Abstract and single-variable traits have already led teacher
education research to a dismal empirical waste-land. We do feel that
the combination of developmental theory and practice does hold
promise as an effective new third-force or even "via media" for
teacher education. We believe on the basis of this first study that it is
possible to help teachers become more complex in their understanding of themselves, their pupils and their own professional competence. We also think that the teacher's repertoire of teaching skills,
particularly the application of counseling and supervision skills to
their own classrooms, can be learned in such a manner as to promote the human growth of the teachers.

Thus we do claim that effective teaching can be defined largely
in developmental terms. The complex act of teaching comprehends
the ability to think abstractly and complexly about human behavior.
Also requisite is the ability to remain cognitively flexible, aware of
individual differences and empathic to a wide range of human emotions. Open-minded, complex, abstract, empathic, and moral: these

are synonymous with functioning at higher stages of development.

Finally, we also claim that it may be possible to effect the psychological-cognitive-maturity of teachers. Good teachers in this view are neither born nor made. We need to find the conditions to foster developmental growth. Educational psychology in general has remained for too long on the side-lines in this effort. Dewey and James long ago identified the problem area and the need to promote a linking science for teaching.

Neither born, nor made, perhaps developed?

The Counselor Applies the Kohlberg Moral Development Model

Thomas C. Hennessy, S.J.

For decades counseling has taken over and put to use the main findings of other disciplines. For instance, vocational counseling has been considerably influenced by the predictions of economists regarding prospective growth or decline of certain industries; personal counseling has benefited from the insights of Freud, Adler, Rogers, Allport, Maslow, to mention just a few favorites. Counselors have a history of interdisciplinary debt and are the richer for it. I am going to suggest a change in the credit and debit line, specifically regarding Rogers and a relative newcomer to counselor education, Lawrence Kohlberg.

Counselors owe a great debt of gratitude to Carl Rogers. He writes perceptively about the individuality of the human person and he models his teaching in numerous audio and video presentations. Furthermore, he pioneered in the area of research in counseling. For these and numerous other aspects of his dedicated life, counselors should be thankful that Rogers attained the greatest professional honors in our field.

Yet I believe that counselors made a great philosophical error when they accepted the main thrust of Rogers' original teaching, his "non-directive" counseling. (To be fair to him, Rogers no longer uses the term "non-directive" and consistently urges the "client-centered" term, but the original term continues to be used by counselors and others.) The "non-directive" approach seemed to be very attractive since the responsibility for the sessions and for all decisions was clearly that of the client. The counselor was absolved of responsibility for the counseling hour and for the decisions that were made. Perhaps some counselors felt comfortable about referring their clients to other counselors who used the "non-directive" approach. Of course, later research showed that the "non-directive" counselors, including Rogers, were indeed indirectly influencing the counseling sessions through various subtle ways, such as the choice of feelings and ideas that were reflected. The majority of Rogerian counselors accepted and vigorously proposed in schools and educational circles the idea that the counselor is "non-directive" not just in methods of counseling but in the area of major, personal life-choices. In a sense such counselors were taking over the ideas of existential philosophy about the overwhelming importance of just one person, myself, and either not grasping or not vigorously proposing the urgency with which most existentialists write of responsibility not only to self but also to others. At the same time that this was occurring, certain sources that were props to ideals and values in society were being gradually eroded, such as supernatural religious influences (the positive and negative aspects of the Ten Commandments) and what used to be everywhere highly regarded, patriotism to country. Of course, humans do not live in value vacuums, and so many who dropped out from accepting and imparting to others the supernatural religious and/or patriotic approach turned to an existential-personalistic one, often not thought out in any depth. Especially lacking, in my view, was the awareness of responsibility to others, particularly those outside one's own orbit, that is, those in the larger society of city or state or nation.

This lack of concern for society at large, in turn, could account for the great increase in violence and white collar crime in society. If I just want to get mine, I'll stop at nothing to obtain it. I'll use violence or craftiness to obtain my personal satisfaction. It's the mentality of those who say, "Sue for damages, though the claim is fraudulent, because only the insurance company gets hurt." In fact, in this case many individuals get hurt, not least of whom are the claimant whose sense of morality is undermined, stockholders whose profits are decreased, the policy holder who in future must pay a higher rate, and the general public whose cost for insurance becomes increased.

Even if this reasoning in placing at least some responsibility on the "non-directive" counselor for the present morality crisis is not accepted, a glance at some of the current crime statistics should be convincing that there is truly a crisis situation facing us, and that whatever our comfortable past behaviors, a change is called for on the part of "non-directive" counselors. The crime statistics show that all elements of society are involved in various kinds of injustices. A summary of business crime in the Feb. 21, 1977 issue of *U.S. News & World Report* indicates that "A \$40 Billion Crime

Wave Swamps American Business." The crime wave is increasing by 10% a year. How department stores react to the pervasiveness of theft is indicated by their marking up their merchandise by an additional 15%. This business crime affects everyone. An authoritative source, the FBI *Uniform Crime Reports,* gives data on U.S.A. reported crimes. In 1975, for instance, there were 20,510 murders in the country (one every 26 minutes), an increase per 100,000 population over 1960 murders of 88.2%. There were 56,090 forcible rapes (one every 9 minutes), an increase per 100,000 population over 1960 forcible rapes of 174%. There were 464,970 robberies which involved use or threat of violence (one every 68 seconds), an increase per 100,000 population over 1960 robberies of 263%. The pattern is the same for aggravated assault, burglary, larcenty-theft, motor vehicle theft; the increases reported over the 1960 statistics are respectively, 164%, 200%, 171% and 156.5%.

My contention is that at a time when our crime is vastly escalating we cannot continue to be "non-directive." If counselors refuse to be "directive" in any sense, clients will go elsewhere and receive the direction they seek. Many of the clients will not go to the clergy for direction but will go to charlatans of various kinds.

Before making specific proposals, I would like to point out that most counselors have two characteristics that are very advantageous for the behaviors I am going to suggest: 1. they are sensitive to value and moral issues, and 2. they are deeply interested in human psychological growth. A word about each.

The effective counselor is sensitive to human feelings. That's an essential prerequisite for acceptance as a student into a graduate counseling program and it's an area which programs successfully develop. Counselors do have sensitivity to the whole range of human feelings. Indeed, they are very concerned about moral and value problems in the initial phases of their education. However, they often become ambivalent in the area of moral feelings and behavior unless they happen to be members of the clergy. Many fear that they may enter into an area in which special education is needed and which would require their taking a stance in controversial issues and thereby jeopardizing their school or agency position. The result is that, while the interest and the sensitivity remains, most counselors are indeed non-directive to the point of being non-verbal in this area. If they are verbal they refer the client to someone else.

Another characteristic of counselors is their interest in human psychological growth. Indeed, this factor explains the interest that many take in existential counseling and the works of authors such as Rogers, Maslow, May, Van Kaam and many others. Counselors themselves want to grow psychologically and they want to facilitate similar growth in others, including their clients and their friends. Another indication of counselors' interest in this direction is their acceptance and experimentation, often without enough critical examination, of projects in the recent, variegated human potential movement.

The counselor who has developed a sensitivity to human feelings, has maintained an active interest in moral and value positions and has a concern for human psychological growth may go to the psychological cupboard and find the pickings skimpy. Yet I propose that he take a close look at what Lawrence Kohlberg and his associates have to offer. The main elements of Kohlberg's work are summarized elsewhere (e.g., Duska and Whelan, 1975). Here I will only highlight some elements from his writings that seem to satisfy the counselor's need for material and procedures which provide for the sophisticated, moral, psychological growth in counseling sessions.

Before making suggestions regarding the application of the Kohlberg writings to the counselor's work, I would like to give a word of warning to any who may rush into this area. Counselors and teachers have been known to read an article or two by Kohlberg or about him and immediately attempt to make applications in counseling and in the classroom. I submit that attempting to make the application, without considerable previous study and discussion, is a sure guarantee of failure and disillusionment in this as in other important endeavors.

The proposals that I make regarding the use of the Kohlberg writings pertain to two general areas: orientation to counseling, and strategies used in counseling. Regarding orientation, I suggest that rather than being non-directive the counselor view the work more positively. Perhaps calling it "involvement" or "personal growth" counseling expresses well the overall orientation.

Regarding strategies that would be recommended in this approach, the following will be considered: 1. positive welcoming (not mental flight, fright or immediate referral), and special sensitivity to issues involving moral and value decision-making; 2. focused moral-value discussion; 3. an emphasis on cognitive methodology for a deep understanding and analysis that precedes decision-making; 4. use of mental exercises, based upon the Kohlberg dilemmas, to evaluate formally or informally the moral stage or level of the client and to stimulate growth in moral level, especially when there is a marked disparity between the client's mental age and moral stage or level; 5. the use of models in the stimulation of moral and value growth.

We will examine the proposed counseling orientation in each of the five techniques or methodologies and make applications to counseling. Then we will attempt to apply this approach to a well-known filmed demonstration of counseling.

The Orientation

The orientation, viewed as flowing from Kohlberg, is one of marked distinction from the "non-directive" stance, though it is somewhat influenced by it. The counselor welcomes moral and value-dominated issues and does not hesitate to indicate his own position in these areas. But in the final decision-making, the norms, the standards and the reality conditions of the client take precedence. The counselor is willing to model a position but does not attempt to prescribe it, such as often happens in non-counseling personal dialogues. Hence the interaction we are discussing is true counseling in the sense that two or more real persons are involved in the attempt to work together to assist one person to understand self and make a decision. In no way is there anything resembling a prescription for the client.

What was mentioned up to now pertains mostly to personal counseling that is not related to vocational decision-making. But involvement counseling has important implications for vocational considerations. Since one of the criticisms offered of non-directive and existential counseling is that in practice the orientation is too ego-centered, this involvement counseling takes a different tack. The counselor emphasizes the importance of particular occupations, especially in those cases where there is congruence among inventoried interests, tested aptitudes and personality characteristics. But he does not stop there. The counselor does not hesitate to investigate with the client how the occupations will relate to the social interest, spiritual and other needs of the individual and of society (Frankena, 1976). Non-directive counselors have been hesitant to volunteer discussions on these latter areas. But the involvement counselor sees these topics as needed for the growth of the client in cognitive and in moral areas.

Lest there be any confusion about this orientation, let me say that no preaching, no urging, no pressuring, and certainly no psychological manipulation is involved on the part of the counselor. Furthermore, the counselor is open and authentic about this orientation when there are inquiries in or out of counseling. He welcomes the opportunity to present his counseling views at professional meetings such as faculty gatherings and does so also before meetings of students, parents and community groups.

In summary of the counseling orientation: involvement counseling aims at bringing out the client's moral and value stance or lack thereof; it fosters the individual's growth in these and in other psychological areas; it sponsors an awareness of the moral-value implications of all decision-making, especially in life-long choices such as vocational counseling. The counselor's concern is not that the client become a carbon copy of his moral and value views but that there be focused discussion and cognition about the stance and level of the client's own moral growth and values.

The Strategies

Welcoming Moral-Value Discussion

Having briefly analyzed the orientation of the involvement counselor, let us briefly examine some of the strategies that we would expect of him. The first of these is the positive welcoming and special sensitivity to issues involving moral and value decision-making. I wish to cite two segments of counseling and supervision sessions as illustrations of the strategy that I suggest.

The first case was brought to a counselor by a student who had falsified data in an application for a scholarship grant-in-aid. The grant was awarded subject to the client's producing copies of the parents' income tax forms. During the course of the session it became obvious that if the copies of the tax forms were produced the grant would be dropped and the student would have to leave college. The counselor was non-directive during the course of the whole session. The only contribution of the counselor was that of helping the client to consider the likely results of the revelation of the fraud that had been committed. That was the whole session. Yet a great counseling opportunity had been missed. The involvement counselor would make sure to learn about the norms or standards of the individual with regard to personal honesty. Would he steal or in what circumstances would he steal from relatives, from friends, from a corporation, from the government? While some rationalization for the fraud under discussion would be undoubtedly presented, the counselor would engage the client in a collaborative, friendly analysis of the rationalization. It is quite possible that the client will remain convinced of the rationalization and continue in the fraud. But it is also possible that the client exercise freedom to act in a way that demonstrates responsibility as a person and as a citizen. In any case, he will not leave the session as he would have left the non-directive session saying that the counselor felt his fraud was all right since nothing was said against it.

The second case involves the supervision of counseling. A doctoral candidate reported his observing a counseling session in which a young girl spoke about her anxieties and concerns about her out-of-wedlock pregnancy. The supervisor held a conference with the counselor during which he praised the general skill and sensitivity that was demonstrated. However, he asked, why didn't she urge an abortion as this was clearly the simplest way out of the problem. He noted, and reported to his professor, that the counselor had made no response and seemed very embarrassed by the question. All this took place after the 1973 Supreme Court decision legalizing abortion. The professor pointed out that the counselor was a black woman and many blacks oppose abortion; furthermore, the professor happened to know that she was Catholic and it is well known that Catholics oppose abortion. By the end of the conference the supervisor appreciated the importance of learning the moral-ethical-values stance of counselors and clients especially when there is a question of life-and-death issues such as abortion. Furthermore, in the interest of the true freedom of the client, the supervisor learned that an abortion clinic is not the only source of referral in cases of this type, but that another type of referral exists, the Birthright type, which encourages a woman to choose for birth rather than for abortion. Obviously, those who are convinced about the importance of freedom of choice recognize without difficulty that these two options, and not just one, should be proposed.

The involvement counselor differs from the non-directive counselor in openness, willingness, even welcoming discussion regarding moral and value issues. Of course, not all non-directive counselors eschew this type of discussion. But a concern regarding taking a position or revealing a position in effect influences many to enter this area very gingerly. They hope the topic is covered very fast.

Focused In-Depth Moral-Value Discussion

Whether using the Kohlberg dilemmas or not, the counselor who welcomes moral-value discussion will be faced with behavioral problems involving stealing, infidelity, lying, illicit drugs, illicit sex, cheating, child or other human abuse, and all other possible types of human behavior. One result of the counselor's welcoming this type of discussion is that he must be ready to participate in this work through a deep analysis of the problems involved and through continued reading about them. An interest and background in psychology is not the only requirement for this kind of counselor. There must be an abiding interest in the developments in the whole range of human behavior, including the study of contemporary morality.

The involvement counselor is willing to focus upon the various types of moral-value behavior and will do so from both a psychological and philosophical framework. While many counselors assume a psychological stance, some have a fear of entering into philosophical areas because of a hesitation to face head-on the real issues involved in all these problems. The involvement counselor, like other counselors, wants to learn details of the problem and the feelings of the counselee. But the involvement counselor also wants to delve deeply into the real meaning of the behaviors being used and into their effects on loved ones and on society in general.

On occasions the involvement counselor assumes a confrontation style. An example is the rare occasion when the client is about to act upon a moral position in such a way that grave harm is likely to befall the client or others. Obviously the danger has to be immediate, and the position taken is not just a theoretical one that can't be acted upon unless one has leadership of a country. The matter of just what is "grave harm" calls for an act of judgment and prudence on the part of the counselor, but there are some positions most people could accept as dangerous. For instance, an attitude that declares: "Because I am a member of race X, I am clearly superior to race Y and Z. Hence I can take every possible advantage of members of the other races, including taking their possessions and their self-respect." Surely the counselor upon hearing this bold racial nonsense cannot be non-directive and if his indirect approach of modeling and a more direct instructional method is not effective, he should not just wring his hands but be more confrontational to correct the errors involved in the statements made. Confrontation may not be successful in dealing with the client but when it is used the client can hardly feel that the counselor agrees with his ideas. So confrontation can be incorporated into this approach but is rarely necessary.

In focused moral-value discussions the counselor abides by the same injunctions as those that protect the learner in areas of controversy, especially regarding indoctrination. Indoctrination is regarded as a one-sided approach to an issue wherein one presents only the preferred way of thinking or brings in the other side's position with a straw-man type of argumentation. While avoiding indoctrination, the counselor does not hesitate to declare his own position and also exemplifies in words and thought the cognitive approach he has adopted.

Cognitive Emphasis

Another characteristic of involvement counseling is the emphasis on the cognitive aspects of the interaction. While there has been a long tradition in counseling that accepts the primary importance of logic and epistemology (what's true, what's false), the acceptance of this trend has been slow when compared to the many schools which have emphasized the importance of recognizing affect as primary. Of course, proponents of both trends have acknowledged the importance of the other one, but the question has been that of seeing cognition vs. affect as of primary importance for the counselor's focus.

The involvement counselor regards clients' thoughts and thinking process as of primary importance in counseling. Values and moral positions are viewed as developing primarily from the contents of the client's thoughts, not from feelings.

Kohlberg's writings show the importance he attributes to the cognitive nature of man. For one thing, his writings attest his debt to and interest in the great philosophers, who are the models of human cognitive achievement. He speaks of the writings of Plato, Aristotle, Dewey, all of whom he studied when philosophy was emphasized so much in the bachelor's program at the University of Chicago. He said: "I knew that Plato and Dewey were right . . . Essentially, what we have been trying to do in moral education is warmed-over Plato and warmed-over Dewey."

The involvement counselor works toward the client's verbalizing reasons for his position and for his decision. He is not inclined to accept the client's statement that "I just have an intuition." Instead, he tries to probe like a truly involved friend (sometimes like Socrates) into the basic thoughts and basic reasoning process of the client. Habitually he would not take the type of adversary stance that Ellis assumes, but like a friend "hand to hand" would try to explore the motivational and reasoning process, as Rogers would explore the affective conditions of the client.

Basically, the work of the counselor in this framework is that of the philosopher, delving into goals, difficulties, options, and results of each of the options. Kohlberg wrote of the child as philosopher, and surely the counselor should be viewed as a philosopher provided the counselor is involved in cognitive matters and has adopted the overall approach of the philosopher.

Does the involvement counselor argue or debate with the client when their positions are poles apart? Generally, this kind of activity is avoided. The counselor does not seek to persuade but is willing to explicate and model his own position.

It is obvious that the involvement counselor who seeks to model and apply cognitive procedures should have personally reached a condition of considerable development in this area. Hence, an abiding interest in philosophy, especially moral philosophy, and questions related to philosophy should characterize such a counselor. The counselor need not seek to match the qualifications of the professional philosopher, but does need a grasp of the philosopher's methods, as illustrated in the writings of some of the great philosophers. In view of the importance of philosophy and the philosophical method, admissions committees for counselor education programs should in the future welcome not only individuals with strong records in psychology and other behavioral sciences but also those with courses in philosophy, particularly moral philosophy.

An illustration of the counselor's approach in this framework can be gathered from *Assessing Moral Stages: A Manual* by Kohlberg and others (1976). Here the focus is on the reasoning of the individual. Further, the emphasis is also developmental in the sense that the reasoning expected of the very young is quite different from that expected of the mature adult, especially the principled adult.

Kohlberg's emphasis on the client's cognitive processes can be seen in the method used for scoring responses to the dilemmas. The score is not assigned because of the side one takes in solving the dilemmas. Rather the scores and hence the total moral development stage reflects the reasoning offered, the response to the consistently repeated question, Why?

Exercises for Measurement and Growth

The fourth special technique or method that this approach utilizes is the application of exercises, primarily dilemmas based upon the Kohlberg tests. The dilemmas are directed toward ascertaining the client's current Kohlbergian moral stage and toward stimulating growth to the next higher stage.

In order to make use of the dilemmas and to ascertain the exact level of the client, it will be necessary that the counselor spend some time in motivating the client to take the test and commit to writing the choices and options available in the test. Thus typically some time would be required between the period when the client is tested and the use of the test results. During that interval the counselor scores or has scored the materials that the client produced. The result of the scoring would indicate that the client is predominantly in one stage, let us say Stage Four, in moral reasoning.

In the interview that follows the scoring of the dilemma materials, the counselor reports the results and the implications of the results to the client. In passing, I should say that I oppose the dissemination of moral reasoning scores to classes in groups as this kind of reporting may result in fixation or stagnation of moral reasoning stages because of group pressures. In reporting the test results of moral reasoning to the client during the interview, it is important that the counselor try to be factual and try to avoid making an individual feel inferior if his Kohlberg level is low.

After the reporting of the client's level, the really important problem has to be faced, that of stimulating growth. I would like to suggest two possibilities along this line, one counselor-based, and the other audio- or video-based. In either case, the goal is specific, that of making the next higher stage of moral development (beyond that actually attained) seem attractive to the client.

The approach which is counselor-based develops in either or both of two possibilities: the descriptive or the evocative. The descriptive consists of the counselor's narrating in a focused but attractive, reasonable fashion the details of the way the people at the next higher stage of moral development think about the dilemma that had been posed. In addition, the specific reasoning processes and habitual approaches to problem solving of these people is attractively described. The purpose of the counselor's descriptive efforts is to open up to the client an alternative and better pattern of reasoning.

The "evocative" approach of the counselor means helping to raise the client's level of thinking on the basis of the knowledge and method of reasoning that was already demonstrated. The foundations of the better reasoning are already there but the counselor helps the client see that there's a better way of seeking the solution or the truth. Whether the counselor has in mind the recent literature of decision-making or the approach of the Socratic dialogue, the fundamental idea is the same: the client has within himself the potential for cognitive growth and the counselor can stimulate that growth.

The counselor may find it more stimulating for the client to see or hear an audio or video recording of others discussing the pertinent dilemma. For this purpose it will be necessary to have available audio or video recordings of different groups at middle or higher levels of moral reasoning. For instance, if the client is predominantly at Stage 4 in the Kohlberg test, the counselor would use a recording of Stage 5 reasoning. The participants should be of approximately the same age as the client, and if possible, they should be individuals who would be held in high esteem by peers. In a college or high school the discussants might be the leaders of student government or successful athletes. Adult clients might be attracted to discussions among high level officers in government, professors, film or TV personalities, professional athletes and the like. Obviously, recordings for the more mature adults will be difficult to obtain but should be sought nonetheless. The goal of the peer-age recording is to challenge and stimulate growth in moral reasoning. After the recording is heard, the session returns to the counselor-based activity with the counselor attempting to evaluate growth informally through clarifying questions. The session may also develop into an evocative session as was described above.

Models of Moral Behavior

Bandura (1969) and Krumboltz and Thoresen (1976) have written effectively about the importance of modeling to effect change in behavior. The involvement counselor takes a method suggested by behavioral counseling, the use of models, in the stimulation of moral growth. Since mention was made just above of recorded modeling done by peers, this section will be devoted to the use of adults as models, particularly the counselor. Of course, when we suggest adults as models some may say that this poses the problem that so few adults are models that young people have become disillusioned, "turned off", regarding adults as hypocrites. My response is that as with all groups, there are far more who represent the good condition of mankind or adulthood than those who represent the corrupt condition. Even if the proportions are not correct, it seems obvious that the human standard set by the best elements of society should be sought out and followed.

Where can the young find the models they need and so often desperately seek to learn about? Actually in our own generation there are plenty of such models in particular areas. The difficulty arises when we propose a person as a model in the fullest sense. After all Homer nodded and most humans are found to have feet of clay. But for particular moral strengths we can produce models. Today as I write this paper, the media carry accounts of the new administrator of the Veterans Administration, Joseph M. Cleland, called an "authentic hero" not only for his wartime attempt to block a grenade (which actually blew off both his legs and his right arm) but for his tireless efforts to help veterans and the handicapped. In spite of his personal handicap, a senator called him "More full of life than any person I know." There is Bishop Lamont in Rhodesia who is facing prison or exile for his humanitarian efforts for revolutionaries. There is the story of the man who saw another unjustly arrested and stayed in the courts all day until he succeeded in righting the wrong. These individuals are models of particular behaviors, not necessarily models in the full sense. Actually, the *Readers Digest* and other magazines are filled with examples of real life stories that can be used to illustrate that moral behavior is being demonstrated each day in our lives.

It is also important that the counselor have available at least in printed form the stories of the great moral personalities in the history of the human race: Jesus, Moses, Abraham, Jeanne d'Arc, Thomas More, the Buddha, Gandhi, Albert Schweitzer, Dorothy Day, Mother Teresa of Calcutta, to name but a few.

I submit that there is one more element to the availability of adults as models, the counselor as model. We may not like that role and it is understandable that we do not since we are the foremost authorities concerning our own inadequacies. Yet we would not be in this kind of work, I submit, if we did not hope and plan in the direction of our being fully functioning persons which surely includes being completely moral persons. Furthermore, whether we like it or not, those with whom we deal will subject us to considerable scrutiny. There will be awareness of any apparent discrepancy between our profession and our behavior. We should consider being willing to cite to clients our moral reasoning and behavior, especially if our frailty and weakness are part of the picture. Egocentric boasting, "ego trips", should be avoided like the plague.

Kohlberg declares that the principled reasoning towards justice is the characteristic of those in the highest level of moral thinking. (I would establish a higher level for two other areas but we can leave them aside in this presentation.) Is it not appropriate that the counselor who will make use of Kohlberg's ideas examine carefully his own reasoning and behavior in the lifelong pursuit of justice? Justice to my employer, to the various levels of government (including payment of taxes), to clients, to family, to friends and neighbors. Is the counselor willing to go out on a limb, clearly opposing the administration, in cases of injustice in the school? In the community?

If we counselors do not deliberately set about the personal quest for growth in the area of justice in our own lives, I submit that we will be leading a schizoid existence, saying one thing and living another; we will be inauthentic. In the long run we will be failures as counselors as the lack of congruence between our words and our deeds becomes obvious to ourselves and to others.

Application to the "Gloria" Film

Many counselors are acquainted with the film series, Three Approaches to Psychotherapy, in which the same client, Gloria, is interviewed by Carl Rogers, Fritz Perls and Albert Ellis. The series illustrates the great variation in philosophy and techniques that exists between three outstanding representatives of counseling viewpoints.

Here we would like to focus on the first film of the series, the one which features Carl Rogers with Gloria. We will first look at Gloria, her personality, behavior and presenting problem. Then we will examine the philosophy and strategies which Rogers demonstrated in the film. Finally, we will try to apply at least some of the strategies and the orientation which have been described above as characteristic of the involvement counselor.

Gloria

Gloria's presenting problem was that she wanted to learn the best way of dealing with her nine year old daughter concerning her extramarital sex affairs. In addition, she sought help in accepting herself in spite of her being "ornery, sexy and devilish." Further-more, she wanted to know how she could effectively decide between her impulses and her really best interest, "what I want to do" vs. "going against myself." A theme that recurred during the interview was her sense of guilt concerning her relationships with men and her concern about her lying to her daughter regarding her sexual behavior.

She had at least two children, though only the nine year old, Pam, is mentioned. Pam is the object of much of Gloria's concern not only because of her present emotional problems which are not explained, but because Gloria wants to be regarded as her "good mother" now and later on. Yet there is a problem about her being truly a good mother: she has very strong sexual desires and there is mention of the extra money earned by being a waitress late at night. When she brings men home she's afraid of being discovered by Pam. And Gloria has complicated things by asserting clearly to Pam that she did not "make love" to men since her father left.

At one time Gloria stopped engaging in affairs because she realized that she didn't "like herself" when she had them. However, that plan didn't last very long. Even her concern for the children's respect was disregarded with the observation, "Why should they stop me from doing what I want, it's not *that* bad?"

A norm for her behavior that Gloria mentions several times is that when there is a choice and you're not comfortable with it, something is wrong. This is especially the case if you feel bad after you did it. On the other hand, if you're involved in a sexual relationship and there's a real sense of love, everyone including the children would see that the relationship is all right. She has a feeling of disquiet if she enters into the relationship just for the physical attraction, though she was apparently informed in therapy that this situation is natural and so is acceptable.

One value that distinguishes Gloria is her sense of the importance of honesty and truthfulness. She hopes to be able to tell her children later on that, no matter what her behavior, she was at least honest and open about it. "I hate myself if I'm bad and I also hate myself if I lie."

She regards herself as in a double bind: not being able to change her sexual behavior and lying about it. The result is that she sees no way of getting out from the bind and regards the situation as hopeless.

From the film presentation she appears to be highly verbal, intelligent, aware of contradictions, reflective of her own behavior and of the parental influences that still concern her. She is well groomed, generally attractive as a person and very sensitive to others (particularly their thoughts about her).

Rogers

At the beginning of the film Rogers gives an excellent summary of his approach. He says that if he can succeed in establishing a proper psychological climate, his experience has shown him that therapeutic movement can take place. The climate requires his being genuine (real, congruent), accepting (prizing, caring, showing non-possessive warmth), empathizing (moving around in the client's surface and subsurface feelings). If he can create this kind of climate, he believes that the client will explore her feelings more deeply, prize herself more highly, and understand herself more successfully. In addition, he believes that the client will likely move from a locus of evaluation outside self to recognizing greater self capacity for making judgments within herself and for drawing conclusions, including evaluations of herself. These factors could be said to be elements of his philosophy or perhaps better (because less pretentious) his orientation to counseling.

Did Rogers' session with Gloria demonstrate the elements of his orientation? In the areas of being genuine, accepting and empathic, he merited very high grades indeed. As a result of this climate she really did explore her feelings at a surprising level for a first interview, she accepted herself at the end of the session far more than she did at the beginning, and she seemed to understand more about herself. Of course, there were still the lurking questions of uncertainty about her behavior and her conscience (a word that was not used in the session). Rogers expected that she would be more answerable to herself than formerly and the session turned out that way. An interesting indication of the development that took place in the half hour can be judged from something Gloria said at the beginning and from something Rogers said at the end. At the beginning she said she had a concern that he would not "be so harsh on me." What a difference from that concern when at the very end Rogers says, "I am feeling close to you at this moment," and she apparently agrees with him.

A doctoral student's report on some of the techniques Rogers used to achieve his goals included the following: Reflection of feelings; Interpretation of feelings with permission for Gloria to accept or reject; Gloria accepts most interpretations but rejects several and tries to restate or clarify; Rogers reinterprets and she accepts; Assistance in formulating choices; Acceptance of her was noteworthy; Emphasis on self-evaluation. The student noted that Gloria wanted specific answers in the beginning but seemed more self-guided at the end.

It seems to me that the key to the reason for Gloria and Rogers' "feeling good" about the outcome of the interview was her realizing that on the surface at least her problems will be solved if she accepts herself as she is. Gloria felt that Pam would accept her being imperfect and if that happened Gloria could accept herself. She seemed to feel very enthusiastic over that prospect.

In spite of the admitted strengths of the interview, I am convinced that this session, like so many "client-centered" ones, really represents counseling failure and missed opportunity for real growth. Gloria came to Rogers as she had gone to other therapists ostensibly for help in dealing with her children, especially Pam. Yet the session was so filled with the word "guilt" and confusion about her personal behavior, it seems that her real quest was centered around her style of life. But Rogers doesn't focus on that, doesn't read between her lines and hear her saying that she really wants to be a better person. She has been condemning herself throughout the interview but he leaves her with the idea that he accepts her and that probably Pam will accept her and so she can continue as she is. And attractive as she seems on the film, she herself used the word "trollop" to describe her behavior. She had many personal assets but much of her behavior was "devilish" (her term) and contact with Rogers had the net result of self-acceptance, her type of sex behavior and all. His statement at the end of the interview that "You look to me like a pretty nice daughter" probably had the net result of reinforcing her behaviors. So great an authority was very accepting of her as she had portrayed herself. Surely she wouldn't be expected to change her behavior, to become a better self or a better mother to Pam.

Lest there be unnecessary confusion about the above evaluation of Rogers' Gloria interview, let me say that in it Rogers achieved his goal, the climate or "the necessary and sufficient conditions for therapeutic growth." But fundamentally what I am challenging is the sufficiency of these conditions. Something more is needed, including at the very least, an orientation toward the growth and improvement in the client beyond the areas of self-concept and self-acceptance. With this criticism of Rogers' work in mind, and still within the half hour framework of the Gloria interview, let us see what the involvement counselor would attempt to achieve (orientation) and the techniques that could be utilized.

The Involvement Counselor with Gloria

If asked to state his orientation prior to seeing Gloria, the involvement counselor would express his viewpoint somewhat like the following.

> I want to be of service to Gloria. That means that I'll first try to find out why she's seeing me. I'll realize, however, that her "presenting reason" for coming may be quite different from her real concern. So I'll be very careful to listen for themes, which could be expressed by recurring words or phrases and I'll note non-verbal communication whenever the themes are mentioned such as bodily tensions or a change in tone of voice.
>
> If the client's message reveals a concern for her moral situation I'll try to reinforce the importance of this part of her life rather than downgrade it or flee from it. I'll try to be stimulating and creative in helping her grow and develop in her moral behavior. Of course, I'm convinced of the importance of her personal freedom, and so I will not pressure or manipulate her in any way. But I will not hesitate to make known my own stand. My prayer is: Lord, help me to help Gloria. May she become her best possible self.

The first technique mentioned above is that of welcoming moral-value discussion. In practice, the counselor would not rush into this area until it became clear that Gloria truly had a concern about her promiscuous living. After about ten minutes of the session the fact that this aspect of her behavior was a cause of concern became clear. At this point, the involvement counselor could state quite clearly: "Gloria, you said you came to discuss your relationship with Pam, your lying to her and your self-acceptance. I think that behind these problems, you have another one, the promiscuous sexual relationships that you have with men. I suspect that one part of you says that you want to continue, and another part of you says, let's stop this because it's wrong." Note that no attempt is made to deny the fact or the legitimacy of the presenting problems, but that they are seen as centering around the moral one.

Assuming that Gloria would accept the suggested focus, the counselor continues in a predominantly cognitive style. Of course, the counselor is sensitive to feelings and seeks to elicit them and does reflect them. But the distinctive human dignity is in the cognitive realm and so real growth, while using affect, flows from cognitive advances. So the involvement counselor invites the client to analyze carefully the real meaning of her promiscuous sex life. She could try to see what's happening to herself, to the men involved, and to her children. While the counselor presents this kind of outline for discussion, he hopes that the actual details will come from her. For instance, regarding what's happening to her, he could suggest that she think about what she'll be like ten or twenty years from now if she continues in this kind of activity. Whether or not she has a religion, what is this aspect of her life doing to her own standards, her moral code? What's becoming of her view of the real meaning of love? Regarding her thoughts on the men involved, the analysis could call for her specifying what she really thinks of them. Are they just means for her goals? Are they just things and really not persons? Is each episode a demeaning and not a human experience? The discussion regarding the effect of her behavior on her children should be particularly fruitful, especially since she feared being discovered by Pam. Her role as teacher and guardian of her children could be reviewed, especially in the area of preparing them for ideas of love and marriage.

Alternatives to her current behavior could also be discussed. Possibilities for reentry into married life could be a fruitful area of analysis. An important goal for the counselor is that of attempting to draw out from Gloria the attractive elements of what she herself considers a really good life style. This may be a source of stimulation for her to take realistic efforts to achieve the changes that would precede her moving in that direction. This view of a higher stage of living is comparable to the view that a person at Stage 3 in the Kohlberg terminology takes, when ready to move, of ideas received from those who are in Stage 4.

Limitations of the half hour allotted with Gloria make it impossible to administer and score either the Kohlberg or the Rest test. Yet it is likely that she would be found to be at Stage 3 in the Kohlberg test ("good girl," a term from others; "if an authority tells me, I'll risk it"). In this stage, "What is right?" is associated with what people expect of you from your role, e.g., as mother. The time limitation would also prevent focused moral-value discussion beyond that which is indicated above since she really accepted the fact that her actions were "bad." Furthermore, there would be no time to survey with her the models whom she could look to in regard to her growth and development as a woman. Were there time, it is very likely that she herself could speak more of possible models, such as the woman who admires her at work.

Gloria praised Rogers and criticized her parents because she could be open with him and could not be open with them. In the film, Gloria appreciates Rogers' helping her to accept herself as she is. I have often wondered if she ever realized that Rogers could have helped her to become a better person, and could have helped her to accept herself as a person striving to become better. Of course, I also wonder if Gloria would accept the invitations of the involvement counselor to analyze more realistically her present situation and then change her behavior.

Other Applications

Everything said above about the work of the counselor was directed primarily to work in the one-to-one situation. In a sense, that's more difficult work when compared with group work since stimulation can be usually expected from the members of the group who have reached higher levels of reasoning. We will not further consider the application of the Kohlberg material to the group since the literature is filled with that aspect of his work (e.g., Blatt, 1966; Sprinthall, 1976; Kavanagh, 1976). Suffice it to say that what has been said of the one-to-one sessions is also applicable to group sessions.

Outside of work with groups and individual clients, the school counselor has an indirect influence on the classroom. Some counselors, for instance, are on school curriculum committees. And all counselors seek to establish good relationships with other professional workers in the school, especially with the classroom teachers. In these kinds of contacts the counselor can impart information and enthusiasm for the Kohlberg moral development model. Various types of consultation with teachers and administration enable the counselor to suggest the need for professionals to have a definite commitment and sensitivity to value and moral issues and to incorporate them into curricula, such as literature and social studies. The counselor could also encourage the initiation of programs such as Mosher and Sprinthall's deliberate psychological education (which contains a strong moral education element). The counselor could emphasize the importance of securing the services of a specially qualified instructor for these units and programs.

In conclusion, I suggest that acceptance of the non-directive approach was a serious mistake for counselors. They followed the leadership of many who set the stage for a normless society or for a completely self-seeking segment of society. If counselors accept the invitation to profit from the research and labors of Lawrence Kohlberg and his associates, they can help turn or at least tilt the direction of society. The clients will still set their own norms but we counselors will not be giving the message that we will be of no help in this quest. Our orientation will be that of involvement with the personal needs of the client so that we will not be non-directive in providing help. Our strategies will include that of welcome to moral considerations, not fear and flight as some counselors displayed in the past. We can offer focused, in-depth moral and value discussions. Our emphasis will be on the cognitive approach, even though we recognize the importance and the need to bring to awareness the feelings of clients. We will not hesitate to make use of pertinent moral exercises and tests, such as the Rest test and the Kohlberg dilemmas; these can provide scores for the stage placement of clients and for stimulation towards further moral development. Finally, we will actively search our own times and the past for the pertinent models of moral development for use with clients. Though shying away from the implication of the word, counselors will recognize that we are regarded as "models." While we see ourselves as still "becoming," at the least we can attempt to grow in areas which the moral philosophers have emphasized, such as in our pervasive sense of justice and in the practice of justice in our personal lives. Thereby we will develop personally and provide our clients with additional models.

Numerous benefits will accrue if we succeed in the goals which are urged in this paper. School counselors will be able to show more tangible results of their works and, as their contributions to society will become more obvious, their positions will not be cut from school budgets. Counselors in private practice, in colleges and agencies, will be able to offer to clients and administrators a better description than they now can of their proper role and function. Counselors themselves will have a clearer sense of their contributions to clients and to fellow citizens. Confusion regarding accountability should be decreased. Competence evaluation should be facilitated. For all these benefits, let the non-directive counselor out and the involvement counselor in!

What the Value/Moral Educator Can Learn from Piaget

Frank W. Lewis, S.J.

"Apart from our relations to other people, there can be no moral necessity. The individual as such knows only anomy and not autonomy." (*The Moral Judgment of the Child,* p. 194)

My task here is both challenging and frightening. The challenge is both difficult and pleasant—difficult because of the immense volume of the Piagetian corpus; pleasant because it is an opportunity to share with educators some of the fascinating findings of the most authoritative expert on child development, Jean Piaget. But the task is also frightening. It involves scrutiny of complex researches meticulously designed and executed, and then reported in considerable detail, in a vocabulary no longer standard and a syntax long since fallen into desuetude. The fright is assuaged, however, because Piaget himself has synthesized for us many of his key discoveries. Most of Piaget's publications are focused on cognitive development, but there are some in which he has focused directly on moral development. These shall be our main concern here.

But first a caution. In an era of instant-on television, instant photoprints, and instant foods, it is necessary to recall that in at least some areas of inquiry, there is no instant wisdom. To understand Piaget or the problems of moral education, the learner must investigate for himself. Piaget constantly reminds us that learning is inventing, creating, discovering, or re-inventing, re-creating, re-discovering for oneself. These few pages of condensed comment on Piaget are no substitute for the exciting experience of directly studying his work.

There is also a paradox in this attempt to use words to understand what Piaget has learned about moral development. He would prefer, I suspect, that we replicate his experiments and discover these truths for ourselves. We shall find him, moreover, saying

strong things about the dangers of verbalism in education. I hope
that the contradiction is only apparent here, and that my exposition
of his insights which have produced cognitive dissonance in me will
be the occasion of similar stimulation of you, with the result of an
improved understanding of both the learners we seek to help and
our role in fostering their development.

Uncovering hidden assumptions and articulating unstated implications are among the philosopher's key tasks, but they are ancil-
lary to his main project, which is obstacle-removal. If we are to see
at last what is really already there we must clear away the clutter of
naively assimilated attitudes, unexamined beliefs, and culturally-
transmitted myths which interfere with clear vision, filter and distort
our perceptions, and secretly influence our inquiries. After his more
than half a century of scientific inquiry into human development,
what Piaget has to say will challenge many of the ideological under-
pinnings of our educational institutions and methods. Piaget can help
free educators from programmed frustration only if they have the
humility to put aside defenses, and look at what he points out with
the unguarded, trusting wonder of the children we all care about.

Expositions of Piaget's moral development research and theory
can be found in many places: general introductions to his thought
(e.g., Pulaski, 1971), general discussions of moral development or
moral education (e.g., Wilson *et al.*, 1967; Duska & Whelan, 1975;
Graham, 1972), symposia on practical applications of Piaget's work
(e.g., Lubin *et al.*, 1975), and in Piaget's own publications. His own
expositions include numerous cursory observations in his cognitive
studies extending from 1928 to 1972, summaries of his findings and
theory for general audiences (e.g., 1970, 1973, 1969), and especially
his classical research report, *The Moral Judgment of the Child*
(1932/1965).

Drawing principally from his own expositions, I propose here to
offer the moral educator the following areas of discussion: A.
Piaget's generic conclusions about learning and the learner (applicable to moral as well as cognitive learning); B. some specific conclusions about cognitive development of special interest to moral education; C. specific research data about moral development; and D.
implications for moral educators.

Learning and the Learner

Piaget views the human learner as a living organism in dynamic
interaction with the environment (which includes object, events,

subjective experiences, and other persons), striving to maintain a dynamic equilibrium ("equilibration") through a twofold "adaptation" which is simultaneously an 'assimilation' of the environmental input to already formed structures and 'accommodation' of the structures to new elements of the environment. The person enters the world capable of creating or constructing for itself, through the adaptive interaction with its world, a progressively more complex series of interrelated structures which regulate its functioning interactive behavior and are, in turn, modified continually by this interaction. The structures and functions specifically characteristic of the human person are the cognitive and moral ones. Structures and their organizations are inferred from observed functioning. Structures are internal regulatory principles which both maintain the person (preservation) and regulate its developmental adaptive interaction with its environment.

Piaget clearly distinguishes his own explanation from the two most widely accepted types of human development theory, by insisting that the person is its own chief architect, the primary creator of its own structures, the "master of his destiny" (1932/1965, p. 99). Without denying the respective contributions of heredity and of environment, Piaget insists that the evolution of the person is neither the unfolding of innate programming, nor mere conditioning by external influences (the prejudice of most contemporary social science and of many social welfare programs). He will not allow himself to be bracketed with either the maturationists (e.g., Rousseau, Freud) or the social conditioners (Skinner, a variety of learning theorists, etc.). Piaget argues that there is a third alternative to maturationsim and neobehaviorism: interactionism. He is interested in new thoughts, predetermined neither by nervous system maturation nor by environmental encounter, but constructed within the individual through an internal process of reflexive abstraction on the external process of experience. It is education, he argues, that makes this possible. (1972, pp. 25-26)

Emphasizing the crucial importance of education as a necessary factor for intellectual and moral formation, Piaget views it as a unified process, stretching from birth to the end of adolescence, responsible for the transformation of 'rough outlines' (the biological and aptitudinal givens) into efficient behavior patterns. These 'rough outlines', which can be neglected, developed, or destroyed, require social and educational interactions for their maturation (1973, p. 55; 1932/1965, p. 94). The neonate is a bundle of possibilities or 'potentialities' (his expressions remind one of Aristotelian Scholastic 'potencies') which depend, for healthy development, upon appropriate educational milieus (1973, p. 101). In the formation of the individual, social factors are especially important in the matter of learning customs, rules, and behavior patterns which are "acquired by external transmission, from generation to generation, by education, and develop only through multiple and differentiated social interactions" (1973, pp. 44-45). External educational action is a necessary (but not, of itself, sufficient—the person is the prime agent) condition (whether one thinks of familial surroundings or of the school) of the person's development. Through social interactions the growing person learns not only the language in which collective values are expressed, but the values themselves, "as well as the rules applicable to them, beginning with the two most important systems of values and standards for the later adaptation of the individual to its surroundings: logic and ethics" (1973, p. 46).

Neither logic nor ethics, he insists, are innate. The growing person forges or constructs his own logic and ethics through appropriate social experiences. To be able to do this he must be able to function in a milieu which, besides giving him the opportunity to acquire knowledge, to listen, and to obey, offers him adequate scope to exercise his autonomy in the construction of his own norm systems—in short, a "social environment, not made exclusively of submissiveness" (1973, p. 52).

The structures which the individual so forges are inevitably to some extent idiosyncratic, since there are inescapable differences in individual aptitudes and interests, in social experiences, and in the individual's formative activities whereby he forms his structures. There will thus be an inevitable pluralism of logics and ethics, a pluralism of ways of being rational and of being moral. Sincere people may, therefore, fail to agree about truth or values without one or another being 'wrong,' 'irrational,' or 'immoral.' This view has far-reaching consequences for educational discussions about 'truth' and about 'morals.' It suggests that the widely-shared expectation that prolonged discussion will produce substantial agreement about facts or norms may be less reasonable than we are wont to think. It suggests, too, that many ameliorative social action projects (including compensatory education programs) are ill-conceived. The problem of an inevitably pluralist society would not be how to get different people to agree in ideology and behavior, but rather how to get differing people to live cooperatively in matters of the 'common weal' while retaining differing beliefs and values.

In the development of the learner, Piaget discerns a kind of "teleology". We expect acorns to mature into mighty oaks, and kitten embryos to grow into furry, bewhiskered cats, not giraffes. What is the *TELOS*, or mature fulfillment, of human neonate? Piaget views human development as a complex evolution from the self-centered individual to the mature "person"; he defines personality as "reciprocal rapport" (1973, p. 90). The self-centered child's moral/intellectual egocentrism is an obstacle to the inherent relations of reciprocity that all evolved social living contains. The maturing "person", however, helps create and accepts a kind of discipline by voluntarily subjecting himself to a system of mutual "norms" that subordinate his liberty in respect to that of others.

Personality is neither the absolute autonomy of egocentrism nor the heteronomy of being governed completely by outside pressures, but a reciprocity which preserves individual autonomy (because freely entered into) and guarantees social cooperation (because the autonomous person regulates his activity by norms in the creation of which he has freely collaborated). In this view autonomy and reciprocity are correlative aspects of the personality. The person is an individual who has learned to situate his own ego in true perspective in relation to others' egos. He enters into a reciprocity-system which requires simultaneously that he adopt an independent discipline (autonomously self-imposed) and that his own activity undergo a basic "de-centering" (shifting from a self-centered focus to a viewpoint that includes consideration of the different perspectives of others). For Piaget, "the two basic problems of ethical education are, therefore, to assure this de-centering and to build this discipline" (1973, p. 111). Education must aim at the creation of persons capable of intellectual and moral autonomy and of respecting this autonomy in others by agreeing on reciprocal norms which legitimate the activities of all. Such personality development "really requires a free and spontaneous activity in a social milieu based on collaboration and not on submission" (1973, p. 92). Hence, Piaget continues, "the right to education is not only the right to attend schools, but also "the right to find in these schools all that is necessary to the building of a questioning mind and a dynamic moral conscience."

"Spontaneity" and "collaboration" are two key elements in Piaget's generic definition of learning: spontaneous, collaborative investigation by interaction and experimentation with the environment (including objects, events, persons, and subjective experiences). "Spontaneous" in this context means, not uncaused or unexpected, but freely chosen by the learners out of their own interests; it is therefore the opposite of pre-packaged, pre-programmed, mandatory, prescribed, coerced, or cajoled. Piaget explains that this stress on the spontaneous activity of the child, required by his constructivist theory of development, is one of the characteristic features which distinguish his view from that of the neobehaviorists (1973, p. 5-6, 10-11). He also urges that the knowledge achieved through free investigation and spontaneous effort will be retained, that the learner will have acquired a methodology useful for life, that his curiosity will be stimulated without the risk of being exhausted (1973, p. 93).

The second element in Piaget's definition of learning is the insistence on its collective or collaborative nature. He emphasizes the necessity of free collaboration among the students themselves (and not only between the teacher and the student), and of "collective living" and a "collective milieu" as "essential to the full development of the personality in all its facets" (1973, p. 109). Focusing more specifically on the requirements of moral learning, Piaget concludes:

> It becomes evident that neither the teacher's authority nor the best lessons he can give on the subject suffice to engender living, dynamic relationships, comprised of both independence and reciprocity. Only a social life among the students themselves—that is, self-government taken as far as possible and parallel to the intellectual work carried out in common—will lead to this double development of personalities, masters of themselves and based on mutual respect (p. 110).

In *Biology and Knowledge* (1971) Piaget reiterates his thesis that knowledge is an interindividual as well as an intraindividual achievement, and that the more generalized forms of knowledge are forms of cognitive exchange or of interindividual regulation that result from common functioning in a living organization. These nonhereditary social regulations are the antidote to the egocentric distortions of the individual and a necessary condition for the formation of a decentered epistemological subject (p. 360-1, p. 368). The strong emphasis on collaboration in learning challenges the view that an individual learns solo, raises questions about competition's role in promoting learning, suggests a need to re-appraise the "individualized instruction" movement, dethrones the self-sufficient achiever (in school or in the marketplace) as emulation model, and is pregnant with implications for the selection of in-school or out-of-school learning opportunities for children. What happens, for instance, to silence and fixed seating when collaborative learning is encouraged in the school?

"Investigation" is the third element in Piaget's definition. It highlights the process of searching as much as the satisfaction of finding, and includes no suggestion that the solutions to problems are already known. It has much in common with the Progressivists' "experience-learning", with the "discovery method" of teaching sciences, with the procedures of the "open classroom", and with the "action-learning" demands of recent high school reform reports.

By adding the elements of "interaction" and "experimentation" Piaget intends to emphasize, in contrast to the passive, book-centered, or lecture/note-taking features of traditional school experiences, an active manipulation of things and events—often by attempting the untried (a characteristic of the genuine experiment). There are at least two noteworthy points here. The first is the demand that the learner interact with the real world. The second is the expectation that some experiments will fail. Does this view have implications for our traditional views of what is success and what is failure in education? The unsuccessful experiment is still a source of knowledge to the scientist!

Requiring that education provide ample opportunity to interact with the real world will obviously include escape from the confines of the school building; there is only so much of the real world that can be reproduced inside the school building, especially in later years as students move from a preoccupation with physical objects to the investigation of social, economic, and political institutions. Even where classroom discussions are appropriate, Piaget insists, they require "a collective atmosphere of active and experimental investigation" (1973, p. 95). Action-learning is essential because, for Piaget, thinking is internal operating which presupposes adequate external operations. Furth suggests that "thinking and acting need not be conceptualized as two separate activities; rather, thinking should be taken as synonymous with 'intelligent' action" (1970, p. 23).

Cognitive Development and Moral Education

Obviously, cognitive factors are crucial ingredients of morality. Moral judgments decide and guide personal actions; with moral judgments we evaluate our own and others' decisions and behaviors. "Moral judgment" has been, in fact, the special focus of most of Piaget's own moral development research (1932/1965, p. 7). He has, moreover, always insisted that the cognitive and the moral are inseparably correlative aspects of a unified human development, that there is a parallelism in their respective structures and in their evolution, and that there is a kinship of logic and ethics (1932, p. 398, 404).

In the course of his cognitive researches Piaget has uncovered countless phenomena of interest to moral educators. There is, for example, the moral character of the child's early notions of physical causality, wherein the "child endows things with consciousness principally in order to explain their obedience to a hierarchy. It credits things with a moral nature rather than with a psychology" (1929, p. 224). The young child is a moralist before becoming a physicist!

Those who ask of the very young child or hear him give reasons for his behavior, are reminded that "until he reaches a certain age (7-8, at least), the child is insensible to contradiction" (1928, p. 163). The very young child, not conscious simultaneously of the multiplicity of factors in a complex notion, is able neither to combine them nor to arrange them in a hierarchy, but reasons only by proceeding from particular to particular. Within a short period of time the child may blithely offer conflicting and even contradictory reasons for the same behavior.

The young child's inability to remember from one day to another, or to relate a new instance to a previous similar one, means that the adult must be resigned to repeating again and again what he wishes the child could remember. Whether because of inability to recall or because of inability to perceive relations of similarity, the child does not recognize the present situation as an instance of what was previously forbidden or commanded.

The egocentric child's inability to take someone else's viewpoint makes it unreasonable to expect the very young child to consider the feelings, the convenience, or even the situation, of the adult (or of another child, for that matter).

Given the dependence of moral reasoning on cognitive development, Piaget's cautions about logic are important to the moral educator. Piaget found that formal logic (in the sense of the capacity to reason according to such logic—not the knowledge of such a discipline) is not innate (1973, p. 48-50; 1932/1965, p. 398), does not really begin to be formed until the child is 11-12 years of age, and can take till the age of 14-15 years for complete achievement (1973, p. 49). There are obvious implications in these research data. One implication concerns the kinds of reasons or arguments to be used in discussing moral issues with children of different ages, and about the kinds of answers and explanations one can properly expect children to give. Another implication pertains to the understanding of mathematics, an abstract discipline which "is nothing but logic" (1973, p. 96). Piaget says it is "first of all and most importantly, actions exercised on things, and the (cognitive) operations themselves are more actions, but well coordinated among themselves and only imagined instead of being materially executed" (1973, p. 103). Admitting that it is both necessary and natural for cognitive development to reach abstraction in all areas during adolescence, Piaget warns of the dangers of abstraction not rooted in "a series of previously uninterrupted concrete actions." This caution applies to the use of abstract moral reasoning or argument with the young child. Just as the understanding of basic mathematical concepts requires ample experience of material objects, in different shapes and sizes, with their multiplicity of movements and interrelations, so too does effective moral development and intelligent moral discussion presuppose extensive experience and experimentation with social living, with collaboration and cooperation. Where this experience is lacking, abstract moral discussion is vacuous.

Piaget has strong criticism for the premature or excessive verbalism of the traditional school. "The true cause of failures in formal education," he argues, "is therefore essentially the fact that one begins with language (accompanied by drawings, fictional or narrated actions, etc.) instead of beginning with real and material action" (1973, pp. 103-4). Piaget insists that language comes after understanding, that it is the expression rather than the source of cognitive activity. He does not believe that all verbal teaching is useless, but emphasizes that preliminary concrete activity must prepare the learner for verbal exchange, which must take place in an appropriate social/ethical milieu. If "lessons are given without social experience to support them, their practical results risk being of little worth" (1973, p. 130).

Verbal exchange with the young must not only be rooted in concrete experiences; it must be a response to questions that emerge spontaneously in the learner, and it must take his interests into account (1973, p. 129). Piaget explicitly indicates his agreement with John Dewey on this point (1932/1965, p. 367-370).

A careful study of Piaget's investigations of cognitive development and of his conclusions about the stages of normal cognitive growth will be very rewarding to the moral educator. A good starting point is his U.N. essays (1973) and then any one of the many fine summary expositions of his theory (e.g., Brearley & Hitchfield, 1969; Pulaski, 1971).

Moral Development

For the moral educator, Piaget's classic investigations of moral development, reported in *The Moral Judgment of the Child* (1932/ 1965), are a goldmine of information about growth and of clues to appropriate attitudes and coping procedures, suitable learning experiences, and apt teaching materials and methods for fostering the developmental process. His investigations are focused on moral judgment, not moral behavior nor moral sentiment (p. 7). His method throughout is the interrogatory clinical interview, supplemented by observations of child behavior, though he warns often of the many pitfalls in such a method. Admitting that the only good method in the study of moral facts is the closest observation of the most individuals possible, he argues that it produces only a small number of fragmentary facts and must therefore be completed by questioning. He promises, however, to give as valid only such results (of questioning) as do not contradict observation in family life. He reminds us that questioning in the moral sphere can only be "about reality once removed." ("You cannot make a child act in a laboratory in order to dissect his moral conduct.") Nor is it possible to investigate directly, by interrogation, the moral rules the child receives from the adult. He limits himself to the examination and analysis of the child's judgment of moral value—"not the child's actual decisions nor even his memory of his actions, but the way he evaluates a given piece of conduct."

Within these limits, there is still a major problem: in what relation does the verbal thought of the child stand to his active and concrete thought? What relation is there between moral reflection and moral practice? Is the judgment of value given in answer to my question the same as the child would give in practice, independently of the actual decision he himself would make? Piaget believes he has ample evidence of a correspondence between the action and the theory of the child, which, if not simple, is at least definable. There is, however, a time-lag between the verbal and theoretical judgment and his concrete and practical judgments; verbal thought, even in the adult at times, lags behind active thought. Piaget concludes that the children's verbal and theoretical responses correspond with their concrete and practical judgments made on the occasion of their own actions during the years preceding the interrogatory. (There is an advantage to this limitation—it enables the investigator to find out from the older child something about the value judgments of the young child unable to respond to questions yet). There is a second limitation to Piaget's interrogatory method: the verbal evaluations are not of actions the children authored or witnessed, but of stories told to them; the child's evaluation is, therefore, verbal to the second degree. Evaluations obtained from stories may also lag in time behind the direct evaluations of daily life. (p. 112-120) Children's games offer the investigator a better chance to analyze reality in the making, and it is the study of such games which is the first part of Piaget's four-part inquiry. We will discuss only the first three parts as these contain the experiential data and analyses.

The Rules of the Game (p. 1-108)

Piaget begins with studies of the practice and the consciousness of the rules of the game. He believes that "all morality consists in a system of rules, and the essence of all morality is to be sought for in the respect which the individual acquires for these rules" (p. 13). He chose the game of marbles, both because it was so universal among children and because adult intervention was minimal. He expected that the relations between the practice of and the consciousness of rules would "best enable us to define the psychological nature of moral realities" (p. 15).

Through a complex series of questions Piaget sought to find out:

(a) how the individuals adapt themselves to these (transmitted) rules, i.e., how they observe rules at each age and level of mental development; (b) how far they become conscious of rules, in other words, what types of obligation result (always according to the children's ages) from the increasing ascendency exercised by rules (1932/1965, p. 24).

With respect to (a), the practice of rules, Piaget discerns four successive stages: 1') a purely motor and individual stage; 2') egocentric imitation of others' use of codified rules (from 2-5 to 7-8 years old)—even when children play together, each one plays on his own; 3') incipient cooperation (7-8 to 11-12 years) in which each player tries to win, and everyone is concerned with mutual control and unification of rules; and finally 4') the codification stage (from 11-12 years on) in which every detail of the game is fixed, and the mandatory code of rules is known to all. Piaget cautions here that the division into stages is an expository device; "the facts present themselves as a continuum which cannot be cut up into sections" and which is not linear in character (p. 27-28).

With respect to the second inquiry, (b) the consciousness of rules, he discerns a different progression through three stages: 1') rules are non-coercive because purely motor, or because non-obliging models (lasts till some time during the egocentric stage mentioned above); 2') rules are regarded as sacred and untouchable, emanating from adults and lasting forever—a suggested alteration is viewed as a transgression ("apogee of egocentric and first half of cooperating stage"); 3') rule is seen as a law due to mutual consent—loyalty demands you respect it, but it can be altered by enlisting general opinion in support of the change. Piaget then contrasts the mystical or magical respect for rules which characterizes the second consciousness stage with the "rational and well-founded respect" of the third. He observes that as soon as there is reciprocal imitation (end of practice stage 2' and all of stage 3') "we have the beginnings of a rule." The early experiences of cooperation do not erase the magical attitude toward rules which is a joint product of child realism and adult constraint. "Cooperation has to be practiced for a very long time before its consequences can be brought fully to light by reflective thought" (p. 64). It is in the third consciousness stage that we find the conjunction of cooperation and autonomy succeed the conjunction of egocentrism and constraint. Rules, hitherto seen as imposed by older children and thus assimilated to adult commands,sacred and untouchable, come to be conceived as the free pronouncements of the actual individual minds themselves, no longer external and coercive but able to be modified and adapted by the group. "Law now emanates from the sovereign people and no longer from the tradition laid down by the Elders" (p. 72).

The difference between the second and third stages of consciousness of rules is striking. Is it, Piaget asks, a difference in kind or a difference of degree? His answer anticipates by almost half a century the now popular Transactional Analysis:

> There is an adult in every child and a child in every adult. The difference in nature reduces itself to this. There exist in the child certain attitudes and beliefs which intellectual development will more and more tend to eliminate: there are others which will acquire more and more importance. The latter are not simply derived from the former but are partly antagonistic to them. The two sets of phenomena are to be met both in the child and in the adult, but one set predominates in the one, the other in the other. It is, we may say, simply a question of the proportions in which they are mixed; so long as we remember that every difference of proportion is also a difference of general quality, for the spirit is one and undivided.
>
> Between the various types of rules which we shall give there will therefore be at once continuity and qualitative difference: continuity of function and difference of structure. This renders arbitrary any attempt to cut mental reality up into stages. (p. 85)

Language and discursive thought, Piaget reminds us, tend to lay too much emphasis on discontinuity; over-sharp discontinuities (e.g., between "stages") are analytical devices and not objective results of research (p. 87). This caution must be kept in mind when studying his division into stages of social attitudes (the asocial baby, the egocentric child subject to external constraint and uncooperative, the civilized adult cooperating with equals), behavior (motor, egocentric and constrained, cooperative), rules (motor, those due to unilateral respect, and those due to mutual respect). "Things are," he urges, "motor, individual, and social all at once" (p. 86). He explores the relations between motor rules, coercive rules, and rational rules, and concludes that although "the social element is to be found everywhere," it is "not just one thing" (p. 88-90). There are differences between the unilateral respect of the little child and the mutual respect of two adolescents, with room for any number of intermediate stages—"the qualities in question are not more important than the proportions in which they are mixed." Different proportions of constraint and cooperation produce different results.

As the egocentric young child grows, "communal life alters the very structure of consciousness by inculcating into it the feeling of respect" (p. 101); rules, conditions for the existence of a social group, become charged with obligation. At first this sense of obligation is rooted in the unilateral respect of dependent child for adult, of young child for older child, of inferior for superior. Progressive liberation from adult supervision and from the domination of older children, exposure to a variety of different customs, and experiences of cooperation with peers lead to a transformation of respect from unilateral to mutual. What was the fruit of external constraint (unilateral respect) is metamorphized into the collaborative product of reciprocating autonomies (mutual respect); obligation freely adopted is subjective, personal, "autonomy."

Adult Constraint and Moral Realism (p. 109-196)

In the second part of his investigations of moral judgment, Piaget studies the related problems of adult constraint and children's moral realism which surfaced in the first part. He limits his focus to one aspect of the consciousness of moral norms—the theoretical moral judgment (as opposed to that which occurs in actual experience). Others have collected data about the child's practice of rules and the conflicts which take place in the child's mind (e.g., research on lying) to which he can compare his results. He set out to examine, not the child's actual decisions, nor his memory of his own actions, but the way he evaluates a given conduct, his judgment of moral value. He uses the interrogatory interview, reminding us of the time lag between the child's practice and his theorizing about it, and between the child's initial theoretical speculations about a problem and his confident verbalization of a theory.

Questioning children about anecdotes involving clumsiness and stealing, Piaget uncovered two distinct moral attitudes—one that judges actions according to their material consequences (objective responsibility) and one that only takes intention into account (subjective responsibility). Both are found in all age groups, but on the average objective responsibility diminishes as the person grows older, and subjective responsibility gains correlatively in importance.

The phenomena of children's lie-telling hold special interest for Piaget, because here the egocentric child's natural tendency to lie clashes with the adult moral constraint. He uncovered three stages in the evolution of the child's definition of a lie. For the very young child (till 6-7 years) to tell a lie is to commit a moral fault by means of language, with no clear distinction between telling a falsehood and uttering interdicted expressions ('naughty words'). Later (from 8 to 10-11 years) a lie is defined in a purely objective manner, as an affirmation which does not conform to fact, whether deliberate or involuntary. At about 10-11 years of age the correct definition of a lie emerges: a statement that is intentionally false. Although the idea of intention appears very early (about 3 years), it is a long while before the child learns to distinguish between intentional acts and others as clearly as adults do.

Exploring children's evaluation of lies (the problem of responsibility, viewed either as a function of the aim of the lie—subjective, or as a function of its degree of falseness—objective), he observed that younger children ignore "intention" and think only of the relative improbability of the lie's content or its actual results, while the older children pay more attention to motives. Among children 6-12 years old, there is a perceptible transition from the objective responsibility of the younger (average age—7 years) to the subjective responsibility of the older (average age—9 years).

Until 7/8 years of age the child tends spontaneously to alter the truth (for its own satisfaction) until adult intervention, usually with strong affective ingredients, arouses obligations of conscience not to lie, which, because they are not rooted in the child's natural impulses, remain "stuck on," "external," heteronomous. The letter of the law must be obeyed; the spirit of the law is not grasped. The child's primitive realism, under the pressure of adult constraint, promotes an "objective" view of morality. An understanding of the spirit of the law, of "subjective" morality, requires experiences of thought-exchange between equals. (Such exchanges are impossible between adult and child because of their initial inequality and the child's unilateral respect.) These mutual exchanges lead to mutual respect and liberate the child from moral realism.

Asking children why people should not lie reveals an evolution with age in the direction of reciprocity. At first the lie is wrong because it brings punishment, then because it is wrong in itself, and finally because it is in conflict with mutual trust and affection.

Piaget analyzes concrete instances of situations involving departures from adult-imposed norms in matters of cleanliness, food-handling and clumsiness. He indicates how very early a strong and spontaneous moral realism fosters notions of "objective" responsibility. He also shows how this attitude, even when it diminishes progressively with regard to the child's own conduct, may very well develop elsewhere, "first in the evaluation of other people's actions, and finally in reflection concerning purely theoretical cases" (p. 185), and may persist in these other areas long after it has been abandoned in personal evaluation.

This moral realism, the effect of both the child's spontaneous realism and adult constraint, is the major obstacle to the child's smooth transition from an early egocentric individualism to a state of progressive cooperation which characterizes the mature person. The dynamics of this realism should interest all who wish to encourage child growth. The child is a spontaneous realist, i.e., he tends to consider as external, to "reify", the contents of his mind (e.g., dreams, names, isolated objects), including the moral laws imposed on him. Till about 7-8 years of age he always regards the notion of law as simultaneously moral and physical; physical regularity, moral obligation, and social rule are all the same—"a part of things, a characteristic feature, and even a necessary condition of the universe" (p. 188-9). Intentions do not matter; the problem of responsibility is simply to know whether a law has been respected or violated. Cooperation leads eventually to the primacy of intentionality, by forcing the individual to be occupied constantly with the point of view of others so as to compare it with his own. Adult constraint, combined with the child's spontaneous realism, produces moral realism. Adult demands are part of the child's experienced world order from the very beginning, and they act, most of the time, in such a way as to strengthen the child's egocentrism and inhibit spontaneous social development toward cooperation. Adult moral commands are usually external and incomprehensible to the young child. Adults, furthermore, are often poor psychologists who by their interdicts and impositions reinforce the notion of objective responsibility and consolidate childish moral realism, while establishing affective response mechanisms which become lifetime liabilities for too many persons.

Piaget finds in the child two moralities: adult constraint and childish realism produce a morality of the right and of duty, of heteronomy and moral realism characterized by unilateral respect; progressive experiences of sympathetic peer cooperation produce a morality of rights and of good, a reciprocal autonomy characterized by mutual respect. Between these two moralities which, "broadly speaking, follow on one another, without, however, constituting definite stages" (p. 195), there is an intermediate phase during which rules are interiorized and generalized, while still experienced as imposed from without.

The Development of the Idea of Justice (p. 197-325)

Piaget directs his investigation to the morality of cooperation by studying the evolution of the child's notion of justice. He studies, in turn, seven aspects of this evolution: (a) children's ideas about punishment; (b) the issue of collective responsibility; (c) the notion of "immanent"justice; (d) the conflict between retributive justice and distributive justice; (e) the relations between distributive justice and authority; (f) justice between children; and (g) the relations between justice and cooperation.

(a) Piaget summarizes what children think of punishment:

Some think that punishment is just and necessary; the sterner it is, the juster, and it is efficacious in the sense that the child who has been duly chastised will in the future do his duty better than others. Others do not regard expiation as a moral necessity; among possible punishments only those are just that entail putting things right, a restoration of the *status quo ante,* or which make the guilty one endure the consequences of his deed; or again, those which consist in a purely reciprocal treatment. Indeed, apart from such non-expiatory penalties, punishment, as such, is regarded as useless, reproach and explanation being deemed more profitable than chastisement. On the average, this second mode of reaction is found more frequently among the older children, while the first is oftener to be found among the little ones. But the first, favored as it is by certain types of family life and social relationships, survives at all ages and is even to be found in many adults. (p. 201)

(b) He asks next whether children consider it just to punish the whole group for the misdeed of an individual member? The question of collective and communicable responsibility interests educators because collective punishment has long been resorted to in schools. Children were asked to evaluate three types of situation, i.e., to state whether it is fair to punish the whole group and why. The situations are:

> 1′) The adult does not attempt to analyze individual guilt and punishes the whole group for the offense committed by one or two of its members. 2′) The adult wants to discover the transgressor, but the latter does not own up and the group refuses to denounce him. 3′) The adult wants to discover the transgressor but the latter does not own up and the group is ignorant of his identity.

In the first case, 1′), not the least trace of collective responsibility was found; children of all ages consider collective punishment to be unjust. The individual, not the group, should be punished for the individual's misdeed. Even young children, prejudiced strongly in favor of adult fairness, reject here the idea of collective responsibility.

The second case, 2′), introducing a group solidarity willed and accepted by each member, elicited two kinds of response from every age group: those advocating that the whole group should be punished and those advocating that it would be more just to punish no one. Advocates of punishment included those who believe, not in collective responsibility, but in a combination of the necessity of punishment and the individual guilt of each member who does not do his duty by informing (generally, the youngest children), and those who believe that the voluntary solidarity of the group constitutes a kind of collective responsibility (generally, the elder children). This last group, along with those who advocate no punishment, regard the punishment of the innocent as more unjust than the impunity of the guilty.

The third case, 3′), that of the unknown offender, elicited two conflicting types of response: the little children advocated group punishment, not because of collective responsibility, but because there must be punishment; the older children wanted no punishment because penalizing the innocent is more unjust than failing to punish the guilty. Piaget concludes that collective responsibility, in its usual sense, is missing from the moral makeup of the child.

(c) Investigating children's belief in "immanent" justice, Piaget discovered that the belief that natural events punish misdemeanors, though very strong in the very young, diminishes proportionately with increase in mental age. He argues that this belief in immanent justice is neither inborn, nor the result of direct parental teaching, but an indirect product of the child's naturally magical mind, fortified by a transference to things of feelings acquired under the influence of adult constraint. The belief diminishes or is abandoned not through mere maturation, but through moral experiences of a certain sort (including the discovery of the imperfection of adult justice which leads the child to question a universal and automatic justice), and the person's general movement away from a morality of constraint and towards that of cooperation.

(d) He next studies the positive effects of cooperation and the possible conflicts between distributive or equalitarian justice (fostered by cooperation) and retributive justice (focused on expiatory punishment).

Since the terms distributive and retributive justice are used often in this section, a word about their Piagetian meaning seems appropriate. Distributive justice is, for Piaget, a more developed form of justice; it is characterized by equality, rooted in mutual respect, fostered by cooperation; distributive justice would reform transgressors through reproach and explanation, calling attention to the fracturing of social solidarity and the need to restore it. Retributive justice, on the other hand, is more "primitive;" it is characterized by a close proportion between transgressions and punishment; it is rooted in unilateral respect, fostered by authoritarian constraint or heteronomy; retributive justice tends to transgressors through vindictive expiatory punishment.

To assess the child's sense of distributive and retributive justice he chose to use stories about children. In the stories, the obedient, well-behaviored child is favored at the expense of others by parents or teachers—an instance of inequality of treatment, fair from a retributive point of view, but unjust from a distributive one. Among the younger ones the retributive point of view prevails, whereas the distributive one prevails with the older children.

How can we explain the increasing acuteness of the growing child's desire for equality (with corresponding diminution of his desire for retribution for its own sake), especially when life at school adds more experiences of adult-inflicted retributive punishment to those furnished by the home? Neither parents nor teachers are directly responsible, Piaget insists. It is the contact of children with one another, their reactions to one another, their experiences of cooperation which promote the change, "sometimes even at the adult's expense." By the last phrase he wishes to indicate that adults often play an indirect role in this moral evolution. "It is very often the injustice one has had to endure that makes one take cognizance of the laws of equality" (p. 275). Noting that he discerned among advocates of equality "a delicate sense of moral distinctions," he adds that "this feeling of theirs seems very often to be the product of reflections made on the moral clumsiness of the adult" (p. 276).

(e) Studying children's evaluations of instances of conflict between adult authority and the sense of justice, Piaget found little children defending adult authority and identifying justice with the law, whereas older children defended equality out of respect for an inner ideal, even when the latter is in opposition to obedience. He found, too, that some older children subordinated strict justice to a higher form of reciprocity ("equity"), requiring that the solution of particular cases of conflict between obedience and justice include consideration of special relations of affection (e.g., between parent and child). In this perspective an unjust tedious task becomes legitimate as a free manifestation of friendliness. There are thus three broad stages in the development of distributive justice in relation to adult authority: the first, in which justice is indistinguishable from the authority of law, i.e., "just" is what the adult commands; the second, in which growing equalitarianism outweighs any other consideration; and the third, in which mere equalitarianism yields to a more subtle conception of justice, "equity," which involves never defining equality without taking into account each individual's situation. The development is accompanied by a diminution of blind obedience to authority and a correlative increase in equalitarian solidarity among the children themselves.

(f) Piaget seeks next to discover to what extent justice between children is retributive or distributive, by questioning them about punishment between children, and then about equalitarianism among them. Whether punishing one another in games or in other kinds of norm-violation, the children were neither vindictive nor expiatory; revenge or arbitrary punishment were condemned. Even those who thought a little boy should retaliate for ill treatment by a bigger boy were "far more concerned with justice and equality than with revenge properly so called" (p. 305). Some (especially younger) children would appeal to adult authority for justice and hence view between-children punishment as usurpation of adult authority.

Asked why one should not cheat at games, children furnished four types of answers: 1') because it is naughty or forbidden; 2') because it is contrary to the game's rules; 3') because it makes cooperation impossible; 4') because it is contrary to equality. As the children get older, appeals to cooperation and solidarity (3 & 4) gain preponderance over those which appeal to authority (1 & 2).

Questioning children about the distribution of service roles or foodstuffs among a group, Piaget discovered that the children were unanimous in demanding equality among peers. Presented situations involving age-differences, the younger children favored either equality or (chiefly) granting precedence to the bigger ones out of deference for their age, while the older children favored either equality or (chiefly) precedence to the little ones out of equity. Justice and solidarity develop correlatively and as a function of the mental age of the child.

(g) To examine the relationship between justice and cooperation, Piaget then asked children what they regard as unfair. From their responses, he discerns three periods in the development of their sense of justice: the first (till 7-8 years) in which justice is subordinate to adult authority; the second (from about 8 to 11 years), a period of progressive equalitarianism; and the third (from 11-12 years on) during which purely equalitarian justice is tempered by considerations of "equity". This evolution of distributive justice in the child is due, he suggests, to a number of factors: 1') the individual or biological roots (necessary but not sufficient conditions for this evolution—equalitarianism is neither instinctual nor spontaneous in its origin); 2') a long period, until 10-12 years of age, of progress in cooperation and mutual respect between children, and then between child and adult as the child approaching adolescence begins to consider himself as the adult's equal. As children get older, their social groupings manifest more organic unity (with laws and regulations, and even division of labor), a far stronger moral solidarity between members, less simple imitation and more shared discussion and interchange of ideas, and a far stronger sense of equality.

The idea of justice evolves in a similar fashion. Ideas of expiation and reward are rooted in the individual's reactions and in the experiences of adult constraint. Through later experiences of cooperation, the focus shifts from punishment-reward to the idea of reparation or of restoring the bonds of solidarity; progress in cooperation and mutual respect changes the focus from expiation to reciprocity.

Piaget concludes his book, as we shall conclude this exposition, by pointing to some of the educational consequences of his observations.

Implications for the Moral Educator

In the final few pages of *The Moral Judgment of the Child* (1932/1965), Piaget points out that his findings discredit both authoritarian and purely individualistic pedagogies. Against authoritarian method he argues that

> It is . . . absurd and even immoral to wish to impose upon the child a fully worked-out system of discipline when the social life of children themselves is sufficiently developed to give rise to a discipline infinitely nearer to that inner submission which is the mark of adult morality (p. 404).

Trying to transform the child's mind from outside is idle, he argues, "when his own taste for active research and his desire for cooperation suffice to ensure a normal intellectual development." He concludes, "The adult must therefore be a collaborator and not a master, from this double point of view, moral and rational" (p. 404). Against purely individualistic methods he urges that

> it would be unwise to rely upon biological "nature" alone to ensure the dual progress of conscience and intelligence, when we realize to what extent all moral as well as all logical norms are the result of cooperation. Let us therefore try to create in the school a place where individual experimentation and reflection carried out in common come to each other's aid and balance one another. (p. 404)

The educational methods which would best correspond with his psychological results, he explains, are "Group Work" and "Self-government".

In "Group Work" the children are allowed "to follow their pursuits in common, either in organized 'teams' or simply according to their spontaneous groupings." The strictly individual work of the traditional school reinforces the child's spontaneous egocentrism and is contrary to the most obvious requirement of intellectual and moral development. In group work, cooperation is recognized as an essential factor in intellectual and moral progress. "The initiative," moreover, "is left to the children in the actual conduct of their work." As for "Self-government," Piaget refers us to the published works of others which explain the principles (theory), describe the experiments (practice), and catalog the possible modes in which self-government may operate. His final word is a challenge to educators: since "pedagogy is very far from being a mere application of psychological knowledge," only experiment, not deduction, can prove the value of various methods, and such experiments are the task of educators themselves (p. 406).

Piaget has not spelled out all of the implications of the study. In the following pages we shall suggest some more of these implications, complementing what the early study has to say with Piaget's later reflections and with some remarks from commentators on his work.

Piaget defines the general goal of moral education: promoting a de-centering of the ego and building an independent or self-imposed discipline (1973, p. 112, p. 117). In promoting this development the educator must always remember that "growth in moral judgment is a developmental process. It is not a process of imprinting rules and virtues by modeling, lecturing, punishing, and rewarding, but a process of cognitive restructuring" (Duska & Whelan, p. 100). In this development, "the relationships between the child and the various other persons in his environment play a basic role" (Piaget, 1973, p. 114).

Piaget's emphasis on the role of others in the person's moral development contradicts innatist and maturationist development theories; it also suggests that peer influence is greater and earlier than many parents and teachers might suspect. When Piaget, for instance, points out the crucial role of communal life in the development of the sense of justice, he is speaking primarily of the communal life among the children, not of communal life shared by adults and child. "It is essentially cooperation and mutual respect among children that develop feelings of justice" (1967, p. 57).

Given a clear vision of the goal, the moral educator's challenge is to provide "a certain formative social milieu" and to determine "by which methods this social milieu will achieve the best formative results" (Piaget, 1973, p. 52-54). For example, Piaget sees the ideal school as "a center of real (and experimental) activities carried out in common, so that logical intelligence may be elaborated through action and social exchanges," where the learner has "the right to find . . . all that is necessary to the building of a questioning mind and a dynamic moral conscience" (1973, p. 47-48, p. 92). Creating such a milieu is "the pedagogical problem" (1973, p. 91). Piaget's findings give us many clues as to the appropriate ingredients of an optimal social milieu for moral growth.

It is obvious that there must be adequate scope for collaborative practice in developing, administering, evaluating, and reformulating the learners' own rules and norms. There must be minimal adult constraint and maximum opportunity for the learners to cooperate and develop mutual respect—a respect learned, not through verbal activities focused on 'respect', but as a natural by-product of collaborative projects.

The moral educator must respect the differences between children at different stages of moral development, if the educator is to make sense of children's questions, remarks, responses, evaluations, etc. School personnel must be aware that in any group of learners there is an inevitable pluralism of cognitive and moral stages, and that even persons at the same stage will be developed to differing levels within that stage. How this evaluation can be done, and indeed whether it can be done satisfactorily at this time, can be judged from other chapters in this book.

To Piaget the good teacher is one who speaks to the child in his own language and induces him "to rediscover as much as he can rather than simply making him listen and repeat" (1973, p. 19). He is a mentor who stimulates initiative and research, minds and consciences (1973, p. 16, p. 74). "He should be an elder collaborator, and, if he has it in him, a simple comrade to the children" (1932/1965, p. 364). It is, after all, not the educator but the learner who is the principal creator of his own personality. Traditional images comparing the teacher, for example, to the god-like creative sculptor molding mature personalities from formless clay, or to the omniscient physician diagnosing and prescribing, must be replaced by a new self-image in which the educator sees himself as comrade, collaborator, and milieu manager. The educator is not, however, a mere gardener, watering and fertilizing, as the innatists and maturationists would have us believe. The child's inter-personal relations are not accidental, but formative elements in his self-construction. Adult constraint or a limited environment can arrest or retard the learner's growth; dense and diversified interpersonal relations can enhance it. Nor is conditioning by educator or environment the all-powerful factor in human development, as the neobehaviorists and many social theorists would have us believe. It is the learner who, interacting with his world, creates himself.

The learner's own activity is thus the central focus of any genuine concern for learning. The learner must discover the truth for himself, by his own activity. Piaget emphasizes this when he warns of the dangers of programmed instruction (which "is indeed conducive to learning, but by no means to inventing, unless . . . the child is made to do the programming himself") and of audio-visual presentations which "may lead to a kind of verbalization of images if they only foster associations without giving rise to genuine activities" (1973, p. 7-8). This same point is reiterated when Piaget insists that learners and educators alike must do research. "Children," he says, "should be able to do their own experimenting and their own research" (1972, p. 27). Likewise, he warns educators that they can learn child psychology only

> . . . by collaborating in new research projects and taking part in experiments. . . . It is even truer in the case of psychology than in other fields that the only way to understand the facts involved and their interpretation is to undertake some research project of one's own. (1970, p. 125, p. 129)

The crucial role of cooperation, thought-exchange, and mutual respect between equals, which Piaget uncovered at every phase of his lifetime of psychological investigations, is clearly applicable regarding moral growth. Of course, moral education must provide adequate scope for the exercise and development of cooperation and interchange. Since Piaget believes that adults have only limited ability to deal with children as equals, and that children find it all but impossible to accept adults as equals, the kind of necessary collaborations and interchanges here suggested must take place between the children themselves. One of the ways in which the concerned educator may evaluate the extent to which a curriculum, method, or learning opportunity is fostering cognitive or moral development is by asking the simple question: how much scope is offered for these cooperative activities of the children themselves?

Piaget's research findings indicate clearly that purely expiatory, arbitrary, or collective punishments should be avoided completely, and that the children themselves should collaboratively determine and administer the rules and norms which govern them, and decide what reciprocal restorative recompense will be expected of the norm-violator.

Piaget's data reveal, too, the crucial importance of the child's progressive exposure to a diversified community of persons and values. It is the variety of perspectives, viewpoints, opinions, and evaluations which trigger the individual's activities of comparing, criticizing, and evaluating in an atmosphere of mutual respect—which activities produce a moral autonomy-in-reciprocity, a mature moral person.

What Piaget has to say above about the connection between his pedagogy of "self-government" and the requirements of citizenship in a contemporary democracy gives every educator plenty to think about, for instance, the learners' need for adequate opportunities:

1. To develop internal self-discipline and mutual interpersonal controls (in contrast to large group obedience to adult constraints);

2. To experience the need for and the reality of mutual respect through sharing in small-group projects;

3. To practice the responsibilities and exercise the rights of democratic citizenship through participation in genuine self-government at every stage of development.

Additional areas suggested by Piaget's work include educators' and students' need to examine the "hidden curriculum" of the schools' structures, procedures, expectations and norms, whether formally promulgated or vicariously experienced in the attitudes of school personnel. Piaget would have educators examine whether each school activity fosters rather than frustrates the development of the "habit of internal discipline, of mutual respect, and of 'self-government' " (1932/1965, p. 363).

Silberman (1970), reporting on a major study of American schools, exposes two basic pervasive faults: "mindlessness" and "mistrust." The educator who heeds Piaget will be more 'mindful', will know better both what to do and why it should be done. But he will not have the courage and perseverance to do it unless he has also learned from Piaget to "trust," to trust the inherent thrust of the growing person. Educational theory and practice have been handicapped by the warping influence of a pessimism about human nature and its potential for development. Piaget tells us he has discovered, and invites us to discover for ourselves by pedagogical experiment, an inner dynamism in the human person to know and to do what helps it grow.

The Value/Moral Education Movement and Alfred Adler

Leo Gold

"Individual Psychology educates for a real community for which one must work and strive. Among the present day community efforts it will give recognition only to those which lie in the direction of an ideal community, which, although never attainable, will still be effective as a goal" (Adler et al., 1964, p. 305).

"Thus we would accept as worthwhile only the kind of 'education community' which offers preparation for being the fellow man of the future" (Adler et al., 1964, p. 306).

Some Key Concepts of Alfred Adler

The Adlerian approach to education is a system that concerns itself primarily with the relationship of the individual to society. It gears itself to a view of social responsibility and clearly bases itself on a set of moral values. Its concern transcends the acquisition of skills and knowledge and in addition stresses a concept of social interest. The student is to be trained to effectively contribute to the welfare and betterment of society. The teacher is to be trained to recognize and correct the mistakes of each child that could lead to later social maladaptation. The teacher is also expected to create a realistic democratic atmosphere in the classroom that encourages the development of social interest (Ansbacher, 1956, p. 399).

Core Concept

A core concept in Adler's thinking is the training of the child toward the useful side of life. Here there are definite ideas of social responsibility including ideas about what are fundamentally decent in human relationships and why these are important for human survival. Inherent within this education system is an interpersonal caring which leads to one experiencing oneself not egotistically but rather as a fellow human being who devotes his creative activities to the social matrix. He sees education as a significant means of training the individual to carry out the life tasks of work, community participation, love and family.

The foundations for becoming an effective, creative, socially responsible individual do not occur by themselves but are learned in the home and at school. Adler establishes positivistic means of achieving this through encouragement and creating experiences of success for the child. An atmosphere which is inhibiting, restrictive or punitive produces discouragement which interferes with both learning and the development of social interest. Within this context mistakes are not seen as "bad" but rather as a means of developing judgment that leads to better understanding. This in turn leads to growth rather than the production of feelings of inferiority that inhibit social development.

No Education without Moral Judgment

Unlike other psychological schools of his period, Adler put great stress on values and education. His thinking very much reflected the enlightened trends of his time. There is a social idealism and utopian view of what society could become that reflects itself in his social understanding of humankind. In keeping with this construct, let us begin with a basic hypothesis that there can be no education that lacks a concept of moral judgment. Let us interpret the word "moral" as that which is in keeping with what Adler defined as "social interest" and let us interpret the word immoral as that which is not beneficial to humankind.

Democratic Education

In defining social interest Adler perceived human behavior, whether individually or in groups, as moving always in the direction of upward development and toward the welfare of humankind. Social interest is that force within the individual which when applied encourages him and leads him to contribute constructively to social welfare. Meaningful education not only trains the individual in skills but stresses the importance of utilizing these skills as a means of participating in the betterment of society as well as the effective functioning of that society on a day to day basis. The individual, as he matures, contributes to the maturation of his society. In this sense both individuals and societies should evolve from positions of inferiority to positions of increasing enlightenment. Adler believed that this is best achieved in education through positive, democratic concepts which stress a sense of equality rather than through punitive, authoritarian systems which stress competitiveness and inequality. In contrast to other schools of thinking he did not see moral development as achieved through repression and sublimation but rather through cooperation and sharing.

A Basic Clash

The modern world appears to be in a period of transition with tremendous confusion between authoritarianism and democracy. Some cultures stress concepts of cooperation and freedom and others demand obedience and belief without question. One world has the concept of self-actualization and the respect for differences while the other demands the individual submit himself to the authoritarian expectations of society at the cost of his individuality.

The same problems exist in our educational system where there is also a process of transition which produces much confusion for both educators and students. It is safe to assume that the confusions of any given society will reflect themselves in the educational process. This confusion is not new but has plagued society as humankind became restive under traditional regimes and sought change.

The Authoritarian Approach

The democratic process which the Adlerian position espouses stresses the relationship of equals. The authoritarian process stresses the superiority of one group or individual at the cost of another. A system of education based on the autocratic method defeats a large number of people in the end because it reinforces feelings of inferiority and creates a sense of discouragement. It creates an elite who justify their position on the basis of the inferiority of others. The rationale that supported the slave system and its belief in the basic inferiority of the black that existed in the 17th through the 19th century in the United States clearly reflected this mode of thinking.

Positive Motivation

Autocratic processes, particularly in education, are discouraging to the greater bulk of students and prevent meaningful learning or moral maturation. Within our educational system we talk of democracy and tend to practice autocracy. This is seen in the teacher who spends more time in disciplining than in teaching and in the principal who is seen as the ultimate punisher rather than as a creative planner. Moral education and development cannot occur well in such a system since it gives only lip service to democracy but does not practice it. The student reacts to the actions of the faculty and responds to the hypocrisy inherent in the system. The system turns out cynics or relatively uneducated individuals rather than people trained to function in a democratic society.

Rudolf Dreikurs points out, "Our educational orientation lags far behind political concepts of democracy which has been, at least theoretically, well established for some time" (Dreikurs, 1971, p. 5). He points out the futility of systems of reward and punishment and stresses the need for inner motivation and a sheer sense of understanding what is right or effective on the part of the faculty and the students. The need is clearly for new educational approaches which depart significantly from current models. The need is for those which encourage rather than pressure students to learn. One learns because one is motivated to learn. The process of education contributes significantly to the moral development of the individual. The motivated student works from a sense of responsibility which is basic to the democratic society. Individual differences do not become barriers in such a situation but rather permit all to work together with diversity which enables a rich educational process to develop. In the democratic method each student and teacher has a sense of significance and relevance to the school.

To achieve optimum ends in education, Adler stressed the need to move away from those concepts of moral values which emphasized authoritarianism, competition, and punishment. He did not see moral development as a repression, but as achieved through cooperation and sharing.

In keeping with Adler's teaching, in the 1930's Oscar Spiel developed a working system of education within a school that did away with the concept of punishment. In agreement with Ferdinand Birnbaum, he felt that a child who makes difficulties, suffers from difficulties (Spiel, 1962, p. 27). Inherent in this concept is the idea that the individual is responsible for his own behavior and can choose to learn or not learn in terms of how he perceives his life situation.

It becomes important to discard the concept of punishment and authoritarian control and find more creative ways of educating the child. The experience of punishment inhibits the learning process because the resultant psychic pain and anger causes the individual to lose focus on the educative process. It is difficult to concentrate on learning when one is distracted by feelings of anger and rebellion. The child, like the adult, is readily distracted by negative emotion and becomes unmotivated to learn since the greater the anger and rebellion the more withdrawn the child becomes from the process.

The Teacher's Attitude

To educate the child, one must first educate the teacher to the value and purpose of education. The teacher has to acquire those skills of relationship to his students which make unnecessary the need for punishment. He has to learn how to motivate and encourage children so that they are prepared to work cooperatively with him in the mastery of curriculum and its application to everyday life. Where the child experiences difficulty in the school situation, it is more important for him to recognize incorrect attitudes toward education which he can be encouraged to modify rather than rely on traditional modes which stress his failures and are directly or indirectly punitive. Methods which discourage class participation and belonging are rejected. From the Adlerian viewpoint, let us consider those attitudes which interfere with learning on the part of the teacher and the student as error. Errors are permissible and can generally be corrected in a reasonable fashion. Within education, the greatest degree of learning is accomplished when one is willing to take the risks that may result in error so that understanding can develop and one has the courage to pursue richer insights into the nature of the world. Let us further assume that these insights lead ultimately to the development of skills and attitudes that contribute to the welfare of the individual and to humankind.

Increasing Independence

An additional goal of Adlerian education is to encourage increasing independence on the part of the student. Independence is best understood, not as separating the individual from others, but rather that he becomes increasingly self-motivated in his pursuit of growth within the social system. An effective educational system is one which stimulates the individual to further educate himself formally and informally so that he can contribute toward social interest efficaciously.

Equality, Sharing

Inherent in the Adlerian classroom is the concept of democracy and equality. Students and faculty cooperate in establishing the goals of education and share in the means of achieving these ends. Within this system the teacher does not give up his role as an expert, but shares his expertise with his students in order to develop a sense of cooperation and collaboration which brings them together and does away with feelings of distance and alienation. The best learning occurs in an atmosphere of mutual respect. One is more likely to have a greater sense of motivation when one feels a distinct identification with the activity because one is a sharer in its creation and operation. The greater the sense of alienation experienced by the student from the educative process the more he withdraws from it, the more he inhibits his learning and moves toward increasing experiences of failure. Conversely, when the student develops a sense of belonging and participation in an atmosphere of encouragement, he develops a sense of accomplishment and more readily seeks to carry out the tasks of life in society. A discouraged child moves toward mischief or negative modes of behavior characterized by failure. An encouraged child moves toward increasingly effective social adaptation through the mastery of skills. Encouragement is based on a belief in the ability for growth that is inherent in each individual. In a productive classroom atmosphere each individual seeks to activate the others toward achieving common educative goals. Togetherness and sharing are stressed in contrast to the competitive model which, because of its stress on superiority at the cost of others being less, produces in many the feelings of mediocrity and inferiority. It creates a situation wherein a handful at the top look down on the others, forming an elite who oftentimes vie with each other as well. Success at the cost of others is antithetical to learning and certainly does not create a world of mutual respect. Where we educate to a sense of equality, there is a respect for difference and each individual contributes in keeping with his ability. This concept of mutual respect enhances not only the learning of academics, but at the same time educates the student toward achieving effective human relationships so that the entire process becomes preparation for life. Education must be holistic in that it is consonant with life rather than so specialized that it loses sight of this integration and educates for failure.

Moral Level and Contributing to the Community

In keeping with the above ideas, Spiel says: "The class as a working community is a training ground for the individual child enabling him on the one hand to perform tasks demanded of him, and on the other, to solve the problems of his relations with his fellows" (Spiel, 1947, p. 55). This is a functional view and based on our understanding of the interpersonal, interdependent nature of human existence. Spiel further states: ". . . the moral level of the individual can be judged and confirmed only by his achievements on behalf of the community" (Spiel, 1947, p. 55). This is most important because it sees morality as a functional concept and not as an abstract ideal.

The purpose of education is not merely to enable the individual to acquire personal skills and amass knowledge, but also to train toward finding a rational role in society. Education, if effective, directs the individual to those modes of functioning which enable him to contribute toward the overall operation of society. An Adlerian would take the position that it is the responsibility of each individual to contribute to the social welfare and development of society. He would recognize the educational system's responsibility, like the family's, to train the child to a concept of social usefulness. Education is seen as a major means of preparing the individual for the social tasks of life which will confront him as he develops and matures. Adler states: ". . . there is . . . a tendency among many children and adults to unite themselves with other human beings, to accomplish their tasks in cooperation with others and to make themselves useful from a social point of view" (Adler, 1949, p. 115).

Values: Teaching and Practice

The values important in sustaining an effectively developing society must clearly influence the educational process and become part of what meaningfully shapes the life of the child in a constructive direction. Where this is lacking or fails, the school fails in its task and both the child and society may suffer. Within the Adlerian construct the child is trained to cooperative sharing, since values derived from sharing offer the greatest possibility for society to survive and for mankind to achieve ongoing goals toward the future. Certainly it is true that what the world can become is largely dependent on the values which we transmit to children. An educative system that teaches positive social values through both theory and methodology of teaching is a potent force for civilizing humankind. A school system that stresses common sense through practice develops not only scholarship but also the pragmatic application of that scholarship to further the survival of the species rather than its destruction.

Goal Orientation

Learning, to be meaningful, must be goal oriented. From a moral point of view, learning is purposive since it should enrich the individual in his capacity to contribute to the community. This quality is not inherent in the individual, but rather derives from "common sense." All learning is preparation for the future, and it is the pursuit of the fictive ideas that one has about what that future should be which motivates an individual to learn. Man's relationship to nature creates a moral imperative since it commits him to evolving concepts of survival if he is rational, and dooms him to destruction if he is not. We might postulate that to survive and assure the survival of others is moral, and to be destroyed or to destroy others is immoral. The developing child must be trained to the art of survival since at birth he lacks this ability. The parent and teacher, through the application of their skills, create the moral atmosphere necessary to achieve this state.

When the parent or teacher educates toward destructive modes of behavior, these modes become immoral in that they interfere with the social development of the child. Immoral, here, could be defined not necessarily as bad but as misguided, since the educator/parent has clearly not thought through the consequences of his teaching on the child's functioning in the future. Dreikurs has indicated that in negative atmospheres very often the child and the parent/teacher do not perceive each other as fellow human beings, and by their inability to achieve rapport, create atmospheres which are contrary to social interest (Dreikurs, 1971, chap. 1). Understanding and positive feelings are core factors in achieving moral development. The education process can in no way ignore the psychological needs and development of the child and still positively train him to be a morally effective participant in the process of everyday living.

Group Discussion

Within the school situation, if one believes in democracy and equality, a range of pragmatic methods are available which ensure the achievement of positive development. Group discussion, which encourages honesty and communication, is a major device for dealing with a range of problems that occur in the school situation. There is no reason why teachers and students cannot set up a relationship of open and frank communication which could create understanding and bring them closer together.

The teacher and the student are cooperators in the same process, and at different levels are seeking personal growth. Through discussion they should reach agreement on a concept of values and modes of relationship that they can all share and pursue. Values are important since they clarify the purpose of education. Student and teacher also share in confronting faulty values in relationship to society and move together toward modifying these values. This is incumbent on both as either can have faulty values. Both should agree that there are few beliefs which are so exact that they cannot be modified or changed as life itself changes. Agreement is more useful than the moralizing of a superior to an inferior. Things are not arbitrarily right or wrong but are understood on the basis of sound discussion and judgment.

Punitive methods must be replaced by approaches that clarify the nature of the individual's behavior so that he can return to creative participation in the learning process. Learning cannot occur efficiently without participation since it is an active and not a passive process. Unresolved problems interfere with learning and their resolution becomes a major factor if learning is to occur. The child, through receiving understanding in the learning process, develops a sense of belonging, and wishes actively to participate and contribute to the social good. Within the construct of social interest, his participation increases his sense of personal worth which is a necessary aspect of moral development.

Change in the Community

If the school, like the family, is to be a major force for moral development, its approach cannot be only an intellectual one. Rather, it must of itself become a model atmosphere where the concepts of morality can be lived and experienced meaningfully. The experiencing of it as well as the talking about it become the means not only of acquiring pragmatic moral values that can be lived, but can also be generalized onto the life pattern of the individual in society. Education, to serve as a moral force, must be relevant to life. To be relevant, the relationship of faculty to student must reflect life in the community and both must have the courage to innovate what might result in meaningful change in the community where behavior is not consonant with social interest.

To be potent in this sphere, the school has to determine what is social interest in the pragmatic sense. Not that we should do good and contribute to the social welfare of society, but rather what practical programs can be developed that will serve this purpose. In essence, we need a workable ideal of what should be and then a practical program of practice within the educational process that makes this possible. I do not doubt that this will result in a revolutionary concept of education since it will require radical departure from traditional educational models which historically focused more on the learning of facts than the education of the individual for social living. Simply acquiring facts and grades is one thing. But what a difference there is in actualizing the concept of responsibility toward society where the facts have to be utilized.

Basic Skills and Social Context

From the very beginning of the school process, the basic skills have to be learned within a social context. They have to be relevant to the needs of the individual and of society. We might state that the individual has to learn early that the acquisition of skills is a pragmatic responsibility which will enable him to participate in and contribute toward social interest more effectively. Thus, he can early acquire the understanding that responsibility does not limit him but, in fact, leads him to greater personal and social freedom. In this sense we see inherent in social interest an effective means for the individual to develop a sense of freedom, a capacity to move through life rather than to be inhibited by it.

Creative Living

Freedom as a concept should lie at the core of democratic moral development. The educational system, in its training of the child, has to move toward a definition of what creative living is about. The purpose of having moral values is to enable individuals and societies to live in harmony. It points to the direction of "becoming." One achieves "becoming" through encouragement. Education, in order to contribute effectively to moral development, has to eliminate discouragement which is a negative value that inhibits the freedom to act meaningfully. The courage to "be" and to "become" establishes the goal of moral development. "Being" and "becoming" must always be understood as a process relevant to both individuals and societies, both aspects forming a unitary whole. Moral development is the means by which we establish the rules of movement that enable this process to occur. Education is part of this process, the same as the family unit, and has the responsibility to see that this process is carried forward toward achieving the greatest benefit for humankind both microcosmically and macrocosmically through the concept of social interest.

Adlerian Theory in Practice

The following is a list of Adlerian attitudes that deal with education and particularly point to moral development. These are ideas that are taught in family education centers and teachers groups both here and abroad. They repeat in part what has been previously stated and in addition illustrate the very practical, optimistic approach which characterizes this psychology of humankind, particularly as applied to the educational process.

- The school is the place that prepares the student for life in society.
- The goal of education is to sharpen the skill of the individual through the development of intellectual, practical and social skills which enable him to contribute to the social process.
- All education should effectively train for social interest and social participation.
- Through the application of a democratic process the individual is trained to a concept of equality and concern for fellow human beings.
- Cooperation is to be preferred to competition.
- To learn this well, all students must be active participants with the teacher in developing the means of achieving these goals.
- Negative behavior is best dealt with through understanding and encouragement toward positive behavior rather than through punishment.
- All students participate jointly through class discussion in dealing with negative behavior.

- Encouragement is the primary way through which students change, adapt and grow rather than through autocratic or punitive methods.
- Negative behavior of a child is considered a mistaken attitude on his part. It is part of the learning process to encourage him to perceive alternatives which are more correct or effective in dealing with his life situation.
- A child's good work is to be respected and valued rather than to be paid off by material rewards.
- The goal of education is in part the achievement of self-realization on the part of the student that leads him to more correct judgments about himself and society.
- Through the educational process the individual matures into a useful citizen who takes his place as a fellow contributor in the community.
- The educator is most effective when he deemphasizes negative behavior and recognizes and focuses on positive behavior.
- Education should not occur in isolation from the community but, wherever meaningful, should involve the community in such a fashion that it encourages each student to utilize his life style and developing abilities for social good.
- Education should also serve a psychological purpose in that it trains the child to move toward life effectively with courage rather than into negative bypaths which are counter-productive and self-defeating.
- The student learns to believe in his own ability through his experience with peers and faculty. Others' belief in him encourages his own belief in self and the achievement of self-realization.
- Self-realization corresponds to moral development and is best understood by how effectively the individual contributes to the community as a fellow human being.
- School should be a training ground for communal living. Here the student continues his moral development through his interaction with fellow students in dealing with the various aspects of everyday living.
- Self-government in school prepares for responsible behavior in society. The school is to be used as a microsociety with students filling the various roles and offices required by that society.
- A weekly class council should be held to create a forum where problems can be explored, projects discussed and personal feelings aired to foster self-understanding and understanding of others. The purpose of the council is to encourage the students to understand and help each other.

- In a creative program the teacher must be as much a psychologist as a teacher. He works to create a positive democratic environment and understanding that enables the problem child to make a transition toward socially useful behavior.
- Within the Adlerian overview an individual is trained to social adjustment and this is a basic part of the educational process. Moral development is thus a learning process and serves to unite the various facets of education toward service to the community.

Further Application of Adlerian Tradition

In keeping with Adler's concept of social interest both he and his followers, through the years, have actively developed community based programs. Theory can only have meaning when it is applied to everyday living. This has been done by Adlerian practitioners both in North America and in Europe. Following World War I, Adler organized some 30 guidance clinics in Vienna. There he applied his theories directly in public demonstrations before audiences. In this way he trained parents, involved communities and displayed the efficacy of the ideas discussed previously. The audience actively participated, drawing from their own experiences in order to encourage and help the child or parent in the demonstration.

Family Education Centers

This methodology laid the foundation for the family education associations which were pioneered by Rudolph Dreikurs in the United States and Canada. The family education method dealt with the family and then the school. The Adlerian literature was studied and parents and teachers sought to apply the concepts to everyday life in encouraging children and students to participate creatively and evolve an effective set of values in their relationship to others.

As it exists today, the family education center begins very simply. Usually a group of lay people, parents or teachers decide to have a study group. They utilize either of Dreikurs' texts, *Children: the Challenge* or *Maintaining Sanity in the Classroom*. The study group will have ten 2 hour sessions when each chapter of the book is discussed and compared to the practical application of the ideas to child rearing. The study group becomes a nucleus for other study groups in the community and generally leads to the establishment of a local Adlerian Society.

The society tends to function at a broader level, sponsoring larger numbers of study groups, advanced study groups, etc. With continued growth a Family Education Center is developed wherein families and teachers can be counseled in practical ways of dealing with family life. The society at this point also develops trained staff drawn from the Alfred Adler Institutes in New York or Chicago or from universities where Adlerian methods are taught in the guidance programs. A broad range of study materials in terms of texts and manuals is available, and consultation services are offered to the community to educate in regard to democratic methods in the school and in the home. Many thousands of North Americans, Hawaiians and Europeans are currently involved in applying these principles to everyday life. A number of schools in the United States and Canada are now actively involved in applying Adler's system of thought to the school. The beauty of the system is that it involves both lay and professional people democratically working together to make the programs effective.

What is unique in the system is that Adler's method of public counseling has been continued in the family education center and everyone participates. When a child has a problem, the teacher as well as the family takes part so that from a holistic point of view all of the significant figures in the child's life are brought together. The method of operating such centers is clearly defined and when put into operation appears to be generally productive. Their basic philosophy is to educate and train both parents and teachers in effective child development. The philosophy is geared to the development of social interest which includes a creative concept of values that will lead to a more humane world. Adler's contribution is that he does not assume innate goodness but stresses that individuals and societies must be trained to creative social living. The process at any level deals with direct and practical application of corrective measures to erroneous behavior which lead to change. The centers try to teach better ways of resolving and correcting errors in social living rather than resorting to punishment.

Training Institutes

At a more sophisticated level there are the training institutes where students are professionally trained at the graduate and post-doctoral level in Adlerian therapy and guidance. The Alfred Adler Institute of Chicago in particular has trained many leaders in community work. With the Adler-Dreikurs Institute of Bowie they have developed active degree granting programs in counseling and a range of sub-specialties in child guidance, family therapy and community education. The Alfred Adler Institute of New York and the University of West Virginia have for many years also had special programs in guidance and teacher training programs. The proliferation of centers training a broad range of people in Adlerian concepts has been most impressive in our hemisphere.

Application in Schools

Vienna: Oskar Spiel

When the theory has been applied to school systems the results are notable. Oskar Spiel in Vienna, in 1931, established the Individual Psychology experimental school in an impoverished working class community of the city. The philosophy of education expected each child to participate actively in the educative process. They were expected to find out things for themselves, take part in school affairs, be responsible for the atmosphere of the school, etc. Teachers were seen as having a therapeutic as well as scholastic role. Dialogue is important in this system of learning and the discussion method dominates. The method of discipline in the school was not based on punishment but rather on insight. Spiel states: "We shall seek rather, with the insight which we have won by our observation and our interpretation of the erroneous aims of the child to bring him to greater self-realization, to reveal his fundamental errors and to show him how his wrong attitude has developed." He further states: "The final aim of all this will be to make the child independent. The acid test of any educational system is the extent to which it brings the child to educate himself" (Spiel, 1947, p. 30).

The concept of the class council which was now fully developed by Dreikurs in the United States, was begun in this school. Students and teachers met, discussed problems of work and discipline and democratically, through consensus, worked out practical solutions utilizing the concepts of sharing and mutual respect rather than the more traditional authoritarian approach. Though his school was designed for normal students, Spiel reported that 60 out of 63 severe problem children who were sent to the school returned to normal functioning. It is hard to feel oppressed in a setting where one shares a responsible role.

Elk Grove, California

The Adlerian ideas used by Spiel in the 1930's continue to be applied today. The Elk Grove School System in California has applied the same type of approach and John Platt, a counseling psychologist in that system, has reported the same type of results. The important stress on democratic values, social responsibility, sharing and cooperation are inherent parts of the moral development of the child in the school. The stress is on practice. It is a workable philosophy and is happening today not only in California but in schools and classrooms throughout the country.

From the very beginning of school at Elk Grove the class is organized around democratic concepts in a clearly structured fashion. Students meet, set rules, plan meetings, work at problem solving and actively participate in every aspect of classroom life. Methodologies are worked out in keeping with Adlerian thought that lead to clarification and meaningful structure. The students are trained in techniques of problem solving. This permits a spirit of cooperativeness and helpfulness which are significant concepts in moral development.

At Elk Grove responsibility is clearly defined cooperatively by parents, teachers, counselors, students, etc. The following is a partial list of concepts taken from one of their memoranda:

- Children have rights as well as responsibilities.
- Children should be consulted about jobs that need to be done.
- Allow children a choice in which jobs they would like to do.
- Allow the consequences to follow naturally from uncompleted jobs.
- Place appropriate time limits on when a task should be completed.
- Vary the tasks to be done.
- Use common sense in the number of tasks expected of each child.
- Do not expect of a child what you are not prepared to "model" in yourself.
- Examine own standards. Learn to accept the classroom as a place of work or communication for the members, and not as a reflection of your own personal worth.
- Never do anything for a child that he can do for himself.

It is interesting to note in the above the very pragmatic and practical approach that is used. This is consistently carried out through every aspect of the school experience from grade to grade. Responsibilities are clearly defined and the methods discussed and worked out in the daily experience of the classroom. The value system is clear and the goal of effective social participation is recognizable in the above ten rules. Democratic development is not haphazard but requires rules that are flexibly developed and applied. Very basic to the entire system is the concept of encouragement. To be productive there has to be an optimistic belief in each individual and that no matter what the basic lifestyle of the individual it can be directed to the betterment of the individual and society. Even encouragement itself is not an abstract ideal but requires very specific techniques to be effectively carried out.

Adler's Holistic Approach

While we can only touch briefly on the structure of the Elk Grove program spearheaded by Dr. Platt, this type of program is being increasingly explored in other schools. At its core it deals with pragmatic methods of achieving effective moral development. Most important in the Adlerian approach is not that these qualities exist abstractly but rather are learned and must be created within a logical and meaningful situation. Its goals are clear-cut and full moral development is equated with a concept of social interest. Ultimate maturity is determined by how well an individual integrates and contributes to society and functions as a fellow human being, with a realistic ability to be concerned for others. He or she must be both a giver and a taker. The gist of the Adlerian approach is holistic in that its aim is the integration of the individual to society in a way that ensures the increasing growth and survival of humankind.

An Interview
with Lawrence Kohlberg

1. Biographical

Father Hennessy: When I first heard a sketch of your personal background, I was particularly struck by what happened to you in your internment. It became an opportunity for you to ponder deeply on ethics, morality, what makes people moral or immoral in their lives. I was reminded of the forced confinement of Ignatius of Loyola. His battle wounds on his leg after the siege of Pamplona kept him abed for months. His readings and meditations brought it about that his life changed from being "one of the boys" to one with high personal goals, including his own education, and high hopes for changing the world of his time. How do you react to this comparison?

Dr. Kohlberg: I agree that some moral educators come out of peculiar backgrounds. Without claiming to be in Ignatius' league (he was, of course, one of the world's great moral educators), I guess I do share a certain similarity with him—that of starting out as a mischievous boy. Recently I gave a lecture to teachers at my old boarding school, Andover. Some of my old teachers were still there and they must have been shocked at my speaking about moral education since I was on probation all the time I was there. I think that I was trying to emulate the school behavior of the institution's most distinguished alumnus, Humphrey Bogart, who was "kicked out." And I think that as a high school student if I had thought that I would end up in the area of moral education I would have been absolutely incredulous. So the world does funny things to you.

H: What happened after you completed high school?

K: I went to the Merchant Marine, after a period of reflection about my life. This was just at the end of World War II. As a rather unreflective Jew, I reacted to what had happened in Europe in the war and in the Holocaust by working on ships that were bringing Jewish refugees through the British blockade under the auspices of the Haganah. We did that for two or three years and were captured and put into internment in Cyprus.

H: What happened in Cyprus?

K: I consider that period as one of enforced reflection. I became aware of the limits of my own moral thinking. I realized that a mixture of late adolescent idealism and late adolescent egoism and egocentrism had led me to do what I was doing. I had acted on the idea that ends justify the means. I reflected also on the morality of the Haganah leaders who for years were engaged in actions that were getting people killed for what we considered a justified cause. But I had never really faced up to the morality and the dilemma in the controversy about the ends and the means. The upshot of my reflection was that I decided to go back to school. I had been glad to get out of school and did not think I would want to return. But now I had made up my mind that in college I would concern myself specifically with moral and political philosophy.

H: You went to the University of Chicago. Did the special curriculum there influence you in your later work?

K: I think it gave a philosophical emphasis to my thinking and writing—philosophical in the technical sense of being influenced by the writings of Plato, Aristotle, Dewey and others. Actually, my desire to steep myself in moral and political philosophy was easy to pursue during Hutchins' time. In that period at the University of Chicago Aristotle was read and regarded as right, Dewey was read and regarded as wrong. Elsewhere everyone knew that Plato was right and Dewey was wrong. Somehow I struggled to combine. I knew that Plato and Dewey were right and that everybody else was wrong. And essentially what we have been trying to do in moral education is warmed over Plato and warmed over Dewey.

H: Does an example come to mind of your work vindicating a theory or approach of one of the great philosophers?

K: Yes. Dick Fenton and I worked with a group of teachers and kids in Pittsburgh. We wanted to test ways of leading people to a higher level of moral awareness and a foundation gave us $200,000 for the project. We instructed twenty social studies teachers in the theory of the Socratic question. In the classes where the teachers used the Socratic method we found that most of the kids moved up in their moral awareness and that where the teachers did not use this approach the kids had not moved at all during the year in this area. So for the large grant our results indicated that Socrates was right in his method and was right at a statistically significant level.

H: One aspect of your writing that appeals to me is the fact that you integrate philosophy and psychology, particularly Piaget. Can you trace Piaget's first influence on you?

K: Piaget was not mentioned in psychology in the early '50s. My first exposure to him came in a philosophy course. And having a good Chicago humanistic education I could see what Piaget was talking about. It was what Dewey was talking about and I became very enthusiastic about him.

H: Was your main training in philosophy or in psychology?

K: In psychology. But let me tell you a personal anecdote that influenced my career. I was completing a doctoral program in clinical psychology and working as a psychology intern in a Veterans' Administration hospital. I was primarily in a unit with psychotics. Remember this was back before we had tranquilizers. A patient was in my office for therapy. She started talking very loud, making inflammatory complaints about the chief ward psychiatrist, and did this just as the ward psychiatrist happened to be in hearing distance. He told her to get out of the office and he put her on shock treatment. I protested at that kind of treatment and it led to my ultimately resigning from the Veterans Administration program. One result of this experience is that I became really convinced that you could not help adults or children in the context of injustice. Another result was that I started to work again on my thesis which had been lying dormant until that time. And I have been working in the line of my dissertation ever since.

2. Philosophical Influences

H: You mentioned that you really liked Plato. How did he influence your moral education work?

K: The notion of morality levels that I use goes back to Plato. The other fundamental notions that we work with also go back to Plato. For instance, we talk about the importance for moral education and moral development of living in a just community. Related to that idea is that of the just school community and ultimately the just whole society. This is the theme of Plato's *Republic*. Of course, Plato's idea of justice was different from ours in the sense that his was hierarchical and ours is democratic.

H: Did Dewey have a strong impact on you?

K: Very much so. For instance, in the area of the democracy and the just society. He reformulated Plato's *Republic* in terms of the notion that the just society and the just school was a democratic one.

In fact, our approach is very much that of John Dewey. Let me quote him:

> The aim of education is growth or *development*, both intellectual and moral. Ethical and psychological principles can aid the school in the *greatest of all constructions—the building of a free and powerful character*. Only knowledge of the *order and connection of the stages in psychological development can insure this*. Education is the work of *supplying the conditions* which will enable the psychological functions to mature in the freest and fullest manner.

He's making two statements. The first statement is that the aim of education is development, a concept that sounds like a cliche, but is so radical that it completely transforms what we are doing in the schools. It says that education is not teaching information skills and attitudes (he's not saying that we shouldn't teach them) but that its ultimate purpose is development, both moral and intellectual. His second statement is that what schools are doing isn't a set of specific things that are very different from what goes on outside the school. Obviously, for instance, in terms of moral development the family, the church and the peer group are all involved in activities that stimulate or perhaps retard moral growth.

3. Research and Its Application

H: You have mentioned your indebtedness to Piaget, Dewey and Plato. What have you added to their contributions? What's the novelty of your approach?

K: It's not in the area of teaching or instruction in the usual sense. Instead we investigate the conditions in the family, in the school and elsewhere that stimulate moral development. Then we try to see that the schools create similar conditions. One of these conditions that I already mentioned is the usage of the Socratic dialogue as most favorable for moral development. Another is the importance of democracy, the chance to control the decisions made in your regard and to elaborate the decisions in terms of fairness and justice. These practices are emphasized as more effective than instruction in the usual sense, although instruction is also involved.

H: You mentioned the importance of your doctoral dissertation research and its influence on your life. Would you offer a summary of it?

K: Using the Heinz dilemma (editor's note—cf. Introduction), we worked with a group of 75 boys, fifteen years of age and in "working class" families when first studied. They were interviewed for responses to the Heinz dilemma, and the Stages of Moral Development were based on analyses of their replies. Actually, we have been able to follow up the young men on the basis of a twenty year longitudinal study. The group is now down to 60. We have found that as adults some of them are at Stage Two, some are at Stage Five, and in our particular sample we have found none who have reached Stage Six up to this date. Remember they are now in their thirties and so it is possible that in our interviews every three years we may find that some of them later on in their lives may reach Stage Six. We don't know if this will happen. Whether as adults they are at Stage Two or at Stage Five they went through the same order of stages. The Stage Fives went through Stage One, Two, Three, Four before they got to Five. The Stage Two never went through Stage Three or Four or Five. They went through Stage One and Two and then stopped. The rate and terminal point of moral development is very variable but the order of sequence is the same.

We have also conducted cross-cultural studies to match the Chicago one in Taiwan, Turkey, India, Israel, Mexico, and so on. And we have done longitudinal work in one other case, Turkey.

From all this research we think that we have vindicated the idea of the concept of moral development in stages. Of course, the concept of stage means a sequence of steps such that if change in moral thinking occurs it is always forward, never backward, and the forward movement is always to the next stage above it (stages aren't skipped).

H: The longitudinal aspects of your study are important. Would you illustrate the changes that took place in the thinking over the years of one of your subjects?

K: In 1955, I got this response from Tommy, age 10: "Heinz should not steal. He should buy the drug. If he steals the drug he might go to jail and would have to put the drug back." He also said: "Again, Heinz' wife might be an important lady like Betsy Ross who made the flag. The police would make the druggist give her the drug if she was an important lady." Tommy at this time could be either at Stage One or Stage Two. If he's at Stage Two, it is because of his rational calculations of gains and losses. If he's at Stage One, it is because of the irrational sort of view that punishment makes something wrong. Punishment is tied to authority. Whatever the powerful people say is right. Because Betsy Ross is powerful and important, she comes first. Pursuing this point further with Tommy, I asked: "Suppose you could save either one important person or a whole bunch of unimportant people?" His reply: "Well, that is really hard. Maybe you should save all the unimportant people because maybe they have more furniture." So he was equating the value of life with how much property they had. That is Stage One thinking. At age 13 he moved to Stage Two. Here he had a rational concern about punishment, saying: "Heinz should steal the drug to save his wife's life. He might get sent to jail but he would still have his wife." So he treats punishment as a rational consequence to be weighed with other self-interest consequences. His approach now is egocentric but there is a sense of fairness at Stage Two as reciprocity or back scratching: you do something for me and I will do something for you. Tommy was asked: "Should Heinz steal the drug if it was his friend dying instead of his wife?" His answer: "That's going too far. He could be in jail while his friend was alive and free. I wonder if his friend would do it for him. If you do it for your wife, she will do it for you."

Three years later Tommy has moved to Stage Three, saying: "If I were Heinz I would have done the same thing (stealing). You can't put a price on love. No amount of gifts make love. You can't put a price on life either." Now he has moved into "conventional" morality. For the first time his morality has moved from the dimension that emphasized self-interest to a concern for aspects of living that show a shared moral value like love for another person. Later on in his mid-twenties, Tommy says: "Yes, I would steal the drug. I have obligations to my country, my wife, my family and my religion.

There is not only love to my wife but obligation. We've committed ourselves before God to the contract of marriage." Now he's at Stage Four. He has the beginning of a realization of order and obligation in society and the beginning of the notion of the social contract. He says equivalently: "I have a contract to my wife and to God as a husband."

Tommy has reached Stage Four, the "law and order" stage and it's as far as most Americans go. But it's not an adequate level of development, since in the name of law and order you had Stage Four Americans and Stage Four North Vietnamese killing each other. The function of morality is to help resolve conflicts and disagreements among people with fairness and justice. The point is that Stage Four morality doesn't provide universal principles that all men can agree on.

H: Tommy didn't reach Stage Five or Stage Six so far. But since you have given some description of the other stages, how would you characterize the last two stages?

K: As I mentioned earlier, the majority of our adults are at the conventional level, Stage Three and Four. In our longitudinal sample only 20% reached Stage Five as adults. I noted before that the framers of our Constitution were themselves at Stage Five and, without the benefit of research, designed a government which would maintain Stage Five principles even though principled people might not come into power. The machinery they initiated included the checks and balances, the independent judiciary, freedom of the press and so on. They all came into play in the Watergate investigation.

The tragedy of Richard Nixon is the one Harry Truman pointed to long ago, that he never understood the Constitution, a Stage Five document. As far as I know, no public word of Mr. Nixon ever rose above Stage Four, law and order. A number of his transcripts from the White House tapes, indeed, showed rather lower stages. Though he never understood the Constitution, the Constitution understood Mr. Nixon and any who attain power without the Stage Five understanding of commitment to the justice and rights of man.

In dealing with some of the issues of moral education in schools, I found an easy way of getting American students to accept the Stage Five notion. I have tried to get them to understand their political involvement as a social contract in which they are involved and ask them, as it were, to sign that contract with informed consent.

H: In a sense Stage Five is non-controversial. But isn't Stage Six a source of considerable problems?

K: It certainly is. Before discussing it further, I'd like to make the point that in our stages each higher one is a better stage because it provides the ability to resolve problems which lower stages don't. Stage Five, the universal rights stage, helps resolve conflicts not resolved in Stage Four. I pointed out how Stage Four justifies people in different societies killing each other. So where laws and societies conflict you need something that's universal to all society wherein all men can agree, some principle or principles. If we don't reach some principles here we're not resolving the problem of what morality is for. That's what Stage Six is meant to provide. It makes tremendous demands of us and it is very idealistic. But unless we try to at least contemplate that level I don't see how we can resolve any of our great problems that plague mankind.

Relatively few people have reached Stage Six. I have cited Abraham Lincoln and Martin Luther King but lots of lesser known people are at this stage. In it the natural rights of Stage Five are defined by general ethical principles and obligations that are universally applicable to all mankind. For instance, there is the respect for human dignity and human personality which implies a principle of justice. In this stage rights are seen as derived from principles rather than as simply being a notion of some universal fact. There is a hierarchy of these rights.

H: I believe that you make use of philosophy for a deeper analysis of Stage Six.

K: I have turned to moral philosophers like Emanuel Kant and more recently to an associate at Harvard, John Rawls, and I have argued that Stage Six principles formulated by these men have helped resolve conflicts at this stage.

Kant's famous Categorical Imperative is the moral principle to treat each human being as an end, not a means. My application of Kant's Categorical Imperative (human beings are ends, not means) in the Heinz drug dilemma is that he would steal the drug to save the life of a person. In the mercy killing dilemma (see pp. 225-26) the Categorical Imperative principle would be applied by allowing the mercy killing in that particular situation, that is, she herself wanted it, was suffering a great deal and was terminally ill. So in summary, I regard the Categorical Imperative as meaning respect for the human personality as a moral human principle.

H: This type of Kantian principle works well regarding the drug dilemma, but many people including myself turn to theology regarding the mercy killing. The problem seems to demand an even deeper concept of the human person, that is, man's contingency and dependency ultimately for his human life and death on a higher being, that is, God. Hence the admittedly difficult situation doesn't allow direct human intervention. How do you react to that kind of thinking?

K: As you know, my focus is on stages of moral thinking and especially on thinking which is based on principle. The approach you presented is, of course, principled thinking.

I would like to bring up a notion that John Rawls developed. It's an elaboration of the Golden Rule which is another statement of the respect for human personality, "Do unto others as you would have them do unto you." Rawls elaborates his view in a book which I think is the most important volume in moral philosophy written in the twentieth century, *A Theory of Justice*. In this work he says that the principles of justice that should guide society are the ones we would choose if we didn't know who we were going to be in the society, if we didn't know our place or position in society. In that case if we were law makers, the laws that would be enacted would be those that we would contract into, not knowing whether we would be poor or rich, well educated or ill educated or whatever we might be. The principles he reaches and with which I agree are: 1. The principle of maximum liberty (if you don't know who you are going to be in society, you would want to provide the greatest amount of liberty for yourself that's compatible with equal liberty to others); 2. The principle of maximum equality (each of us would accept an inequality if it were to our benefit as an advantage). What does that mean? While still retaining a capitalist society, it says there is no real inequity in society whether a person makes $100,000 or $5,000. The claim is that capitalism is producing a greater benefit for even the worker at the $5,000 level because the person making $100,000 increases the gross national product and that fact makes the person at the bottom better off. While the economic facts of the situation are a little questionable, in any case the principle is clear: the social distribution is one that you would have and live with if you didn't know beforehand who you were going to be.

H: I understand that you see Stage Six thinking in some of the Supreme Court's recent decisions or opinions, particularly regarding capital punishment. How does Rawls' position shed light on the problem of capital punishment?

K: The Court made the decision at the time of the Furman case that capital punishment is a cruel and unusual punishment, prohibited by the Bill of Rights. But the decision rested on a Stage Five notion that capital punishment violated the criminal's right to due process or procedural rights. The argument that the Court used in rejecting capital punishment was that it was being applied without due process. They quoted findings that the application of the death penalty was unequal in that "most of those executed were poor, young, ignorant and black." As a result the states have tried to make laws that meet the Court's procedural objection by making the death penalty mandatory in certain cases, rather than at the discretion of judge or jury. Now the Supreme Court has to decide if mandatory capital punishment is constitutional. In earlier opinions some of the justices proposed that capital punishment was cruel and unusual and violated a basic human right that is nowhere listed in the Bill of Rights, the right to human dignity. Justice Brennan said that a punishment is cruel and unusual if it does not comport with human dignity, if it treats members of the human race as nonhuman; even the vilest criminal remains a human being possessed of common human dignity. The notion of the right to human dignity is of course quite different from the notion of due process.

Now let's apply Rawls' approach to capital punishment. Well, you first ask what's the purpose of capital punishment and the only logical answer is to deter. I wrote a long paper with a lawyer on this question and in the course of the research that we did we realized that it is true that punishment does decrease murder in spite of what many people think. And all of us would contract into society that would have punishment for murder. But would we contract into society that had capital punishment? Not if we didn't know who we were going to be. Not if we were going to be the murderer with possibly some genetic defect that sets us off and makes us murder. So if we would be the murderer we certainly would not expect to contract into a society that has capital punishment. Note that because of justice for the person who might be murdered, we would agree to a deterrent such as life imprisonment for murder. If you view the problem from the position of one who doesn't know who he's going to be and has a roughly equal chance of being a victim or a murderer, there is more or less one murderer for each victim. Some are going to be neither victims nor murderers, but you have to make a decision based on your being willing to live as either murderer or victim. Would you choose capital punishment? You would not!

H: Did your research on capital punishment show that capital punishment is a deterrent to murder?

K: If you look at the statistics alone you see that you save the lives of two possible victims by taking the life of the murderer. If your norm is just saving the greatest number of lives you would come out having capital punishment. But if your norm is that of justice and equality, not knowing who you are going to be in Rawls' sense, you wouldn't have capital punishment.

H: Isn't it possible for a person to object to this position with the claim that one is really preferring the dignity and personality of the murderer over that of the victim? Must one sacrifice one's own dignity for that of another?

K: Stage Six morality is one of justice and equality. It says that my dignity is worth as much as anybody else's and anybody else's is worth as much as mine. This position does conflict with the ethic of self-realization where people say "My obligation is toward my own moral perfection and dignity. I don't have an equal obligation to the dignity of others." Obviously I do not agree with this kind of doctrine since I believe that the only ultimate resolution to conflicts is justice, a very egalitarian notion of not treating your own dignity or perfection as worth more than anybody else's.

There are really three fundamental notions in moral philosophy: 1. Morality is justice; 2. Morality is the utility of the greatest good to the greatest number; 3. Morality is perfection. I should like to say in passing that I am working on and planning a supplementary stage, Stage Seven, to provide for those who reach moral perfection, give up their life for their faith, etc. But there should be a caution mentioned regarding moral perfection that it seems to me that some people feel they are being highly moral in sacrificing the rights of others in a wrong sense of moral perfection, or they may even sacrifice their own dignity. So sometimes the morality of conscience can be misapplied.

H: Are there not some cases where it seems that the rights of two claimants are just about equal and in the pursuit of justice a decision has to be made to favor the one or the other?

K: While we can't get into particular cases, it's my contention that the principles of justice and equality can be maintained in all situations, especially if viewed from Rawls' perspective of not knowing who you are going to be.

H: Are there some possible misuses of the Stages of Moral Development such as the well-known "halo effect" that concern you?

K: There are at least three possible misuses that flow from a misunderstanding of the stages. First, teachers may use the stages for grading students, automatically putting Stage Six at the head of the class, Stage Five just below that, all the way through the class list so that Stage One students are at the bottom. A second misuse is that of grouping the stages together. For example, in a California prison (where ego, interpersonal maturity stages are used, not Moral Development stages), a seventeen year old youth identified himself to me as a Stage Two manipulator. He said: "It's not so bad being a manipulator, but I just don't like being locked up with all those other manipulators." The idea here was to put all the Stage Two manipulators in one unit under a manipulative guard to manipulate the manipulators. That was what they call matching treatment to the stage level of the subject. That is hardly the way I would like to see stages used with any groups. That kind of misuse is also contrary to the theory we propose since you need dialogue and communication between stages if you want growth in the environment.

A third misuse of the stages is that of confusing the stages with a moral judgment about people. Certainly we say that Stage Six thinking is more adequate than Stage Five, Stage Five more adequate than Stage Four and so on. But ways of thinking are not kinds of people. Stages are modes of reasoning and are not behaviors or character or motivation or other psychological factors. And on the moral side, the stages are not a system for awarding or assigning blame. For instance, Stage Six thinking would say that it's all right to steal the drug in the Heinz story. But an individual person who is at Stage Four, law and order, comes along and he doesn't want to steal the drug. Do we say that he is wrong or bad or what? While we recognize that he has not advanced to principled thinking and regards the law as superior to the person's life, we do not have the right to judge the person or assign blame to him. Earlier I said that Mr. Nixon demonstrated Stage Four thinking, but this was not a way of calling him evil or condemning him. We must be cautious in not misusing the stages.

4. The Dilemmas

H: The Heinz drug dilemma is now well known. Has there been any attempt to reach large numbers of the general public for response to the dilemma?

K: We have asked the dilemma in the National Opinion Research Center poll. Seventy-five percent of adult Americans said that it was morally wrong to steal in this case although most said they would do it if they were put into the husband's place. But they wouldn't say that it was really morally right to do it.

Of course, a lot of social scientists have taken a relativistic position and said that what is morally right is what your society says is morally right and what the majority says is right as a rule of one's culture. They say that the morality in children is the internalization of the rules and values of the culture. They say that by that definition those people who say it is morally wrong to take the drug are clearly correct in view of the results of the poll; those who said it is morally right to take the drug clearly never internalized the morality of their culture.

H: The idea of a national opinion poll regarding a moral question is of some interest but doesn't it form a weak basis for moral thinking or in moral decision-making?

K: Of course. Obviously we can't settle moral problems on the basis of the majority opinion. We need to go to moral philosophy to examine why a position is morally wrong or right. Yet lots of adults, sophisticated people, are convinced of the relativistic position, that there's no right answer to the Heinz drug-taking dilemma, that it all depends on his motivation and how much he likes his wife, etc. Now I happen to be a non-relativist, that is, I would claim that in this situation it is universally morally right to steal the drug. People with the relativistic position have been taught in social science classes that all values are relative to one's culture and that as a result there's no universal value and no universally acceptable solution to the

Heinz dilemma is possible. Instead, they equivalently say that the choice is to be made in terms of one's own feelings and judgments since there is no such thing as universal or objective values. The result of this kind of thinking is that we have a great deal of egocentric solutions and egocentric thinking. It undermines the idea of principled thinking. The important matter is present feelings and emotions, not thinking.

H: It's obvious that this kind of approach, the relativistic one, also makes one's self-interest the critical norm. How do you tie the "self-realization" thrust of Maslow and the humanistic school into critiques of high principled moral thinking?

K: I'm afraid that we don't get much help from the self-realization school. It would lead you to say that it is right to steal the drug or it is wrong to steal the drug. It is not clear whether self-realization would rely on Heinz' maintaining his commitment to his wife and the value of human life or on his continuing his commitment to the law and not breaking the property rights of society. As far as I can see, self-realization is no help in this problem. Self-realization emphasizes the notion that one should uphold one's commitment already made to moral principles. It doesn't help us with the content or the determination of moral principles. One needs some moral principles of some sort to make decisions.Self-realization presupposes that we have already formed our moral principles. So for our analysis of the Heinz dilemma we have to get back to the consideration of just what are the moral principles involved.

H: What procedure do you and your associates use when you discuss the theft problem with groups for purposes other than research?

K: Just as in our research interviews, our emphasis isn't on whether people think it's all right to steal the drug. We're concerned about the basic reasoning that they offer for their decision. Typically, I ask two questions: 1. What do you think is the morally right thing to do? 2. Do you think that your answer is just a personal opinion or do you think that your answer is universally and objectively morally right? In other words, I am raising the issue of relativity versus objectivity. I emphasize over and over again that the moral discussion is the difference between asking what is morally right (what *ought* you to do) versus what would you actually do. It's a non-dilemma situation if you just ask what would you do for a spouse or someone loved very much. People just say they'd steal the drug. But if you make the sick person a stranger or friend it becomes somewhat different. In the non-dilemma situation you are getting into the motivation, such as how much he's willing to pay the price of going to jail versus how much you love your wife or friend. In these cases, it's no longer a question of moral reasoning or moral principle but a matter of weighing your own emotions against the dangers involved. While I admit that it is important to consider the emotional aspects of moral dilemmas, an emphasis on them does not help to clarify moral principles or enable us to estimate whatever stage the discussants are at. We discuss the "should" question first (if you don't know what you should do you certainly won't do it) and get into the "would" question later.

H: What are some of the reasons given for thinking it is wrong or right to steal the drug?

K: Let's first look at some reasons given for thinking that it is wrong to steal the drug. Of course, there are some who take an absolute position against ever stealing because it is the law. Some say that the chance of being punished by imprisonment is too great. There are those who think that the right of property or the private right to benefits to one's (the druggist's) hard work and discoveries are of primary importance. Some even urge that the theft would be detrimental to Heinz' own personal, psychological and moral development. A few see theft of any kind, including this kind, as undermining society.

Those who take the position that it is right in the given situation to steal the drug maintain that the human life is superior to property and that when a human life is threatened it is allowable to take a possession, even another's, to obtain the health of the threatened life. Most offer variations of this kind of reasoning.

In oral discussions some individuals want to delve into topics which do not seem helpful to the immediate moral discussion, such as the conditions of medical and pharmaceutical practice, the capitalistic system, etc. This kind of discussion is not encouraged.

H: Would you describe another dilemma that you use?

K: Yes. The next one goes this way: The woman is dying and the drug won't work. She is in lots of pain and the doctors say that she will die within six months or a year. The only way to alleviate the pain is to give her a heavy enough dose of morphine or some other drug that would lead to her death. She knows that and asks the doctor to give her the medicine that will make her die and put her out of her pain. The question is, should the doctor do it or not?

H: In other words, can the person equivalently commit suicide under certain circumstances, and can others cooperate in this act?

K: Yes, but notice that it's considerably different from the recent (1976) case of Karen Ann Quinlan. We really didn't have satisfactory information about Karen's attitudes toward dying in the circumstances that developed. So it was a matter of others making a decision for her. And notice that the doctors in the case didn't object to "pulling the plug" for moral reasons. They were afraid of being sent to jail.

H: I suppose that people again take different sides and that some say that the taking of one's life in this case is acceptable and others say that it isn't. And again, I expect that you seek the reasons behind the choices and attempt to get to basic reasoning such as principles. Would you indicate the type of reasoning that's offered for both positions?

K: Those who oppose the suicide and cooperation in it think that there is a presence, a dignity, a personality with a purpose that the individual even in this case has no right to destroy. It's viewed as a matter of justice to the individual that there be no taking of life.

Those who would allow the woman to take the drugs which would hasten her death think that in these special circumstances she has the full autonomy, the right to weigh both sides and if she makes the judgment in favor of death she should proceed to take the necessary means.

What about the doctor? Those who oppose the death's being hastened also speak strongly of the physician's commitment and oath to preserve and sponsor life and health. On the other hand, those who accept the hastening of death also yield freedom to the doctor. They say he has the right to refuse to cooperate in the sense that he has the right to refuse to go to jail in order to help someone commit suicide. But the really difficult question is this: what is the moral role of the ideal doctor in this kind of situation? Of course, if the woman had a clear moral right to commit suicide in this case, the doctor's situation is much clearer than if the claim is murky. So we again must require those who claim one position or the other to offer a clear statement of the principles on which they base their thinking.

Two additional points come to mind: 1. no matter what one's own moral decisions may be, one must allow other people to exercise their right to disagree with us, and 2. if we make a moral decision based on moral principle from an objective point of view, we must accept the consequences of that decision and this may at times call for sacrifice.

5. Moral Stages and Behavior

H: One of the points that your critics bring up centers around the relationship between moral thinking and moral behavior. How do you react to the statement that just because you think at a high moral level there's no assurance that you'll act in that same way?

K: What I maintain is that moral principles and moral judgment are a necessary but not a sufficient condition for moral action. If someone acts in a principled way at Stage Five or Six, one must be able to reason at that level. On the other hand one can reason at a high level and not always live up to that level. There are many other personality factors that influence moral behavior besides moral reasoning but I say that moral reasoning is a necessary one.

Let me give an example of an additional factor that influences human behavior. By way of introduction, let me recall that one of the things that has been classically considered in moral action has been the will, moral will. That notion had been considered old-fashioned and had been ruled out of psychology. But some students and I are trying to bring it back, following the lead of William James. He claimed that the key to moral behavior was attention: the capacity, the ability to keep your mind on the reasons and considerations of things that were right and keep your mind distracted from the things that were wrong.

In researching some of James' ideas, we looked at kids' attention and their behavior like cheating. Everybody knows that the naughty kids in the school are the distractable ones, those who don't pay attention. Well, we found that there is a very clear relationship between attention (to the brass instruments, pushing buzzers, etc.) and our moral development scores. Let me emphasize that we controlled the variable of mental ability among the young people. In analyzing our results we grouped the Stages One and Two into Preconventional, Three and Four into Conventional, Five and Six into Principled. Among the Principled, only 15% cheated, among the Conventional, 55% cheated, and 70% of the Preconventional subjects cheated.

In working with the pupils' cheating we also divided them according to their being "strong" or "weak" willed. We found that the kids who cheated were the weak willed and Conventional. The strong willed and Conventional as well as the Principled resisted temptation. But with the Preconventional (Stage One and Two) youths, the reverse happened. The strong willed lived up to the courage of their typically Stage Two egoistic principles and cheated even more. The weak willed didn't cheat but for the wrong reasons; they were intimidated and pressured by the situation into not cheating. So will is morally neutral unless it is informed by moral thinking. If you are strong willed and you are a Hitler or someone like that, you have a situation where there is a combination of a powerful pursuit of one's values and goals, together with a low moral level of goals and thinking.

H: In your research regarding cheating and moral will, you said that you controlled for mental ability, that is, you made sure that you had students with the same mental levels in each of the moral groups. However, in spite of the existence of the Professor Moriarity-type criminal, there does seem to be the expectation that the bright person normally will be a highly moral person. It's a kind of stereotype and there are great exceptions, but lots of people think that that's the case. What's your thinking regarding intelligence and moral thinking and stages?

K: While it is true that there is somewhat of a correlation between brightness and moral maturity and that on cheating tests the brighter ones are less tempted, I would like to bring up a parallel between moral stages and Piaget's stages of thinking. In our cheating and moral will research, we found a correlation of .30 between IQ and moral maturity. That's what I call in this case, a necessary but not sufficient relationship. To use Piaget's terminology, to be Stage Two on the moral level you have to be "concrete operational;" to be Stage Three you have to be beginning "formal operations;" you have to have more second sub-stages of formal operation in which you can think in terms of systems to be Stage Four; Stage Four is a social system thinking so for this stage you have to be able to organize variables; for Stage Five you have to be capable of hypothetical deductive reasoning, assuming principles and then making deductions from them.

As an illustration of my contention that moral thinking is necessary but not sufficient for moral behavior, I wish to cite the following statistics. In the adult population in America, about 60% are in Piagetian terms fully formal operational but less than 20% are morally principled. Everyone who was morally principled was formal operational but the reverse is not the case. We all know this intuitively, that is, we can conceive of the genius physicist whose moral reasoning is low but it is hard to think of the reverse, that is, we can't imagine a real saint or a moral leader or moral philosopher who is not cognitively mature. That is why I say that cognitive development is a necessary but not a sufficient condition for moral judgment and moral judgment development is a necessary but not a sufficient condition for moral action.

H: I know that in your concern for moral behavior you and your associates have worked toward molding and studying social environments that encourage moral behavior. Have you met resistance to setting up these environments?

K: In a way, yes, when it gets close to home. For instance, in the late '60s, Mosha Blatt and I were doing moral discussions in a nearby junior high school. The principal wanted to know why we were using fictional dilemmas when there were real moral situations in the school that were worthy of examination like kids stealing, on drugs, getting pregnant. The question was, why don't you help us with these moral behavior problems instead of working with those hypothetical dilemmas. I said I would be happy to try to help with the local moral behavior problems but I want to tell you about how I would do it. I pointed out that according to us, the core of moral development is a sense of fairness and justice. We'd have to not just think about what is fair and just but we'd have to put it into action. That would mean making this a fair and just school. You and the teachers would be more just and fair. His reaction to this proposal was that he was delighted to have us go back to the fictional dilemmas.

H: Under the heading of moral stage and moral behavior, have you noted any interesting development on the part of those you were working with as subjects?

K: There was this prisoner who was what might be called a hard core Stage Two, instrumental egoist. At the end of the program he had moved to Stage Three. He had found and kept in his cell a pet cat. Upon finding this out, a guard ordered him to get rid of it or kill it. The inmate had moved up in moral thinking but had not improved in impulse control and so his argument with the guard ended up with his beating the guard and having three more years added to his sentence. We felt a sense of frustration about this but could do nothing effective to alleviate it.

6. Applied Moral Education

H: You sponsored moral education programs in prisons and in schools. Let's first discuss briefly your work in a prison and then turn to your work in schools. Everybody knows that by and large efforts to rehabilitate or reform inmates of prisons have been failures. Your work seems to be an exception. How did you get started and what happened?

K: We got started with the guards and women inmates at the Niantic Prison in Connecticut. Then we included a male group. We made the first contact with the guards, that is, we started talking with them. We explained our theory and gave them the opportunity to express their feelings. Incidentally, you don't get too many people in a prison who claim that the system is just and fair; nobody is defensive about it; everybody knows that it is unjust. We brought the guards and the inmates together to negotiate a social contract and had them moved into a cottage unit. The basic principle was one man one vote, with all issues that were considered issues of fairness being settled by a majority vote. It's gone quite well in a variety of ways.

I would like to share one experience that is connected with my work with prisoners. A woman prisoner was at a halfway house in New Haven, where there was an opportunity for her to acclimate herself to a job and life on the "outside." It's a fine situation for a person to ease out of prison life if only all the rules are kept. This particular woman was an alcoholic who killed her husband while inebriated. Everyone in the prison felt she had made great progress there. At any rate, she was also doing well at the halfway house but once on the way back from her job she took a drink. Now at the halfway house there was a democratically enacted rule that if you took any content of an alcoholic drink, you would have to return to prison. Well, after she had her drink and returned to the halfway house, it was obvious she had had a drink and was shipped back to prison for two months. At the prison I asked her if she thought that the treatment she received was fair. Her reply was: "It was fair because the group at the halfway house made a democratic decision and besides they were trying to help me with my alcoholic problem." Also at the prison there was a discussion and vote about her being kept there for two months rather than a shorter period. A two month period would mean that she would lose her job. In the discussion I said that I believed that the two month period was too severe. The correction officer said: "You might think that I am Stage Four but these are the rules and they cannot be changed." After a long discussion the case was put to a vote. There was only one vote that said she shouldn't stay for the two months and that was mine. Everybody else including the woman involved thought that it was just that she stay for the two months. I was quite happy to go along with the majority. We have never had a situation where the majority voted what I felt was a violation of anybody's rights.

H: You have mentioned your hopes for the just school. Would you describe your efforts in that regard?

K: Two years ago some people in the Cambridge High School decided to start an alternative school. We started out small, sixty volunteer students and six teachers. There was a very interesting group of students: 10 from academic professional homes, 25 poor black kids, the rest poor white kids. After the moral development interviews, we found out that more than half of the poor kids were at Stage Two, the rest were at Stage Three, and a few of the professors' kids were at Stage Four.

The idea of having a democratic school is far from a new idea. Usually it's part of the planning of the alternative school where there's the romantic ideology of letting everybody do their thing based on the idea that if the children are given their freedom they'll grow. We realized that things were a little more difficult than that ideological approach and we felt that we knew why democracy doesn't work when it is tried in most alternative schools. We also thought that our theory suggested the kinds of procedures that should be developed. I had earlier been involved with an alternative school that emphasized the town meeting and governance system. About two weeks after the school started, the school's video recorder was stolen by some of the students. A town meeting was called and there was a noisy, violent session. At its end, the student proposal that won out was that of buying back the stolen video recorder through a "fence." It was commonly believed that this highly popular "solution" was proposed by the actual thief. Well, the teachers abandoned the democratic approach after their first confrontation with reality. After that incident they made the decisions.

In spite of my own experience with the other alternative school, in the Cambridge one we started off almost as badly as the other. Our theory says that if you want democracy, not mobocracy, you have to provide for moral discussion in which the higher stage will influence lower stage students' reasoning. The whole process has to be worked out so that reasonably fair decisions result and the process takes a lot of careful managing. Yet at the first meeting of our democratic alternative school the teachers came out with this romantic alternative school doctrine that once you got rid of the authority of the traditional school everything would be fine. So at the first community meeting with the students the electives for the last periods in the day were listed. Most of the school day is devoted to English, Social Studies and Math but the last periods of the day were planned for the electives. At the meeting one of the students got up and stated: "I don't like the electives. I vote we go home." That passed with a majority vote, the bell rang and they all went home. We had to get them together again and explain the state law about school attendance through the whole class day.

H: Many other alternative schools have had problems with legal matters. Did you have any other such difficulties?

K: It took us three months to get a rule against marijuana or against drugs in general. During the first two months the kids came in puffing marijuana in the classroom. Luckily we had enough support from the administration to let us work it through in our own way. Vaguely in the back of everyone's head was the notion that if we couldn't work it out in a democratic policy the headmaster would have to bring in the police.

H: You sound as though things are going well now.

K: We feel as though the school has finally developed well. We try to integrate English, Social Studies and moral discussions with both the regular curriculum and the governance of the school. But we have been primarily interested in developing a sense of community and of fairness and doing that at a high stage.

I'd like to give two examples of progress in the moral atmosphere of the school. The first example is about the local stealing rule. When the school first started there was no trouble getting a ruling on stealing but the initial response was pretty much Stage Two ("If someone is dumb enough to leave things around it's his own fault if he gets ripped off"). But after the first year of the school's life, the first real episode of stealing was reported. A girl had ten dollars stolen from her wallet and she took the case to the community meeting. The kids took the view that the school was supposed to be a "fair" community and what kind of place was it if you couldn't leave stuff around. They felt that it was really the community's fault if you couldn't trust each other. They urged that everyone should chip in a quarter to give restitution to the girl who had the ten dollars stolen from her. After the session, the person who had stolen the money, with pressure from friends, did return the money. What I am saying is that at least within the school community, while it is predominantly at Stage Three and far from our limited goal of Stage Four thinking, some progress is being made. Unfortunately, outside of the context of the school community, some of the students are still "ripping off" cars and other things.

The other example of progress that I'd like to cite pertains to the racial membership of our student body. We started by quota with 25% black and 75% white, the white kids coming from what might be called a slightly racist ("Archie Bunker") working class and the black kids being premilitant in their feelings. For a long time there was a real division between the black and white students, which is hardly surprising in view of the "black and white" blocks on community issues in the area. At any rate, a group of black students said that the 25% quota still made them feel unwanted and uncomfortable and they asked that the next six kids who were accepted from the waiting list should be black. After a long and rather violent argument, the white majority did agree that the next six kids should be black on a kind of reverse discrimination policy. The majority said that they wanted the blacks to feel accepted as a part of the community and they could understand why they felt uncomfortable. All this happened last fall. We have had a meeting on the admissions policy for next year and as far as I can tell the black-white tension has dissolved. Black students are now talking about the need to recruit minorities from among the Spanish and Portuguese. They are not just talking about black power. From these illustrations I feel that we are making progress in dealing with moral behavior in terms of making the school a more just community. We feel pretty good about it.

H: When you arrange for legislative and judicial power in the just school to reside in the community meeting aren't you and the teachers remiss in exercising your responsibility and personal obligation? Has your experience with the school community meeting been positive?

K: The turning over of real powers of decision is an important theoretical element of our program. Notice, however, that we require the presence of some individuals at higher stages to assure some disequilibrium that should sponsor conflict and growth among peers. The situation becomes complicated where the teacher or the experimentor has a higher principled sense of justice which conflicts with the students' sense of justice. Your goal has to be that of having them make decisions in terms of the highest level of justice they can currently handle, not in terms of your own hopefully more developed level. Let me say that there were a few times when the community voted to expel kids from the school and I found the experience very painful. Yet I couldn't say that the decisions were wrong or unjust.

H: I have heard of some teachers who became enthusiastic about your work, rushed into class and tried to apply it. Do you have some cautions for such teachers?

K: Yes. I would urge two important elements of preparation, careful study of the theory and a habitual democratic setting in the classroom. Certainly the study that should precede this kind of applied moral education program should amount to lots more than reading an article or even a book. The teacher—and I would hope that a team of several teachers would cooperate in the project—should have spent a long time, a term for instance, in learning precisely what our goals are (including what we're not attempting), our understanding of the stages, what we're really looking for in the dilemmas, etc.

Equally important is the teacher's making sure that there's a democratic climate in the classroom. Students have to feel that they're really encouraged to think and that they're really faced with personal cognitive challenges. I can recall one teacher who squelched the democratic discussion of a dilemma by going to the board and writing: HE HAS AUTHORITY. The dilemma pertained to a military officer's sending others to near certain death. There was no democratic spirit there!

7. The Milgram's Obedience to Authority Experiment

H: Stanley Milgram's experiment with having people administer electric shocks to others at the directions of a psychologist has been cited as an illustration of the Stage Four, law and order mentality. Yet the experiments themselves cause dismay to many people because of the mental anguish of those who give the shocks. Would you comment on the ethics of this experiment?

K: I was at Yale when Milgram began this kind of work. At that time he used Yale students to do the shocking and had not added the element of the weak heart on the part of his confederate who was seen through the one-way mirror and apparently suffering from the electric shocks. At any rate, when I first saw the experiments I shared the feelings of so many others who read or see it for the first time, a kind of horror and nervous laughter about it all. He did deceive his subjects and then later on he did undeceive them. The question of lasting psychological harm to the subjects is really hard to assess. The whole procedure seemed to deny man's moral nature as a thinking, responsible being.

I did have long discussions with Milgram about the experiments and I urged him to change his procedures and goals to make it more morally-oriented. The only tangible effect of our discussions was that I was able to interview his experimental subjects after his work with them was completed.

Another point regarding the ethics of this kind of experiment pertains to codes of ethics for psychological experimentation. I'm not much of a believer in the making of such laws and rules. Instead, I think that we should have the same goal with psychologists and all scientists as we have for the general population, that of raising their personal moral levels. Once that happens their professional activity will be guided by principle rather than by pragmatic considerations as sometimes happens these days.

H: Do you regard Milgram's experiment as helpful toward understanding the adequacies and inadequacies of Stage Four thinking?

K: It demonstrates the inadequacies of this level of moral development on the part of both most of the subjects and on the part of the experimentor. The experimentor shows that he's being obedient throughout his work to the demands of his science, even at the cost of possibly causing his subjects permanent psychological harm. The subjects were obedient to the experimentor in causing harm to another person and their justification was essentially the same as the experimentor's. In his book Milgram explains this justification when he argues that the end justifies the means. Notice that the ultimate persuasion that the experimentor used with those who were wavering was that "I'll take the responsibility." Many of the subjects accepted that argument, even though it was only implied, as the basis for their obedience. Of course, our stage theory requires that for principled action the mature person doesn't hand over responsibility to someone else for his personal, controllable actions.

H: Yet some of the subjects did quit early in the experiment. Was their basic reasoning for stopping their moral judgment that they were hurting other people?

K: We had much discussion in analysis of those who quit and those who didn't. Everyone of the subjects said that they were concerned about hurting other human beings, so the difference isn't the presence or absence of concern. Perhaps it would help if I gave the results of our interviewing thirty Yale students who participated in the study. The interviews were held, as Milgram required, after the completion of his study. We found that of the principled subjects, 80% quit; of the remaining subjects at lower stages, only 15% quit. So we notice that some of the subjects who had not reached the principled level quit and that some of the principled subjects did continue to shock the confederate. There are many as yet unsolved problems about the whole experiment involving the subjects, the experimentor and his "victim", and those who approve and disapprove of the project.

H: Is it possible that the empathy factor was part of the conflict that the subjects who didn't quit felt for the experimentor? They wanted to help him. They also wanted to help the apparently pained₁confederate but were closer to the experimentor. What part does closeness and empathy play in this kind of moral decision-making?

K: First, let's look at the closeness factor. It's true that the closer you are physically and psychologically to a person or to a place that's the object of some kind of treatment, the more concerned you are. So that may have been a factor.

Let's look at empathy in moral decision-making. These days empathy is talked and written about a lot, especially in large urban areas. Everybody thinks it's nice to have empathy. But the Milgram experiment does illustrate how empathy is quite limited as a basis of moral action. The empathic person doesn't want to be mean to the experimentor and spoil his experiment. The empathic person also doesn't want to be mean to the person being shocked. At Stage Three one realizes that it's very mean to hurt another person and you don't want to be mean. But in this case there's the problem of being mean to either the experimentor or the shocked person. The Stage Three person has a real problem. He needs moral principles to solve the conflict of obligations. He needs some principle to move him in the right direction, in this case to follow an obligation to the victim and not to the experimentor. At the principled level the person has to really define rights and obligations in the particular situation. In this case he has to realize that the experimentor does not have the right to order another human being to be shocked and he has to recognize that the individual still has a responsibility for what he's doing no matter what an authority figure is saying.

Milgram makes the point that all of the people who inflicted pain on another person were normal human beings with full capacity to empathize with other human beings. What I maintain is that the problem is not one of lack of empathy or concern on the part of the subjects but one of an immaturity of moral judgment on their part, at least from my point of view. I view this experiment not in terms of the feelings of those involved but in terms of the human rights and obligations of all parties. For instance, did the experimentor have the right to order another person to shock? Did the subject have the right to quit after volunteering and contracting to do this assignment? Did the victim (the confederate) have the right to quit? Did the victim and the experimentor have the obligation to quit when they saw what was actually happening?

H: I appreciate your cautions about the limits of empathy in moral judgment. Yet elsewhere you speak of making use of Rawls' principles which sound somewhat like the descriptions of empathy. Isn't there some relationship?

K: It does sound like empathy when Rawls asks people to put themselves in the other's place. But his meaning is quite different from the meaning of empathy. Empathy emphasizes the feeling aspect of the other person's living. Rawls' principle, on the other hand, is directed toward the whole person and the person's behavior (of course, feeling is included). This comes out clearly when he speaks of the importance of treating other persons as ends and not as means. In fact, that's the point of the Golden Rule, that the emphasis is on the behavior ("do") of ourselves and others; there's no question of limiting oneself to the feelings involved.

Rawls says that you would make the morally right decision if you make your decision as if you didn't know who was going to be in the situation. To return again to Heinz and the drug, if the husband put himself in his wife's shoes he would want to steal the drug. In the case the druggist wants his rights of property to be respected. But suppose the druggist put himself in the shoes of the husband or the wife. What would he then decide? Obviously he would want her to have the drug. If he put himself in the situation of the dying person he would want his own life to be more highly regarded than property. He wouldn't let himself die in this situation even though the cost would be $2000. So a fair decision, one that appears fair, is one that's made when we don't know which person in a conflict of interest situation we would be.

I'd say therefore that empathy pertains to feeling, while Rawls' principle applies to total human behavior including at least feeling, moral and other types of thinking and the moral judgment that precedes action.

8. Current Resurgence in Interest in Moral Education

H: You have criticized the direct teaching of virtues. What's the weakness of this approach? Some newly concerned educators want to use that approach.

K: There are two problems: the approach doesn't work, and there is the difficulty of deciding the virtues you try to instill.

In the period of 1910 to 1930 almost every public school in America had a character education program generally based on what I call, in a rather flippant way, teaching the bag of virtues. They had a set of virtues like honesty, loyalty, obedience and so on and used some combination of teaching and reward to instill the virtues. What happened to this approach, even though every so often people call for its resurrection, is that it was carefully researched by Hartshorne and May. They did a very elaborate study of the character education program in the public schools and elsewhere. They found that all these programs to instill honesty had absolutely no effect in increasing honest behavior among the kids who were exposed to them.

At the time when the Hartshorne and May studies were becoming well known another factor became important. It's the second problem I mentioned above, the difficulty about the virtues themselves. Educators and psychologists became more aware of the relativity of values in a pluralistic society. Though honesty sounds uncontroversial, if you include chastity in the list there's going to be trouble. If you include obedience in the list there'll be even more trouble from those who believe in sponsoring independence and creativity among children. The question is how do you ever get an acceptable consensus or rationale for the virtues you are going to train children in. Are you going to look to the culture of the child? To middle class culture? To Catholic values? To Protestant values? And then the question arises of one's right in a pluralistic society to choose to teach the preferred values.

H: After the confusion about the direct teaching of civic virtues became widespread, the mental health movement took over. What happened?

K: Beginning in the early 1930s a transformation took place as the mental health movement became important in the schools and elsewhere. The result was that we no longer had naughty (a moralistic word) boys, we had emotionally disturbed boys. We developed a whole elaborate system in which teachers could not describe any behaviors that were going on in the classroom by calling them immoral. The children were now referred to the school psychiatrist. The only trouble was that in fact it turned out that the kind of diagnoses that the psychiatrists made had no validity. For example, longitudinal studies were made of children labeled disturbed by psychiatrists and psychologists in elementary schools. As adults these persons were no more likely to be disturbed than those who were not so diagnosed. So the whole mental health approach with all its psychotherapeutic terminology has failed in the schools. The school psychologists and counselors who used this approach are almost the first to admit its failure. So we can't continue to elude the problem by saying that it's a psychiatric problem. We really have to face the issue that there is a role for the school in moral development and moral character growth.

H: Isn't that just what's happening now? Since the early '70s hasn't there been a renewed interest in moral education in the schools?

K: There certainly has been a real resurgence. I think that there are two basic sources or reasons for this change: a realization of the sense of confusion and lack of morality among our children and our sense of the lack of morality in society in general. There is an understanding that if we're dissatisfied with the sense of morality in the wider society and want to do something about it, then the schools have to be the place where more can be done to prepare our future citizens to create a more moral and just society. Of course, events like the revelations connected with Watergate and other investigations seem to be obvious triggers for this kind of concern about moral education.

H: As usual in education, this renewed interest in moral education has produced conservative and liberal blocs. Are the motivations of the groups different?

K: Yes. The conservative group is interested in moral education because they see the increase in crime in the streets, the moral lapses that Watergate revealed in political life, the undermining of what they call traditional sexual morality. They are calling for a return to order and discipline in the school, and to basics in academic and social matters, as well as to moral basics.

Among the "liberals" the current interest in moral education is not only sparked by the Watergate investigations but a kind of rediscovery by liberals of the moral principles behind the liberal faith. For instance, I would say that the liberals in education in the '60s had lost their awareness of the moral principles underlying their liberalism. They rested their faith in technology, educational technology, social science, rational political manipulation. I think that those who professed a liberal faith and who tried to use rational instrumental means have been disappointed and they have come to a growing awareness of the need to have rational or really social ends in education and elsewhere. Ultimately at least in secular education this gets back to the principles on which our society was founded.

H: In this Bicentennial year you suggest that all segments of our society, including the conservative and the liberal, can profit from renewed study of our Declaration of Independence and our U.S. Constitution?

K: Yes. After all America was the first nation grounded on the conception of the principles of justice. The Declaration calls these prin-

ciples self-evident truths, that all men are created equal with inalien-
able rights to life, liberty and the pursuit of happiness. Of course,
these self-evident truths are not so self-evident at all. In fact, every
year the Gallup poll circulates a bill of rights without identifying it as
The Bill of Rights to find whether citizens should have these rights.
The majority of the citizens vote them down.

The reason for citizens' rejecting parts of the Constitution and
the reason for our saying that an appreciation of the Constitution
requires more general moral education is that the framers wrote the
document at an advanced level of moral thinking. It's Stage Five, in
our terminology. That stage is achieved by those who could sign the
social contract with informed consent. Only a short time ago we
realized that it isn't only the man in the street who had not reached
this stage or Stage Four but even the president of the country
couldn't do so.

I think that the original reason why Jefferson and others pro-
pounded the need for free public education was that they wanted all
people to understand the fundamental rights of citizenship. And
today the movement for moral education recognizes that in our society the principles behind our political society are ones that must be
acquired through education. Education will be directed toward the
understanding and acceptance of the principles of justice.

*H: To return for a moment to liberals and conservatives, have you
had a chance to work with both groups?*

K: Yes. In the Cambridge school system I was involved for two
years in a small alternative public high school, the Cluster School. It
was based on the idea of participatory democracy and other elements that liberals usually propagandize. The rule was "one man
one vote." All issues were settled as issues of fairness in a community or town meeting. There was a discipline committee with the
teachers going before it as well as the students. It can be called a
liberal school.

Another alternative school is now being started in the same
district. This one could be called a "neo-traditional" one. It stresses
not only "academic basics" as they call it, but patriotism, respect for
authority and the general emphasis that we might call civic morality.
So we have in the same system two alternative schools, both based
on different aspects of moral education. I hope to do research on
both schools and I expect the results to be most interesting.

H: Though there is a renewed interest in moral development in education at all levels, I would like to know if you discern any growth in moral thinking and judging in American society in general. Are you optimistic or pessimistic in this regard?

K: I am a liberal optimist in terms of where America is going in moral development. I find that there is a slow movement of society toward higher stages. What we have in our time is a crisis of conventional morality but we do have an increasing number of people who are moving up to the Principled level beyond the Conventional level.

In our longitudinal study of the original Chicago boys we find that twice as many of the men, now in their thirties, are at the Principled level as were their parents whom we also interviewed (some of the parents had a college education). There is a more discouraging side to the picture in that more high school students had reached the Conventional stages in the '50s when we began the study than is true today; now more are "stuck" at Stage Two than was true then. The moral and value conflicts of our current history are producing two widely different results. Some people are so confused by the intricacies of the problems that they are perhaps refusing the challenge and not thinking through the issues; as a result we are getting more Stage Two adolescents and adults; they remain at the Pre-conventional level of moral thinking. But on the other hand, the same moral and value conflicts resonate profitably in many others, helping them to move beyond Conventional moral levels to Principled thinking.

I believe that aspects of recent American history that produced moral indignation on the part of our people, together with the resurgence of interest in education and in other institutions for moral education programs should make all interested parties hopeful about the future moral climate of our country.

The Contributors

JOSEPH E. BERNIER, Ph.D., is Assistant Professor, Department of Counselor Education, SUNY, Albany

JAMES J. DiGIACOMO, S.J., teaches religious studies at Regis High School and is adjunct Assistant Professor, Graduate School of Religion and Religious Education, Fordham University

LEO GOLD, Ph.D., is in private practice in South Orange, N.J., president of the American Society of Adlerian Psychology and Dean, Alfred Adler Institute, New York City

RICHARD H. HERSH, Ph.D., is Associate Dean, Teacher Education, College of Education, University of Oregon

THOMAS C. HENNESSY, S.J., Ph.D., is Professor and Coordinator of Program in Counseling and Personnel Services, School of Education, Fordham University, New York City

HARRY B. KAVANAGH, Ph.D., is Assistant Professor, Education, Rider College, Lawrenceville, New Jersey

FRANK W. LEWIS, S.J., Ph.D., is Associate Professor and Chairman, Division of Foundations in Teaching, Fairfield University, Fairfield, Connecticut

DIANA P. PAOLITTO, Ed.D., is Assistant Professor, Counselor Education and Counseling Psychology, Boston College

ROBERT J. ROTH, S.J., Ph.D., is Dean of Fordham College, Fordham University, New York City

NORMAN A. SPRINTHALL, Ed.D., is Professor, Psychoeducational Studies, University of Minnesota, Minneapolis

Bibliography

Adler, A. *Social interest: A challenge to mankind.* London: Faber and Faber, 1949.

Adler, A. *The education of children.* Chicago: Henry Regnery, Co., 1970. (Originally published, 1930.)

Adler, A., Ansbacher, H., and Ansbacher, R. *Superiority and social interest: A collection of later writings.* Evanston: Northwestern University Press, 1964.

Ardrey, R. *The territorial imperative.* London: Collings, 1967.

Atkins, V. *High school students who teach: An approach to personal learning.* Unpublished doctoral dissertation, Graduate School of Education, Harvard University, 1972.

Bainton, R. H., *Yale and the ministry.* Harper & Row, 1957.

Baldwin, A. L. *Behavior and development in childhood.* Holt, Rinehart and Winston, 1956.

Bandura, A. *Principles of behavior modification.* Holt, Rinehart and Winston, 1969.

Bandura, A., Ross, D., & Ross, A. A. Vicarious reinforcement and imitative learning. *Journal of Abnormal and Social Psychology*, 1963, 3-11, 66.

Bandura, A., & Walters, R. H. *Social learning and personality development.* Holt, Rinehart and Winston, 1963.

Barron, F. *Creativity and psychological health.* Van Nostrand, 1963.

Beck, C., Sullivan, E., & Taylor, N. Stimulating transition to postconventional morality: The Pickering high school study. *Interchange*, 1972, *3*, 28-37.

Becker, H. S. *Complex organizations—a sociological reader.* New York: Holt, Rinehart and Winston, 1965.

Becvar, R. *Skills for effective communication.* Wiley, 1974.

Bellack, A., et al. *Language of the classroom.* New York: Teachers College Press, 1966.

Berkowitz, L. *Development of motives and values in a child.* Basic Books, 1964.

Bernier, J. *A psychological education interaction for teacher development.* Unpublished doctoral dissertation, University of Minnesota, 1976.

Beyer, B. K. Conducting moral discussions in the classroom. *Social Education*, 1976, 194-202.

Biddle, B., & Ellena, W. *Contemporary research on teacher effectiveness.* Holt, Rinehart and Winston, 1964.

Blatt, M. *Studies on the effects of classroom discussions upon children's moral development.* Unpublished doctoral dissertation, University of Chicago, 1970.

Blatt, M., Colby, A., & Speicher, B. *Hypothetical dilemmas for use in moral discussion.* Cambridge, Mass.: Moral Education and Research Foundation, 1974.

Blatt, M. M., & Kohlberg, L. The effects of classroom moral discussion upon children's level of moral judgment. *Journal of Moral Education,* 1975, *4*(2), 129-161.

Bok, D. C. Can ethics be taught? *Change,* 1976, *8*(9), 26-30.

Boyd, D. *Education toward principled moral judgment: An analysis of an experimental course in undergraduate education applying Lawrence Kohlberg's theory of moral development.* Unpublished doctoral dissertation, Harvard University, 1976.

Boyd, D., & Kohlberg, L. The is-ought problem: A developmental perspective. *Zygon,* 1973, *8*, 358-372.

Boyer, E. L. A new liberal arts crucial to survival. *The New York Times,* January 15, 1975, pp. 57; 98.

Brearley, M., & Hitchfield, E. *A guide to reading Piaget.* Schocken Books, 1969.

Bronfenbrenner, U. Freudian theories of identification and their derivatives. *Child Development,* 1960, *31*, 15-40.

Brown, C. *Manchild in the promised land.* Macmillan, 1965.

The Bulletin of the Regents 1976 statewide plan for the development of postsecondary education. Albany, N.Y., June, 1975.

Byrne, D. *The development of role-taking in adolescence.* Unpublished doctoral dissertation, Graduate School of Education, Harvard University, 1973.

Carkhuff, R. *Helping and human relations, Vol. I and II.* Holt, Rinehart and Winston, 1969.

Colby, A. Values clarification—book review. In *Harvard Educational Review,* 1975, *42*(1), 134-143.

Collingwood, T. Retention and retraining of interpersonal communication skills. *Journal of Clinical Psychology,* 1971, *27*(2), 294-296.

Conrad, C. University goals: An operative approach. *The Journal of Higher Education,* 1974, *45*, 504-516.

Crittenden, B. Form and content in moral education. Ontario Institute for Studies in Education, 1972.

Crittenden, B. A comment on cognitive moral education. *Phi Delta Kappan,* 1975, *10*, 695-696.

Cyphert, F. Analysis of research in teacher education. *Journal of Educational Technology,* 1972, *23*(2), 145-151.

Cyphert, F., & Spaights, E. *An analysis and projection of research in teacher education.* Ohio State University Research Press, 1964.

Dewey, J. Psychology and social practice. *Psychological Review,* 1900, *7*, 105-124.

DiStefano, A. *Teaching moral reasoning about sexual and interpersonal dilemmas.* Unpublished doctoral dissertation, Boston University, 1976.

Dowell, R. C. *Adolescents as peer counselors: A program for psychological growth.* Unpublished doctoral dissertation, Graduate School of Education, Harvard University, 1971.

Dreeben, R. *On what is learned in school.* Stevensville, Miss.: Educational Service, 1968.

Dreikurs, R. *Children: The challenge.* Duell, Sloan & Pearce, 1964.

Dreikurs, R. *Psychology in the classroom.* Harper & Row, 1968.

Dreikurs, R. *Social equality: The challenge of today.* Henry Regnery, Co., 1971.

Dreikurs, R., Grunwald, B. B., & Pepper, F. *Maintaining sanity in the classroom.* Harper & Row, 1971.

Duska, R., & Whelan, M. *Moral development.* Paulist Press, 1975.

Ebel, R. L. Estimation of the reliability of ratings. *Psychometrika,* 1951, *16,* 407-424.

Elkind, D. Egocentrism in adolescence. *Child Development,* 1967, 38, 1025-1034.

Erikson, E. H. *Childhood and society.* (2nd ed.) Norton, 1963.

Erikson, E. H. *Identity, youth and crisis.* Norton, 1968.

Flanders, N. A. *Analyzing teaching behavior.* Addison-Wesley, 1970.

Flavell, J. *The developmental psychology of Jean Piaget.* Van Nostrand, 1963.

Foster, C. *Developing self-control.* Kalamazoo, Mich.: Behaviordelia Press, 1974.

Frankena, W. K. The philosophy of vocation. *Thought,* 1976, *60,* 393-408.

Frankenburg, C. *I'm all right.* London: Macmillan, 1961.

Freud, S. *New introductory lectures on psychoanalysis.* Norton, 1933.

Furth, H. *Piaget for teachers.* Prentice-Hall, 1970.

Furth, H., & Wachs, H. *Thinking goes to school: Piaget's theory in practice.* Oxford, 1974.

Gallup, G. The public looks at the public school. *Today's Education,* September/October, 1975.

Gazda, G. M. *Human relations development: A manual for educators.* Allyn and Bacon, 1973.

Geoghegan, B. But is it values education? In T. Hennessy (Ed.), *Values and Moral Development.* Paulist Press, 1976.

Getzels, J. W., & Jackson, P. *Creativity and intelligence.* John Wiley, 1962.

Getzels, J. W., & Jackson, P. The teacher's personality and characteristics. In N. Gage (Ed.), *Handbook of research on teaching.* Rand McNally, 1964.

Gewinner, M. N. *A study of the results of the interaction of student teachers with their supervising teachers during the student teaching period.* Unpublished doctoral dissertation, Mississippi State University, 1968.

Glaser, R. Components of a psychology of instruction: Toward a science of design. *Review of Educational Research,* 1976, *46*(1), 1-24.

Goldberg, A. Conceptual systems as a predisposition toward therapeutic communication. *Journal of Counseling Psychology,* 1974, *21*(5), 364-368.

Goodlad, J., & Klien, M. *Looking behind the classroom door.* Worthington, Ohio: Jones, 1974.

Goodman, P. *Compulsory mis-education.* Random House, 1962.

Gormally, J. et al. The persistence of communications skills for undergraduate and graduate trainees. *Journal of Clinical Psychology,* 1975, *31*(2), 369-372.

Graham, D. *Moral learning and development: Theory and research.* Wiley-Interscience, 1972.

Greenspan, B. *Facilitating psychological growth in adolescents through child development curricula.* Unpublished doctoral dissertation, Graduate School of Education, Harvard University, 1974.

Griffin, A. *Teaching counselor education to black teenagers.* Unpublished doctoral dissertation, Graduate School of Education, Harvard University, 1972.

Grimes, P. *Teaching moral reasoning to eleven-year-olds and their mothers: A means of promoting moral development.* Unpublished doctoral dissertation, Boston University School of Education, 1974.

Gump, P. V. Education as an environmental enterprise. In R. Weinberg & F. Woods (Eds.), *Observation of pupils and teachers in mainstream and special education settings.* Minneapolis, Minn.: LTI, 1975.

Haase, R. F., DeMattia, D. J., & Guttman, M. A. Training of support personnel in three human relations skills: A systematic one-year follow-up. *Journal of Counselor Education and Supervision*, 1972, *3*, 194-199.

Hall, R. T., & Davis, J. U. *Moral education in theory and practice.* Prometheus Books, 1975.

Hartshorne, H., & May, M. *Studies in the nature of character.* Macmillan, 1928-1930, 3 vols.

Harvey, O. J. System structure, flexibility and creativity. In O. J. Harvey (Ed.), *Experience, structure and adaptability.* New York: Springer, 1966, 242-262.

Harvey, O. J., et al. Teacher's belief systems and preschool atmospheres. *Journal of Educational Psychology*, 1966, *57*, 373-381.

Harvey, O. J. et al. Teacher beliefs, classroom atmosphere, and student behavior. *Educational Research Journal*, 1968, *5*(2), 151-165.

Hemming, J. The development of children's moral values. *British Journal of Educational Psychology*, June 1957, 77-88.

Hennessy, T. C. (Ed.) *Values and moral development.* Paulist Press, 1976.

Henry, J. *Culture against man.* Random House, 1963.

Hickey, J. *The effects of guided moral discussion upon youthful offenders' level of moral judgment.* Unpublished doctoral dissertation, School of Education, Boston University, 1972.

Hoffman, M. L. Altruistic behavior and the parent-child relationship. *Journal of Personality and Social Psychology*, 1975, *31*, 937-943.

Hoffman, M. L. Empathy, role-taking guilt, and development of altruistic motives. In T. Lickona (Ed.), *Moral development and behavior.* Holt, Rinehart and Winston, 1976.

Hoffman, M. L., & Saltzstein, H. D. Parent discipline and the child's moral development. *Journal of Personality and Social Psychology*, 1967, *5*, 45-47.

Holstein, C. *Parental determinants of the development of moral judgment.* Unpublished doctoral dissertation, University of California, Berkeley, 1969.

Holt, J. *How children fail.* Dell, 1964.

Hudson, L. *Frames of mind.* London: Methuen, 1968.

Hunt, D., & Joyce, B. Teacher trainee personality and initial teaching style. *American Education Research Journal*, 1967, *4*(3), 253-257.

Hunt, D., & Sullivan, E. *Between psychology and education.* The Dryden Press, 1974.

Hunt, M., & Metcalf, L. *Teaching high school social studies.* Harper & Row, 1968.

Iannaccone, L. Student teaching: A transitional stage in the making of a teacher. *Theory into Practice*, 1963, *2*, 73-80.

Jackson, P. *Life in the classroom.* Holt, Rinehart & Winston, 1968.

James, W. *Talks with teachers.* Norton, 1958. (Originally published, 1889.)

Jencks, C., & Riesman, D. *The academic revolution.* Doubleday, 1968.

Jones, V. *Character and citizenship training in the public school.* University of Chicago Press, 1936.

Joyce, B., & Weil, M. The teacher innovator: Models of teaching as the core of teacher education. *Interchange*, 1973, *4*(2-3), 47-59.

Kay, W. *Moral education.* London: George Allen and Unwin Ltd., 1975.

Kohlberg, L. *The development of modes of moral thinking and choice in the years ten to sixteen.* Unpublished doctoral dissertation, University of Chicago, 1958.

Kohlberg, L. The development of children's orientations toward a moral order: I. Sequence in the development of moral thought. *Vita Humana*, 1963, *6*, 11-33.

Kohlberg, L. Stage and sequence: The cognitive developmental approach to socialization. In D. Goslin (Ed.), *Handbook of socialization theory research.* Rand McNally, 1969.

Kohlberg, L. Stages of moral development as a basis for moral education. In C. Beck & E. Sullivan (Eds.), *Moral education.* Toronto: University of Toronto Press, 1970. (a)

Kohlberg, L. Education for justice: A modern statement of the Platonic view. In T. Sizer (Ed.), *Moral education.* Harvard University Press, 1970. (b)

Kohlberg, L. From is to ought. In T. Mischel (Ed.), *Cognitive development and epistemology.* Academic Press, 1971.

Kohlberg, L. *Continuities in childhood and adult moral development revisited.* Address to Life Span Psychology Conference, University of West Virginia, 1972.

Kohlberg, L. The role of the teacher and of the school community in education for moral action. In L. Kohlberg, *Collected papers on moral development and moral education.* Cambridge, Mass.: Moral Education and Research Foundation, 1975, Vol. 2.

Kohlberg, L., Colby, A., Fenton, E., Speicher-Dubin, B. & Leiberman, M. Secondary school moral discussion programs led by social studies teachers. In L. Kohlberg, *Collected papers . . .* (1975).

Kohlberg, L., & Mayer, R. Development as the aim of education. *Harvard Educational Review*, 1972, *42*, 449-496.

Kohlberg, L., Selman, R. l., & Lickona, T. A strategy for teaching values. In *First things: Values.* New York: Guidance Associates, 1972.

Kohlberg, L., & Turiel, E. Moral development and moral education. In G. Lesser (Ed.), *Psychology and educational practice.* Scott, Foresman, 1971.

Kohlberg, L., Wasserman, E., & Richardson, N. The just community school: The theory and the Cambridge Cluster School experiment. In L. Kohlberg, *Collected papers on moral development and moral education.* Cambridge, Mass.: Moral Education and Research Foundation, 1975, Vol. 2.

Kohlberg, L. et al. Assessing moral stages: A manual (Preliminary ed.). Harvard University, 1976.

Kozol, J. *Death at an early age*. Houghton Mifflin, 1967.

Krathwohl, D., Bloom, B. & Masia, B. *Taxonomy of educational objectives: The affective domain*. McKay, 1964.

Krumboltz, J., & Thorensen, C. (Eds.) *Counseling methods*. Holt, Rinehart & Winston, 1976.

Ladenburg, T. Cognitive development and moral reasoning in the teaching of history. *History Teacher, 10* (2), February 1977.

Leming, J. S. *Adolescent moral judgment and deliberation on classical and practical dilemmas*. Unpublished doctoral dissertation. University of Wisconsin, 1973.

Levin, K. *Resolving social conflict*. Harper, 1948.

Loevinger, J. The meaning and measurement of ego development. *American Psychologist*, 1966, *21*, 195-217.

Loevinger, J. Theories of ego development. In L. Breger (Ed.), *Clinical-cognitive psychology*. Prentice-Hall, 1969.

Loevinger, J., & Wessler, R. *Measuring ego development*. Jossey-Bass, 1970, Vol. I and II.

Lickona, T. Piaget misunderstood: A critique of the criticism of this theory of moral development. *Merrill-Palmer Quarterly*, 1969, *15*, 338-339.

London, P. The Rescuers: Motivational hypotheses about Christians who saved Jews from the Nazis. In J. Macavlay & L. Berkowitz (Eds.), *Altruism and helping behavior*. Academic Press, 1970.

Lorish, R. *Teaching counseling to disadvantaged young adults*. Unpublished doctoral dissertation, School of Education, Boston University, 1974.

Lubin, G. et al. (Eds.) *Piagetian theory and the helping professions*. U.C.L.A. Press, 1975.

MacDonald, F. *A behavior modification view of video playback: Microteaching*. Paper presented at AERA meeting, New Orleans, 1973.

Mackie, P. *Teaching counseling skills to low achieving high school students*. Unpublished doctoral dissertation, School of Education, Boston University, 1974.

Maslow, A. *Motivation and personality*. (2nd ed.) Harper & Row, 1970.

Matthews, C. C. *The classroom verbal behavior of selected secondary school science teachers and their cooperating classroom teachers*. Unpublished doctoral dissertation, Cornell University, 1967.

McAuliffe, S. *The differential effect of three training models upon the acquisition and transfer of interpersonal communication skills*. Unpublished doctoral dissertation, University of Minnesota, 1974.

Miles, M. Some properties of schools as social systems. In G. Watson (Ed.), *Change in school systems*. NEA, 1967.

Miller, G. Psychology as a means of promoting human welfare. *American Psychologist*, 1969, *24*, 1063-1075.

Miller, J. School and self-alienation: a conceptual view. *Journal of Educational Thought*, 1972, *7*(2), 113.

Mischel, W., & Geruse, J. Determinants of the rehearsal and transmission of neutral and aversive behaviors. *Journal of Personality and Social Psychology*, 1966, *3*, 197-205.

Mischel, W., & Gilligan, C. F. *Delay of gratification and resistance to temptation.* Stanford University Press, 1962.

Mischel, W., & Liebert, R. M. The role of power in the adoption of self-reward patterns. *Child Development,* 1967, *38,* 673-683.

Morison, S. E. *Harvard college in the seventeenth century.* Harvard University Press, 1936, 2 vols.

Mosher, R. Knowledge from practice: Clinical research and development in education. *The Counseling Psychologist,* 1974, *4*(4), 73-82.

Mosher, R. Funny things happen on the way to curriculum development. In H. Peters & R. Aubrey (Eds.), *Guidance: Strategies and techniques.* Denver: Love Publishing, 1975.

Mosher, R. L., & Purpel, D. E. *Supervision: The reluctant profession.* Houghton-Mifflin, 1972.

Mosher, R. L., & Sprinthall, N. A. Deliberate psychological education. *The Counseling Psychologist,* 1971, *2*(4), 3-82.

Mosher, R., & Sullivan, P. A curriculum in moral education for adolescents. In *Challenge in educational administration,* Department of Educational Administration, Edmonton, Alberta: University of Alberta, 1974.

Mosher, R., & Sullivan, P. Moral education: A new initiative for guidance. *Focus on Guidance,* January, 1974.

Mounier, E. *Personalism.* London: Routledge and Kegan Paul, 1952.

Murphy, P., & Brown, M. Conceptual systems and teaching styles. *American Educational Research Journal,* 1970, *7*(4), 529-540.

Muss, R. E. *Theories of adolescence.* Random House, 1975.

Mussen, P., Conger, J. J., & Kagan, J. *Child development and personality* (4th ed.). Harper & Row, 1974.

Newsweek. Moral education. March 1, 1976, 74-75A.

O'Brien, G. M. Colleges' concern grows over ethical values. *The Chronicle of Higher Education,* February 23, 1976, *11*(22), 5.

Osmon, R. V. *Associative factors in changes of student teachers' attitudes during student teaching.* Unpublished doctoral dissertation, Indiana University, 1959.

Paolitto, D. P. *Role-taking opportunities for early adolescents: A program in moral education.* Unpublished doctoral dissertation, Boston University, 1975.

Peters, R. S. Moral development: A plea for pluralism. In T. Mischel (Ed.), *Cognitive development and epistemology.* Academic Press, 1971.

Peters, R. S. Moral development and moral knowing. *The Monist,* October 1974, *4.*

Piaget, J. *Judgment and reasoning in the child.* Routledge & Kegan Paul, 1928.

Piaget, J. *The child's conception of the world.* Routledge & Kegan Paul, 1929.

Piaget, J. *The moral judgment of the child.* (M. Gabain, trans.). Free Press, Macmillan, 1965. (Originally published, 1932.)

Piaget, J. *The origins of intelligence in children.* International Universities Press, 1952.

Piaget, J. The general problem of the psychobiological development of the child. In J. M. Tanner & B. Inhelder (Eds.), *Discussion on child development.* Vol. 4, International Universities Press, 1960.

Piaget, J. *Science of education and the psychology of the child.* Orion Press, 1970.

Piaget, J. *Biology and knowledge: An essay on the relations between organic regulations and cognitive processes.* University of Chicago Press, 1971.

Piaget, J. Some aspects of operations. In M. W. Piers (Ed.), *Play and development: A symposium.* Norton, 1972.

Piaget, J. *To understand is to invent: The future of education.* Grossman, 1973.

Pulaski, M. *Understanding Piaget: An introduction to children's cognitive development.* Harper & Row, 1971.

Raths, L. E., Harmin, M., & Simon, S. B. *Values and teaching: Working with values in the classroom.* Charles E. Merrill, 1966.

Rawls, J. *A theory of justice.* Harvard University Press, 1971.

Redmore, C., & Waldman, K. *Reliability of a sentence completion measure of ego development.* Unpublished article. St. Louis, Mo.: Washington University, 1975.

Report of the Committee on the Study of Values at Fordham College. Fordham University, November, 1975. Unpublished.

Rest, J. Developmental psychology as a guide to value education: A review of "Kohlbergian" programs. *Review of Educational Research*, 1974, *44*, 241-259.

Rest, J. The research base of the cognitive developmental approach to moral education. In T.Hennessy (Ed.), *Values and moral development.* Paulist Press, 1976.

Rest, J., Turiel, E., & Kohlberg, L. Level of moral development as a determinant of preference and comprehension of moral judgments made by others. *Journal of Personality*, 1969, *37*, 225-252.

Rice, J. M. *The public school system of the United States.* Century, 1893.

Rudolph, F. *The American college and university: A history.* Alfred A. Knopf, 1962.

Ryan, K. *Don't smile until Christmas.* University of Chicago Press, 1970.

Selman, R. *Role-taking ability and the development of moral judgment.* Unpublished doctoral dissertation, Boston University, 1969.

Selman, R. The relationship of role-taking to the development of moral judgment in children. *Child Development*, 1971, *42*, 79-91.

Selman, R. Taking another's perspective: Role-taking development in early childhood. *Child Development*, 1971, *42*, 1721-1734.

Selman, R. L. Social-cognitive understanding: A guide to educational and clinical practice. In T. Lickona (Ed.), *Moral development and behavior: Theory, research, and social issues.* Holt, Rinehart & Winston, 1976.

Selman, R. L., & Lieberman, M. Moral education in the primary grades: An evaluation of a developmental curriculum. *Journal of Educational Psychology*, 1975, *67*(5), 712-716.

Shutes, R. Needed: A theory for teacher education. *Texas Technical Journal of Education*, 1975, *2*(2), 85-94.

Silberman, C. *Crisis in the classroom.* Random House, 1970.

Spiel, O. *Discipline without punishment.* London: Faber and Faber, 1947.

Sprinthall, N. A. A cognitive developmental curriculum. *Counseling and Values*, 1974, *18*, 94-101.

Sprinthall, N. A. Moral and psychological development: A curriculum for secondary schools. In T. Hennessy (Ed.), *Values and moral development*. Paulist Press, 1976.

Stevens, R. *The question as a measure of efficiency in instruction*. New York: Columbia University, Contributions to Education #48, 1912.

Sugarman, B. The therapeutic community and the school. *Interchange*, 1970, *1*(2).

Sullivan, P. J. *A curriculum for stimulating moral reasoning and ego development in adolescents*. Unpublished doctoral dissertation, Boston University, 1975.

Teilhard, P. De Chardin. *The phenomenon of man*. London: Collins, 1960.

Thompson, J. M. *A study of the effect of having a trainee co-counsel with a live model during a micro-counseling practice session*. Unpublished doctoral dissertation, University of Minnesota, 1976.

Three approaches to psychotherapy. Santa Ana, California: Psychological Films.

Torrance, E. P. *Guiding creative talent*. Prentice-Hall, 1962.

Torrance, E. P. *Encouraging creativity in the classroom*. W. C. Brown, 1970.

Turiel, E. An experimental test of the sequentiality of developmental stages in the child's moral development. *Journal of Personality and Social Psychology*, 1966, *3*, 611-618.

Turiel, E. Developmental processes in the child's moral thinking. In P. Mussen, J. Langer, & M. Covington (Eds.), *New directions in developmental psychology*. Holt, Rinehart & Winston, 1969.

Turiel, E. Stage transition in moral development. In R. M. Travers (Ed.), *Second handbook of research in teaching*. Rand McNally, 1973.

Turiel, E. Conflict and transition in adolescent moral development. *Child Development*, 1974, *45*, 14-29.

Veysey, L. R. *The emergence of the American university*. The University of Chicago Press, 1965.

Wasserman, E. R. Implementing Kohlberg's "just community concept" in an alternative high school. *Social Education*, April, 1976, 203-207.

White, R. *Lives in progress*. Holt, Rinehart & Winston, 1966.

Wilson, J. *Practical methods of moral education*. Heinemann, 1972.

Wilson, J. et al. *Introduction to moral education*. Penguin, 1967.

Wittmer, J. & Myrick, R. *Facilitative teaching: Theory and practice*, Pacific Palisades, Cal.: Goodier Press, 1974.

Wright, D. *The psychology of moral behavior*. Penguin, 1971.

Wright, G. History as a moral science. *The Chronicle of Higher Education*, February 23, 1976, *11* (22), 24.

D